THE WEARINESS OF A GHOST

Wae's me, wae's me!
The acorn's no yet
Fa'en frae the tree
That's to grow the wood
That's to mak the creddle
That's to rock the bairn
That's to grow a man
That's to lay me.

[Woe is me, woe is me!
The acorn has not yet
Fallen from the tree
That will grow the wood
That will make the cradle
That will rock the baby
That will grow into a man
Who will lay me to rest.]

The song of *The Cauld Lad of Hylton*,
traditional verse

GHOSTLY SCOTLAND

The Supernatural and Unexplained

GHOSTLY SCOTLAND

The Supernatural and Unexplained

by Lily Seafield

with additional text by Rosalind Patrick

WAVERLEY BOOKS

This edition published 2023 by Waverley Books
an imprint of The Gresham Publishing Company Limited,
31, Six Harmony Row, Glasgow G51 3BA, Scotland UK.

First published in 2006 by Geddes & Grosset
(an imprint of The Gresham Publishing Company Limited).
This combined text was previously published in two separate editions:
as *Scottish Ghosts*, printed 1999, 2001, 2002, 2003,
and as *Supernatural Scotland*, printed 2005.

Text by Lily Seafield and Rosalind Patrick.
Cover design by Mark Mechan.
Piper copyright Shutterstock.
Eilean Donan Castle copyright Photodisc Inc.

ISBN : 978-1-84934-548-4

Printed and bound in Spain by Novoprint S.A.
Typeset in Scotland by Geddes & Grosset using
Bitstream fonts Baskerville and Kuenstler

Contents

Contents

Contents

Hotels and Public Houses: Extra Guests   153

Military Specters   164

Contents

Contents

Contents

Introduction

SCOTLAND is a country with a rich and varied history, a land of strikingly beautiful scenery with a people proud of its traditions and heritage. The years that have passed since the beginnings of its history have seen much conflict and upheaval and many triumphs and tragedies that absorb historians and capture the imaginations of storytellers and their audiences. Scottish folk legends tell of fairies, giants and monsters that have lived (or still do live) cheek by jowl with the mere mortals who inhabit this small country. Where or why these stories began no one can be certain, but they have entertained audience and teller alike for many long years and continue to do so. Whether such stories have any base in fact is a matter for debate, but there will always be those who believe that they have some truth attached to them. The search for the Loch Ness Monster goes on, for example, and probably will for all time.

It is the same with the many hundreds of ghosts that are said to populate Scotland. It seems that wherever you go, whatever stories you hear about a place and its past, there is likely to be a ghost story lurking in the background, ready for anyone who will listen. The specters of sinners condemned to a life in eternal limbo, the tortured souls of those who have been shamefully wronged, victims of cruel and terrible crimes, mysterious "green ladies," "white ladies" and phantoms determined to leave their mark on the living, soldiers, animals and ghastly deformed creatures, all have their place in Scottish ghost stories. Old ghosts, new ghosts, Scotland has them all, ready for those who are willing to hear them, see them or sense their presence. Some ghosts have the ability, it would appear, not only to delight the committed ghost-hunter but also to convince the most skeptical of unbelievers. There are plenty of accounts of people who have been shocked into believing in the existence of ghosts by the appearance of just such a thing, making their hair stand on end and sending them screaming, white-faced, from their beds.

To those who remain dubious, it is clear why some ghost stories have been told. Perhaps a place has a great history of colorful characters who performed gory deeds. The history makes good telling, but people want to hear more. These colorful characters are dead, so what more can be said? The thing to do is to keep them going in ghostly form: a creak in the night, the howl of the wind, a falling leaf brushing past a face—these things can all take on sinister form and be attributed to the mischief of those who have gone before. History comes alive again and is so much more exciting; people will flock to hear the stories and share in the experience.

Other ghost stories, the unbelievers will tell you, are merely the product of over-fertile imaginations. Someone was wakened in the night? It was no more than a bad dream. A shiver down the spine? There must be some normal physiological explanation. And so it goes on. But the tales of supernatural occurrences multiply. Sometimes a rational explanation simply cannot be found. Evidence has been collected of people's experiences and stories have been compared. Books have been written. Television documentaries have been made. Ghosts have really made the big time—and Scotland is full of them.

This book contains details of many of the most famous of Scottish ghosts, some of which are hundreds of years old. It also tells of some that are not so well known and some that are not so old.

Some ghost stories are strikingly similar—older tales of ghosts and the supernatural that have become very much like the modern "urban myth," perhaps because they have been passed from person to person so many times over many years. When an urban myth is told, it is almost always told as something that happened to a friend of a friend, or a relative of a friend. The events in the story are generally said to have taken place in the town or city in which the story is being told. The same story will undoubtedly have been told in several other places nationwide; each time it will be told as something that happened to somebody connected to the storyteller, in the town in which the story is being told. Thus the same story (details may vary but the content will be much the same) finds itself associated with several different locations and groups of people. Some ghost stories are like this—the same basic elements are there but the places and the people involved are different. It must be the case, therefore, that some of the stories will, quite simply, be untrue.

Some of the stories in this book are myths that have their roots in the nature and activities of the personality involved. The stories that were circulated about Bonnie Dundee are a prime example of this, as are the legends that surround Michael Scott of Balwearie. Bonnie Dundee was a figure who was both feared and hated by many people so it is perhaps not surprising that rumors about his supposed devilish associations and supernatural powers were circulated by his enemies. Michael Scott was by all accounts very clever and learned, and great learning can inspire fear and suspicion.

Some ghost stories, inevitably, have their origins in long, dark nights by the fire, when a gifted storyteller with a fertile imagination could easily send a chill down the spines of a willing audience.

In a country in which beliefs in many things supernatural have been widespread for so many years, it is inevitable that there will be many more stories than real supernatural occurrences. This book makes no attempt to separate fact from fancy. Those readers who wish to pursue their interest in the ghosts and supernatural beings of Scotland can follow their own trail. This book can act as a starting point, but each ghost-hunter will find him or herself following a different path. No nation on earth is more inundated with reportings of hauntings and paranormal activity, and people travel thousands of miles to visit our ghostliest centers. There are so many ghosts and so many stories to chase.

In addition to the stories of particular ghosts and eerie happenings, mention is made of some of the beliefs that people in Scotland held, and sometimes still hold, about supernatural phenomena of various kinds—the nameless supernatural "types" that were thought to visit the world of mere mortals, influencing them and sometimes playing havoc with their lives. The devil has also earned his place in this book, for he has been associated with many of the ghostly tales of evil deeds and strange occurrences after death that were told all over Scotland over the years.

A Supernatural Character

Theories abound as to why Scotland should be such a magnet for otherworldy activity. One prominent one being that the Celtic character is more sensitive than most to what lies beyond, is more intuitive and less earth-bound.

Perhaps this instinct explains why Spiritualism and mediumship thrive in modern Scotland, the country that brought forth some of its greatest practitioners, including the legendary Helen Duncan, aka Hellish Nell, the last woman to be tried—and convicted—under the 1735 Witchcraft Act. This war-time physical medium, celebrated for her seeming ability to make the dead walk amongst the living, is written off as the worst kind of fraudster by some, while hailed as a martyr to her art by others.

Gordon Smith is one of today's most internationally renowned Spiritualists, credited with some truly remarkable demonstrations. Yet it would be difficult to find anyone more strongly connected to his Scottish roots, more grateful for his down-to-earth Glaswegian upbringing and the humor of the city which remains his home.

This Celtic sensitivity, if such it is, is doubtless informed by the landscape, which has the ability, not just to change from one ten mile stretch to the next, but from one moment to the next. You can gaze down from the summit of Ben A'an, in the Lomond mountain range, and see for miles, down onto the still surface of Loch Katrine and out across the peaks, then suddenly find your view obstructed, yourself shrouded in billowing white mist and the day lost to sight. But as you descend, out comes the sun again and the long, lavish views, only to disappear instantaneously beneath a freak shower of hailstones. Like all peoples, we are affected by changes in light and atmospheric pressure, our imaginations are triggered by them, and our senses heightened. Perhaps this is what gave rise to our tales of gray giants treading softly behind travelers in remote places, and curious creatures that suddenly appear by roadsides and shores, and vanish in the blink of an eye.

Perhaps too, this at least partly explains why the witch-hunts of the 16th and 17th centuries reached such hysterical proportions in Scotland, where hundreds of innocent men and women were burnt to death by zealots who feared for their newfound religion, Christianity. The horrors of that time have never been completely forgotten. Nor has the ancient, generally benign, belief system that underpinned "the Craft." Today, as secularism continues in its ascendancy, Scotland is witnessing something of a renaissance in pagan rites and Wicca, the modern reconstruction of what remains of the old religions.

The Scottish psyche is also undoubtedly informed by changes in society. The strict doctrine of Presbyterianism and the insistence of rationalism created a hunger for the in-explicable and fantastic. "Plain claes and purridge" (ordinary clothes and porridge, i.e. a frugal existence) leaves little for the imagination to feed on, so it is little wonder the old tales, passed on by word-of-mouth through generations, remained popular even as John Knox railed against superstition and nonsense.

There is also a link with ancient Celtic beliefs, notably that the spirits of the dead remain amongst the living. The neo-lithic standing stones, burial cairns and mysterious straight tracks that cross-hatch the countryside indicate that here was a society that revered its ancestors and regularly paid homage to them. These spirits guarded the living, and perhaps even guided them.

Earth energy investigators, whose specialism takes in ley lines and sacred sites, believe that the ancients had means of communicating with the dead and that certain places, such as standing stone circles, operated as portals to another di-mension.

This finds a modern translation in the science of UFOlogy. Bizarrely, and no-one as yet has posited even a credible the-ory as to why, Scotland clocks up more UFO sightings than anywhere else in the world. And the most popular destina-tion for extra-terrestrial visitors is the unremarkable town of Bonnybridge, in the Central Region.

Could these sightings be related to those ancient portals, or to the ability of our ancestors, some vestiges of which perhaps survive in people born today, to see through the darkness to the worlds beyond?

Fairies, Green Ladies and Devilish Struggles

Fairies

SCOTTISH folklore is populated with a whole host of fairies, demons, ghosts, green ladies and other manifestations. It is hard, perhaps impossible, to separate these into distinct entities, for the stories and beliefs that relate to them are closely intertwined. For example, the fairy and the ghost were much the same according to certain traditions. Some fairies were not so much perceived as "little people" but rather as spirits of people long dead, either imprisoned on earth or left on earth after having been denied entrance to either heaven or hell. Some fairies were believed to be evildoers and mischief-makers, abducting women and children; others were less malevolent, granting wishes and effecting changes for the better in the lives of the mortals who crossed their paths.

Human interaction with the fairy world was fraught with problems. There was always the danger that if you crossed a fairy the consequences could be unpleasant in the extreme. Thus, there are stories of people who have discovered a magic salve that, if rubbed on their eyes, helps them to see fairies. When this facility is discovered by someone in the fairy kingdom, the mortal concerned at the very least has the facility taken away, but more often will have the offending eye or eyes put out.

There are countless tales of people who have seen into the world, or kingdom, of the fairies, whether through gift, by chance, through the use of a magic salve or in a dream. Stories of people who have had such access to, or sight of, the world of the fairies often tell how a living person has looked into the fairy world and recognized relatives, friends or acquaintances who have died and are now living in the fairy realm. Tales such as these reinforce the idea of a link between the ghost or spirit of the dead and the fairy.

The fairy world, much like the world of the spirits, has its own time, which bears no relation to real time. This uniqueness of time, or perhaps timelessness, which is associated with fairyland, is illustrated by one particular story that comes from Inverness.

The story tells how two fiddlers were visiting Inverness, looking for places to perform, when they met an old man who asked them if they would play at a dance for him. This they agreed to, and they followed the old man to a place called Tomnahurich. They reached Tomnahurich, a small hill outside Inverness, towards nightfall. They entered a opening in the side of the hill and found themselves in a richly decorated hall where scenes of great merriment were taking place. A party was well under way, with food and wine laid on in astonishing quality and abundance. The fiddlers found themselves in the company of many beautiful, but very small and fine-boned, women. The men were allowed to eat and drink their fill at the feast before the dancing began. When they took up their fiddles to play, the party got into full swing. The fiddlers played their hearts out but did so with great pleasure as the music was enlivening and uplifting and the dancing ladies were a joy to behold. Time passed, and they hardly seemed to notice it.

At last, when it seemed that morning had come, the dancing came to a halt and the fiddlers packed up, ready to leave. The old man who had hired them paid them generously with a bag of silver and the fiddlers departed from the hillock in fine spirits. It had been a great night and a most profitable one. They wandered back towards Inverness, and it was here that things seemed to take a strange turn. Everything was different. The town itself had changed so much that they hardly recognized it as the same place. New buildings had sprung up, as if from nowhere. The people had changed too. They all wore very different clothes and laughed when they saw what the fiddlers were wearing, calling their attire "strange" and "old-fashioned."

The fiddlers could not work out what was wrong and decided to return to their own home town. Here they found that the situation was much the same. It was as if several tens of years had passed in the real world while the fiddlers had been away playing at the dance at Tomnahurich.

Finally, the two men tried to take refuge in religion and went to their local church. Their appearance caused quite a stir, but the congregation were silenced when the minister started to speak. Then, at the first mention of the name of God, the two fiddlers crumbled to dust in front of all those present.

The fact that the men were said to crumble to dust when the name of God was mentioned bears out another widespread belief about fairies—that their existence was somehow at odds with God and God's world; that they were, in fact, more associated with things demonic. Other stories about fairies often relate how the little creatures disappear at the mention of God.

Glaistigs

The glaistig was another supernatural being, a female who appeared in various forms and was sometimes associated with spirits of the dead (*see* also page 325). Some of the forms that this phenomenon was supposed to take on included half-woman, half-goat, a dog, a sheep, a woman in green and a monster. Whether or not the glaistig was a malevolent being is uncertain. Supernatural occurrences both catastrophic and benign have been attributed to glaistigs in different parts of Scotland at different times. Glaistigs have been commonly associated with water, said to live in places such as waterfalls, lochs and burns. Some were said to be particularly attached to, and protective of, animals, the young and the feeble, herding cows, playing games with children and caring for the sick and elderly. Some stories associate mischief with the concept of the glaistig, and activities similar to those of a poltergeist have been attributed to glaistigs in various folkloric tales. Other tales tell of much more sinister events, however, such as the waylaying and killing of travelers and the pronouncing of curses. Some people, accordingly, saw the glaistig as a manifestation of evil.

Where the glaistig came from or how she came into existence was also a matter of differing opinions, but the link with the dead was never far away. She was sometimes perceived as a human being who had fallen under fairy enchantment; sometimes she was seen as a spirit of a dead person, sometimes a devilish creature with malicious intent. Whatever she was, or wherever she came from, the glaistig was tied in with traditions that link the idea of an afterlife with that of some sort of realm coexistent with the world of the living but inhabited by supernatural beings.

Green Ladies

There are links between the concept of the glaistig and the many tales that are told of green-lady ghosts. Green ladies pop up here, there and everywhere in Scotland, and are often regular visitors and familiar sights to the people and the places that they haunt. Glaistigs, as has been already mentioned, were sometimes said to appear as ladies dressed in green.

Some green-lady ghosts have acquired a reputation for a certain amount of mischief. This links them with some traditional perceptions of the glaistig. In addition to this, certain green-lady ghosts have been said to be able to assume different forms, such as those of a dog or a horse, a feature held in common with glaistigs.

Glaistigs were anonymous creatures, but this is not always the case with green-lady ghosts. Their identities and the reasons for their presence are often known to those whom they haunt.

Wailing Washerwomen

The banshee

The sight or sound of a woman lamenting and washing clothes has for centuries been associated with doom and death in various parts of Scotland.

One such washerwoman was the banshee, who could be seen by streams and rivers, singing mournful laments as she washed the clothes of one or more people who were about to meet with a violent death. The banshee, it was said, could be approached with caution. If a mortal managed to sneak up to a banshee unnoticed, he or she could then take hold of her and ask her who was to die. Some people believed that, once caught, the banshee would also grant three wishes.

It is said that a banshee was heard wailing in Glencoe shortly before the massacre of the MacDonalds by the Campbells.

Some of the MacDonalds heard the noise and, realizing that they were in peril, fled to the hills. This, so it has been said, is one of the reasons why the massacre, awful though it was, was not as bad as it might have been. Forty members of the clan perished, it is true, but given the facts that they were outnumbered by the Campbells and taken by surprise during the night, the numbers of the dead were not as great as might have been anticipated.

The caoineag

The caoineag was another grim spirit who made her presence felt when death was close, but she was less accessible to humans than the banshee. Like the banshee, she was heard to mourn and lament at the edge of a river or stream, but the caoineag was not visible to the human eye. She could not be approached and no one could talk to her. Those who heard the sound of her mourning were said to be doomed to face death or great sorrow.

The third type of ghostly washerwoman was believed to be the specter of a woman who had died in childbirth. It was widely believed that when a woman died in such a manner, all her clothes had to be washed at once. If this was not done, the woman, who had died before her time was due, would be condemned to wash and to wail in some sort of limbo until she reached her "due time" on earth; that is, until a time was reached when it would have been more natural and appropriate for her to die.

Devilish Struggles

There was a certain fascination, verging on preoccupation, with the devil long ago in Scotland. If anything or anyone was particularly feared for any reason, the hand of the devil had to be in there somewhere. Thus it was that men like John Graham of Claverhouse, "Bonnie Dundee," came to be associated with the black arts. He was greatly feared, and the actions he took against his enemies, in particular the Covenanters, earned him widespread hatred. Stories began to circulate that his work was more than human and that he was in some way devilishly inspired. The rumors grew wilder over time. He was said to have consorted with the devil, to have practised the black arts and to have struck a deal with the devil whereby he would become invincible in battle. As the fear and loathing of the man increased in intensity, so the stories about him became more fantastic. Sir Tam Dalyell, a contemporary and ally of Claverhouse, earned himself a similar reputation.

The devil could be a convenient excuse for getting rid of someone who was proving to be a particular nuisance. Many a woman met a terrible death in Scotland in the sixteenth century, condemned for witchcraft and satanic practises. Some of these women might have been guilty of certain unsavory practises; some, undoubtedly, practised the black arts. Nevertheless, it cannot be denied that, as far as many of them were concerned, they had done nothing to deserve their fate. Sometimes it was the case that a woman simply knew too much for her own good—a superior intellect and an inquiring mind were often treated with suspicion and could be enough to inspire a witch-hunt. Some women were too gossipy, others kept themselves to themselves too much, and the remainder simply behaved in a way that somebody, somehow, found offensive.

Those who did practise the black arts, both women and men, were said to be well acquainted with the devil. Those who admitted to such knowledge, or were forced into admission of such knowledge, suffered greatly for it. Some survived the rumors, but their notoriety lived on after them. If the stories that are told about them are to be believed, the spirits of people like these almost always seem to return. So we hear of the ghost of Major Weir, who consorted with the devil and still haunts the Old Town in Edinburgh, and the ghost of Alexander Skene, riding in his coach across the lake every year on Hogmanay to meet with Auld Nick.

The devil made frequent visits to the land of the living, according to tradition. He prowled the world of mortals in various forms, haunting the virtuous, tormenting the indecisive and tempting away the impious. Whether he appeared as man, beast or monster, the devil could always be identified by his cloven feet.

The story of Beardie of Glamis Castle, related later, in Ghostly Castles, is one of the many legends that tells of a visit from the devil to mere mortals—with disastrous consequences for foolish Beardie.

The Highlander and the Devil

Another story, which comes from Galloway, tells of a meeting in Glenluce between a proud Highlander and the devil. Plague was rampaging the countryside, sent by the devil himself, and the Highlander and his family were among the fortunate few who had not caught it. The Highlander had jokingly boasted that he owed his own survival to two things—first, the fine Highland blood that coursed through his body; secondly, the fine malt whisky that also ran through his veins in large quantities.

The devil had been annoyed that someone should have the effrontery to speak of the plague in such a light-hearted manner. He appeared in front of the Highlander one night as the bold man was making his way home from the local hostelry. The devil challenged the Highlander to answer for his cheek, but the Highlander, full of Dutch courage, was undaunted.

He felt up to any challenge that was offered him. After some debate, the devil and the Highlander agreed that they would hold a wrestling contest. If the devil won, he would infect the Highlander with the plague. If the Highlander won, the devil would have to put the plague in a bag and give it to the Highlander to dispose of.

The devil was strong, but the Highlander was a wily fighter. They wrestled with each other for some time without a clear victor emerging, both claiming to have won the tussle. In order to settle the argument, they hit upon the idea of a piping contest. The devil rustled up some pipes for them to play and the contest began. The devil, taking his turn first, played a fine tune, but when the Highlander picked up the pipes and began to play, the devil soon realized that here was a man who could play the pipes like no other. The Highlander's music was powerful and moving. It made the devil laugh, dance and weep in turn. The devil could not fail to be impressed and readily admitted defeat. He collected the plague together, like a big black cloud in his hand, then he sealed it in a bag and gave it to the Highlander as promised.

The Highlander had gambled with the devil, a dangerous pastime if ever there was one. Now he was one of the fortunate few who won. He took the bag that the devil had given him to the abbot in Glenluce to see what could be done to get rid of the plague once and for all. It took all the powers of the monks in the abbey to subdue the dark spirits of the plague but at last they succeeded, and the dreadful disease was gone from Galloway.

The Devil's game

So we know that the devil was a gambler. He liked a game of cards, and he enjoyed pitting his wits against mere mortals. He was also a rogue with a liking for a good party. In whatever guise he appears in story or verse, as man or beast, the most frequent things associated with his appearance are music, dancing and wild times. Those who did choose to dabble in the occult and practise witchcraft may have traded their eternal souls when they did so, but they probably thought it worthwhile for the earthly pleasures of taking part in wild bacchanalian rites. Moreover, these pleasures did not necessarily come to an end with death.

Major Weir

The ghost of Major Weir is said to haunt the West Bow in Edinburgh still. He was executed after confessing to witchcraft, but following his death, the sounds that were said to emanate from his house before it was ultimately demolished were not those of tortured wailing or lament—they were the sounds of wild merrymaking. His earthly demise may have been most unpleasant, but his ghost, it would seem, was still having quite a good time of it.

Burns's deil and other stories

Robert Burns' famous narrative poem *Tam o' Shanter* portrays the devil as:

> ——in shape o' beast
> A towsy tyke, black, grim and large

Burns' devil plays the pipes with gusto as the scantily clad witches dance around him with wild abandon. Tam fears for his life, and indeed his soul, when he comes upon the scene and sees the witches cavorting with the spirits of unchristened children and criminals. But in spite of himself he feels drawn to the sight. The devil and his entourage are having fun!

Other stories of the devil and his encounters with mortals tell of the devil being outdone, not so much by piety or the power of God as by sheer ingenuity. One particular legend that has been told of such a battle of wits between a mortal and the devil has been associated in slightly different versions with Michael Scott, the notorious thirteenth-century philosopher (some would say sorcerer), Lord Reay and another anonymous man. The stories differ only in detail; the essence is the same.

The devil has had encounters with the hero of the story before and is looking for a way to torment him. He gives the hero the use of one of his demonic servants to work for him at whichever tasks the hero chooses. The demonic worker is then set a variety of enormous tasks to carry out (bridge-building, barn-building, etc) and completes each task in record time, returning again and again for more work and giving the hero no peace. The hero finally hits upon a plan and instructs his tormentor to go down to the beach and construct a rope of sand. The demonic worker is then condemned to work forever at this impossible task. No sooner has something resembling a rope been made than the tide comes in and washes it away. The devil has been defeated once again.

The fear of the devil amongst the Scots, therefore, can be seen to have been counterbalanced by a certain amount of humor, and also, perhaps, a little envy. Nor is it always the case that those who have associated with the Evil One in life are seen to suffer for it after death. Ghosts with demonic associations are not necessarily unhappy ghosts, it would appear.

The demon crab

The devil appeared as many things. People saw him in the form of animals and strange monsters as well as in human form. Whenever something mysterious or sinister happened, signs of the devil were sought in case the events might be his work. One particular tale from Dundee illustrates quite well that no matter how ready mere mortals were to see Auld Nick, they were not always right in what they saw.

A tragedy had occurred—a brave ferryman had been caught with his boat in a squall and the boat had gone down with all its passengers. Some time later, when the storm had finally subsided, the body of the ferryman was washed up ashore, just in front of the cottage where he had lived. The body was pulled into the cottage and laid out carefully in order that the locals might come and pay their respects. There was quite a crowd gathered. They stood in respectful silence as they looked at the bedraggled corpse of the drowned man.

Suddenly, someone saw a movement in the sleeve of the dead man's jacket. The crowd gave a gasp—the corpse was stirring! The corpse, however, lay quite still, and out of the sleeve crawled an enormous black crab. To the superstitious fisherfolk present, the crab could be only one thing—the devil himself! Everyone jumped back as the satanic beast scuttled across the floor of the cottage and made for the door. A path was quickly cleared to let the crab move on towards the sea—no one dared impede the progress of the devil!

At that moment an elderly fishwife stepped forward, scooped up the crab and tucked it securely in her pinny. Much to everyone's horror, she announced that it was a meal too good to waste. Stories flew here and there for many days afterwards about the terrible smells that issued from the fishwife's cottage as she cooked the crab. Some people even claimed to have seen a beastly black form flying out of the cottage as the fishwife put the crab in the pot to boil. In spite of the conjectures and rumors, however, no one could deny the fact that the fishwife ate the crab, enjoyed it, and came to no harm from the experience. People might have been reluctant to admit it, but it seemed that they had got it wrong about the Demon Crab.

Death and Dying: Ghostly Hordes and Phantom Lights

MANY superstitions survive to this day concerning the dead and the dying in Scotland. They have their origins in times when people were much more familiar with death, particularly premature death, than they are nowadays, when the country is no longer torn by war and internal feuding and when medical science is able to ensure that most of us at least survive into old age.

The custom of sitting up with a corpse before the funeral—the wake, or lykewake—has its origins in the belief that the body of the dead person needed protection from unwanted spiritual interference before it was given a proper burial. In the past there were several symbolic rites associated with the wake, intended to protect the spirit of the dead and send it safely to the afterlife, and also to protect those who remained living.

Those who sat up with the body at night were provided with a bible, a candle, whisky and food. In some parts of the country it was tradition that there was to be no fire lit in the room in which the corpse lay. The spirit of the dead person was in danger of being interfered with by the forces of evil and therefore no chances were taken with the corpse awaiting burial. Domestic animals were kept well away; if a cat or a dog passed over the body it had to be killed. Mirrors in the room were covered up, and if there was a clock in the room, it had to be stopped.

Those who sat up at night with the corpse had to remain there until daylight. If they left in the dark, it was believed that they might witness something fearful.

When the corpse had been laid out, a wooden platter was placed on its chest. On the platter was placed a small pile of earth—symbolic of the body—and another of salt—the spirit, which lived on after death. Sometimes only a small pile of salt was placed on the body.

In spite of all the precautions that were taken to ensure the safety of the dead person's spirit and the souls of those who had come to keep the corpse company, the lykewake was not always mournful by any means. It could be quite a social occasion. In some parts, the long night was whiled away with storytelling and singing—even dancing was not unknown.

Signs of Death

Signs of approaching death were many. Individual stories of people who have witnessed some of these signs are told in another chapter, Signs, Prophecies and Curses (*see* page 356). The gift (or curse) of second sight has often revealed itself for the first (sometimes the only) time when somebody has seen, or dreamt, of an imminent death. Many other stories record ghostly happenings or sights that then turn out to have been warnings of death. Some of these occurrences are very individual in nature, but there are others that have come to be accepted widely as death warnings, communications from the realm of the dead to the land of the living through a living medium.

Death Lights

Sightings of death lights, or death candles as they were

often known, were quite commonly reported. These were lights that were seen in graveyards, close to the sickbed of a dying person or near the site of an imminent death or disaster. Thus an unfamiliar light seen on water was believed to foretell a drowning or a tragedy at sea, and a light above a house meant that death would take place therein before long.

Ghostly lights, similar to death lights, have often been reported shining at the sites of tragedies, in particular ancient battlefields. Rather than warnings of death to come, these lights seem to be markers or reminders of death that has gone before.

Ghosts of the Living

A ghostly figure of a person still alive might be seen alongside that person or sometimes in another place. This was taken to be an ominous sign. Death was not far away.

Phantom Funerals

Phantom funerals, causing surprise and distress to those who witnessed them, were relatively common supernatural occurrences. Sometimes reports of such funerals record the witness as having merely seen and heard such a ghostly procession. However, there are stories of people who have been pushed aside in the roadway as the phantom mourners make their way past. To witness such an event was never a good sign.

One story of a phantom funeral comes from the fishing town of Wick in the north of Scotland. The story tells how a crofter from Wick was visited every year by his cousin, who was a fisherman and came to the port for the herring run. While his fishing boat was based at Wick, he would spend his spare time at the crofter's house. The two men got along famously in spite of their different lifestyles.

One particular year, the fisherman was preparing to set sail for home after a successful season with the herring fishing. His cousin, although not a fisherman, still had a healthy respect for the sea and his farming experience had given him a keen eye for the weather. He felt that the weather was about to take a turn for the worse and urged the fisherman to stay a little longer in Wick. His time there had shown him a healthy profit—what was the hurry?

The fisherman brushed aside the concerns of his cousin and laughed off any suggestion that the weather was too dangerous to go to sea. He was an experienced seaman and his boat was sturdy enough to withstand any squall. He bade goodbye to his crofter cousin and set off.

During the day, the weather turned worse, just as the crofter had suspected it would. The crofter had spent the afternoon visiting a family some way from his own home and when he saw the skies darken, he decided he had better make his way back.

The weather turned very wild with alarming speed and a fierce storm was blowing as the crofter trudged home, battling against the gale. He was halfway home when he saw a strange sight—three men carrying a coffin in the direction of the graveyard.

It seemed a small number of people for a funeral procession—perhaps the bad weather was keeping the mourners away. Curiosity overcame the crofter, and he followed the somber procession to the cemetery. The three men stopped and put the coffin on the ground for a moment or two. Approaching the silent group, the crofter leaned over the coffin for a closer look. He could just make out the name that was engraved on the brass plate on top. It was his cousin's name. The crofter then looked up at the three coffin-bearers. Their faces were all too grimly familiar—they were the faces of three other men from Wick who had been lost at sea within the last year.

The crofter made for home with dread in his heart. When the news reached him some days later that his cousin had drowned after falling overboard in the storm, he was not surprised at all. He had already learnt of his cousin's fate, the night when he had seen the phantom funeral.

Canine Sense

Dogs are still widely believed to be able to see what many human beings cannot. They are thought to be sensitive to supernatural presences and will often show signs of fear and distress before any human being has realized that anything is amiss. Dogs can sense the presence of ghosts. In times gone by, a dog howling in the night for no other apparent reason would often be taken as a sign of approaching death. Some people believed that a dog howling like this should be able to indicate, by pointing, the direction in which the death would take place.

Birds

Birds, both domestic and wild, were believed be "tuned in" to the world of the supernatural and were said to be able to foretell death. Poultry were observed with apprehension in some places in Scotland. A cockerel crowing uncharacteristically in the hours of darkness was thought to mean the approach of death somewhere in the vicinity. Hens showing signs of fear and panic in spite of the absence of any predator in the vicinity were often believed to be foretelling doom for someone close by.

If a raven flew in front of someone along the road that he or she was taking, it was believed to be a bad sign—death was not far away for that person. Birds tapping on the window of a house were an equally unfortunate sign, as was a seagull standing on one leg on the roof of a house.

Death in Foreign Lands

Oh, ye'll tak the High Road, and
 I'll tak the Low Road
And I'll be in Scotland afore ye;
For me and my true love will never
 meet again
On the bonnie, bonnie banks of
 Loch Lomond.

The lines above, the chorus of a song nowadays more often sung raucously (or drunkenly) than mournfully, reflect another belief about the spirits of the dead. The song is thought to have been written around the time of the Rebellion of the '45. In 1745, some supporters of Bonnie Prince Charlie, retreating from England, were captured by the English. The words of the song are the words of one soldier who faces execution to another who is to be freed. The soldier who is about to die tells his friend that he will take the "Low Road" back to Scotland. The Low Road was the name of a spiritual path that was believed to exist along which the spirits of those who died far from home could return to the place of their birth. The Low Road would speed the executed soldier to Scotland faster than his compatriot, who faced many miles of hard marching, but although he might return to his homeland swiftly enough after death, he would never meet with his sweetheart again.

Phantom Hordes

The dead were never far away. Whatever happened to their bodies, the spirits of those who had died had to go somewhere. Whilst some spiritual presences were believed to be benign, inevitably there were many fears about spirits of the dead who wished harm upon the living. Superstition about such malevolent forces was prevalent throughout Scotland.

The realm of the dead was seen in much the same way as the realm of the fairies. Living persons could be spirited away to either realm, either temporarily or permanently. Those who claimed to have gone through such an experience were usually greatly changed by it. In common with stories of visits to the fairy realm, tales of being spirited away by the dead indicated that time in the realm of the dead was different from earthly time. Great distances were traveled in no time at all, and although several hours, or even days, might seem to pass, the person who had been spirited away, once safely back in the land of mortals, would discover that his or her absence had been very brief in earthly time.

The Sluagh, or host of the dead, was greatly feared in the Highlands. The sight and sound of their grim parades through the realms of the living struck terror into the hearts of those who witnessed them. The Sluagh could bring death to those in its path. Those of a superstitious nature would not leave a window on the west side of the house open at night. To do so was to court disaster, for the Sluagh could then enter and cause trouble.

Poltergeists

POLTERGEISTS are a well-documented phenomenon world-wide. Whether or not they are ghosts as such is a matter of some debate. They are not generally associated with any particular person who has gone into the hereafter. Their activities are generally short-lived, the hauntings of a poltergeist not going on indefinitely. Instead, there is generally a period of some weeks or months when activity is particularly troublesome. After this time, the poltergeist will disappear or at least cease its activities.

Poltergeists are closely associated with adolescents, especially troubled children. The appearance of a poltergeist will often coincide with a time of particular trauma for a teenager in the household, whether the trouble be of a serious nature or the usual adolescent angst.

There have been many reported incidents of poltergeist activity throughout Scotland.

Andrew Mackie's House

Perhaps the most famous poltergeist is that which came to haunt the house of Andrew Mackie, a farmer in Ringcroft of Stocking, Kirkcudbrightshire. This story is particularly unusual because it was documented in great detail at the time by a local minister who was very much involved in the whole affair, the Reverend Andrew Telfair. His report is backed up by the testimony of several witnesses, amongst whom are other members of the clergy.

The story dates back three hundred years to the end of the seventeenth century when, inexplicably, the family of Andrew

Mackie began to be tormented by some sort of devilish spirit. The haunting lasted for a period of some three months.

The strange events began one night in February 1695, when Andrew Mackie went out to check on his cattle. When he got to the byre, he found all the beasts running loose. A little puzzled, he tied them up carefully before retiring for the night. Next morning, however, when he went to attend to them, he found that they had become untethered once more. The next night, the same thing happened again. Andrew tied his beasts with even extra care, only to find them let loose, how he knew not, by the next morning. The next morning again he found one of his cattle suspended from the roof of the cow shed by its tether.

The odd happenings in the cow shed then began to be followed up by disturbances in the house. One night, a basket full of peat that had been standing outside found its way into the house as the family slept. The basket was upturned, and the peat was piled up in a heap in the middle of the house. Somehow, the peat had been set alight. Fortunately the family was wakened by the smell of smoke and disaster was averted.

There then followed a period in the month of March when the house was bombarded by stones. The stones came from no one knew where; no one seemed to be throwing them. At first, the odd small stone was seen to fly through the air outside the house. Gradually, the stones increased in size and number, hurled by some unseen force around the house, hitting the building and its occupants.

The disturbances continued—kitchen implements, furniture and bedding were inexplicably moved, turning up in the strangest of places. On one occasion a child of the family was alarmed to see a figure huddled in his blanket in the corner of the room, close to the fire. When someone had plucked up the courage to investigate and pulled the blanket back, it was found that it was not a person under the cover but an upturned stool.

The flying stones became bigger and better in their aim; the members of the family were being knocked and bruised by them and neighbors coming to call were similarly assaulted.

The house was continually disrupted by bangs, knockings, furniture moving and doors slamming. Over time, the family observed that the activities of this strange spirit, if spirit it was, were more frantic on Sundays or at times when the members of the family were praying together.

As the trouble escalated, the family called in Reverend Telfair. He led the family in prayers, but as soon as he left the house, the stone-throwing resumed. Things calmed down in the following few days, but the next Sabbath saw an increase in the stone-throwing. Reverend Telfair offered to spend the night with the family. The spirit rewarded his efforts with more frantic activity. Telfair himself was struck by stones and a stick. Furniture made strange noises; objects flew at people across the room.

As Telfair knelt in prayer, he felt something on his arm and looking down, saw a ghostly white hand at his wrist.

In the following days, the spirit continued to vent its anger. People were hurled across rooms in the house, scratched, had their hair pulled and were beaten with sticks. The stone-throwing continued relentlessly. The children had their covers torn off them as they lay in their beds. Then they were beaten about the hips by an invisible hand.

The spirit began to make itself heard. As the family were praying, they heard a voice saying, "Whist! Whist!"

The torment continued unabated until April, and the bravery and tenacity of the family must have been considerable, for they remained in the house in spite of it all. In April, Telfair sought the assistance of his fellow clergy, and two ministers, Andrew Ewart and John Murdo, from Kells and Crossmichael respectively, joined the Mackie family in prayer one night. The ministers suffered considerable pains for their efforts; huge stones were flung at them both and they were beaten with sticks. The whole house was in more turmoil than ever. Fires began to break out.

One day, Andrew Mackie's wife was stepping into the yard when she noticed that a stone slab in the doorway was loose. She lifted the slab and found some bones and bloody flesh underneath, wrapped in cloth. She took the bones from the house to the landlord's house, quite some distance away, thinking that the trouble might in some way be associated with the bones. In her absence, the trouble in the house only increased. The children found burning hot stones in their beds. Fireballs flew around. The stone-throwing was worse than ever. Mrs Mackie returned the bones to the house. The Reverend Telfair prayed over the bones and was beaten severely with a stick.

And so it went on. Then something happened that made all concerned wonder whether there was something in the house's past to cause the spiritual disturbances. One day, Andrew Mackie found a note, written in blood, or so it appeared, close to his house.

> "3 Years thou shall have to repent a nett it well," the note read: "Wo be to thee Scotland Repent and tak warning for the doors of haven ar all Redy bart against thee, I am sent for a warning to thee to flee to God yet troublt shall this man be for twenty days repent repent repent Scotland or else thou shall."

Was there a connection between the bones and the message? Had there been a murder in the house? The house was not old; it had been built only twenty-eight years before. An investigation into the past history of the building ought not to be difficult. Accordingly, all previous occupants were brought before a committee consisting of Andrew Telfair, the landlord, Charles Maclellan, and others. They were all asked to touch the bones. Nothing untoward occurred, so the committee sent the bones to Kirkcudbright for examination by an assembly of ministers. Five ministers were then dispatched to Andrew Mackie's house to pray. The spirit, angered as ever by religious intrusion, flew into a fury. Stones broke through the roof of the house, and the whole building seemed to shake. Telfair details some of the spirit's activities as follows:

> It brake down the barne door and mid-wall and
> threw stones up the house; But it did no great
> hurt: it gripped, and handled the legs of some,
> as with a man's hand; it hoisted up the feet of
> others while standing on the ground, thus it
> did to William Lennox of Mill-House, my self
> and others, in this manner it continued till ten
> a clock at night.

The ministers persisted for three days, but the spirit would not give in to their prayers. Other people from the district joined in the effort. At one point a neighbor appeared with his dog. The dog had killed a polecat on the way to the Mackie's house and the visitor threw the dead creature in a corner of the room before joining in the prayers. Three more people arrived and were very distressed when the spirit picked up the dead animal and beat them about the heads and bodies with its carcass. One of the visitors felt something like a hand inside his clothes and pockets and became so distraught that he was sick.

The following Sabbath brought even more upset. The spirit whispered and whistled and cried out at the family in prayer. The family and friends and neighbors were injured with stones and sticks. Praying men were lifted off their knees by the unseen force.

Two days later, on 16 April, the Mackie family had had enough. They decided to move out of the house for a while. Five of their neighbors volunteered to stay in the house in the Mackies' absence. Strangely, the trouble in the house stopped and the guests were not bothered by the spirit at all. Outside, however, the cattle were found to have broken loose from their tethers, and some appeared to have been disturbed.

Thinking that things might be improving, some members of the family moved back in after a couple of days. They spent one peaceful night, but in the morning found that the sheep had been tied together in pairs by tethers fashioned from straw that had been taken from the stable. After two reasonably quiet days, the spirit started again, with a vengeance. The beating and stone-throwing began again, and lumps of peat were thrown along with the stones. The spirit whistled and called out, "Take you that!" as it beat its victims. All present continued with their prayers, but the harder they prayed, the more they suffered.

Andrew Mackie was snatching a few hours of sleep when he was woken by the voice of the spirit: "Thou shalt be troubled till Tuesday," it said.

Mackie decided to try to talk to the spirit.

"Who gave thee a commission?" he asked.

"God gave me a commission," was the reply, "and I am sent to warn the land to repent, for a judgement is to come if the land do not quickly repent and I will return a hundred times worse upon every family in the land. Praise me and I will whistle to you; worship me and I will trouble you no more."

Mackie prayed for deliverance from Satan. The spirit's reaction was contemptuous: "You might as well have said Shadrach, Meshach and Abednego."

Several people heard the conversation between Andrew Mackie and the spirit. One of the company attempted to intervene, but the spirit would not countenance this, dismissing the man for meddling in other people's business. When the spirit became silent once more, the family was no further forward.

The next day, there were seven fires around the house started by the spirit, and the family and neighbors were kept hard at work all day extinguishing them. The spirit appeared to be frustrated at the success of their efforts and began to tear down one of the house walls. The family was forced to take refuge in a barn. As they tried to get some rest, the spirit raised a great block of wood in the air above the heads of the children. "If I had a commission I would brain them!" it cried angrily.

The fire-raising and the exhausting task of keeping the fires under control continued all the following day. Mackie was in the barn when the spirit spoke to him again.

"Andrew. Andrew."

Mackie tried to ignore the voice.

"Speak!" commanded the spirit.

Andrew would not speak.

The spirit spoke again, in a calmer tone: "Be not troubled. You shall have no more trouble, except some casting of stones upon Tuesday to fulfil the promise."

Telfair, Maclellan and some others joined the family late that night in the house and stayed there for some hours. Apart from some stone-throwing, all was quiet.

On Tuesday, the day upon which the spirit had said it would stop its troubles, the Mackie family and others gathered in the barn to pray. Mackie was the first to catch sight of a black thing in the corner of the building. The thing grew, and it seemed as if it might fill the whole barn with its presence. It was like a huge, black storm cloud. Chaff and mud flew out of the cloud at the terrified onlookers, who then felt themselves being gripped painfully hard around the arms and bodies by the blackness itself. Then the blackness subsided. Everything returned to normal. A quiet night followed.

On the last Wednesday, 1 May, there was one final fire. A sheep house was destroyed, but neither people nor animals were hurt in any way. The disturbances at Ringcroft of Stocking were finally over, and no one was the wiser as to what had caused them.

There were some theories as to what might have triggered the trouble. Reverend Telfair put three of these forward in his account of the happenings.

Some years before the house was occupied by the Mackie family, it was the home of a man called McNaught. McNaught was a miserable soul. Desperately poor and in frail health, he wondered if some evil force might have taken ill against him. He had sent his son to ask the advice of a spae-wife, or fortune-teller, some distance away. His son had gone to see the woman but had met some soldiers on his way home, enlisted and gone abroad. He finally sent a message back to Ringcroft relating the spae-wife's advice. Under a slab at the threshold of the house could be found a tooth. When the tooth was removed and burnt, good fortune would return to the house. The message got back to Ringcroft too late, however, for Mr McNaught was dead.

The new tenant of the house, a man called Thomas Telfair (no relation of Reverend Telfair), heard of the spae-wife's words, lifted the stone, found a tooth and burned it. He had had no trouble whilst in the house. Perhaps McNaught's misery, Telfair's trouble-free tenancy and Andrew Mackie's troubles were somehow linked.

A second theory concerned the death of a woman of ill-repute whose belongings had been left in the house after she died. Perhaps the Mackies had taken the things for themselves? Mackie denied this strongly, saying that the woman's things, carefully tied in a bundle, had been returned to her nearest and dearest intact.

The third theory was dismissed outright by Telfair, who knew Andrew Mackie to be a good, God-fearing citizen. The theory was that Mackie, when he became a mason, had dedicated his first child to the devil.

The strange occurrences have sparked off many a lively debate in the years that have followed, but no one has come any closer to finding out what it was that tormented the family of Andrew Mackie for three terrible months in 1695. Why it caused so much trouble is just as much of a mystery and will no doubt remain so.

The Devil of Glenluce

Forty years before the astonishing catalogue of events at Ringcroft of Stocking, the household of Gilbert Campbell, a weaver in Glenluce, was disrupted by a similar presence. This story is more typical of poltergeist activity than that of Andrew Mackie's house, in that the spirit appeared to be closely connected to the children in the family, in particular to Campbell's son, a young student at Glasgow University.

The first indication of trouble to come was given when Campbell's daughter, Jennet, began to complain of strange noises in her ears. The noises were shrill, like whistling. Then

Jennet was heard to utter the words of some unseen spirit: "I'll cast thee, Jennet, into the well."

After that, the house was subjected to continual bombardment with stones. Clothing was hurled from drawers, clothes were ripped to shreds, sleepers were woken as the bedclothes were dragged off them by an invisible force.

Much alarmed, Campbell moved his children out of the house for their own safety. The disturbances ceased as soon as the children had gone. The children moved back into the house with the exception of the eldest son, who was studying in Glasgow. For a while things were quiet, but then Campbell's son returned to the house and the trouble started again with renewed vigor. Stones were hurled around, belongings were damaged, and at one point the house caught fire.

The affair caught the attention of the church, and various attempts were made by ministers to exorcise the spirit. The spirit was apparently quite communicative and claimed to have Campbell's son in its power. It claimed to have been sent by Satan from hell to torment the occupants of the house.

While the spirit was willing to communicate with the religious men, it was nevertheless resistant to all their attempts to banish it from the house. It continued to torment the family, beating the children as they lay in their beds, starting fires around the house, hiding the family's belongings or hurling them through the air.

The family showed remarkable courage, remaining in the house throughout all this. Then, without warning, the activities of the malevolent force stopped, and the family was left in peace.

Although no one could be certain as to the cause of the fearful disturbances, one theory connects them to a beggar who had turned up at Campbell's house some time previously. Campbell had sent him away without giving him a penny, and the beggar had angrily threatened to avenge this cold-hearted treatment. It was said that the man was a certain Alexander Agnew, who was eventually accused of crimes against the church and was hanged some miles away in Dumfries. His death apparently coincided with the sudden return to harmony at Campbell's house in Glenluce.

The Poltergeist of Sauchie

A much more recent case of poltergeist activity was that which concerned a young girl called Virginia Campbell who lived in the village of Sauchie in Clackmannanshire. The story caused quite a sensation in 1960–61.

The child had moved to Scotland from Ireland with her parents, and by all appearances was a normal, bright little girl. The move to Scotland might have been more traumatic for Virginia than people around her had realized. Perhaps this, along with the fact that she was at a vulnerable age—she was eleven at the time—accounted for the strange occurrences that took place when she was around.

The strange events started in the child's home. Unexplained knocking noises were heard when she was around, and objects, even surprisingly heavy ones, were seen to move. The child herself was very distressed by what was happening. Her mother kept her home from school and called the doctor, who prescribed tranquillizers. Virginia seemed calmer, but the strange things went on happening. The doctor had some idea that what they were witnessing might be poltergeist activity. In order to try to eliminate this possibility, Virginia was sent to stay the night with relatives, but the strange events went with her. She was clearly the focus of some sort of paranormal activity. After a couple of weeks, things began to calm down, and it was decided that she should return to school.

Virginia's mother told teachers at the school that odd things were happening at home. Objects were moving; some were flying through the air. It all seemed too strange to be true, but initial skepticism on the part of the teachers soon disappeared when similar things began to happen around Virginia at school. Her desk rose inches from the floor. Other children in her class noticed objects moving from place to place. Once, a door refused to shut behind her. Heavy furniture could be seen to move. Although the activities were less violent in nature than had been witnessed in Virginia's home, they were still happening.

Over the next few months, it became more and more difficult to safeguard the child from the morbid interest of the press. The stories that were circulated were sometimes only tenuously linked to the facts. Surprisingly, the other children in the school were much less hysterical than outsiders in their reactions to events. They became quite matter-of-fact about the situation; when Virginia was around, sometimes things moved—simple as that.

The strange happenings became less and less frequent over time, and after a few months they had stopped altogether.

A Haunted Capital

EDINBURGH is a beautiful city, of that there can be no doubt. Dubbed the "Athens of the North" because of the number of classical style buildings it boasts in its graceful Georgian New Town, it also has a proud and ancient castle and a stunning palace that is still a royal residence. Clustered round the Royal Mile, the street that stretches downhill west to east from Edinburgh Castle to the Palace of Holyroodhouse, are the remains of the Old Town, higgledy-piggledy tenements and closes, along with the Canongate, the Grassmarket and the West Bow, all steeped in history and, so we are told, heavily populated by ghostly presences. Edinburgh has seen it all in its time—conflict and siege, plague and fire, murder, intrigue and witchcraft. Seedy and gruesome characters from the past provide a wealth of great material for tourist guides. It must be a joy to have stories about body-snatchers, witch trials and particularly cruel executions to relate to your audience as you stroll the streets of the city with a crowd of visitors. There is enough to tell based on historical fact alone to keep an audience spellbound, but wise tourist guides will know their ghosts as well. There are plenty of them, after all, and their stories add to the thrill of the place. Visitors to Edinburgh can now choose to scare themselves silly on guided tours that specifically concentrate on the horrors of the past and the ghouls that are said to lurk in their wake.Ghosts can make good money for the entrepreneur, but their manifestations were first recorded long before ghost tours were even thought of, and some of the stories have been passed down through several generations. How did the stories start? Do the ghosts exist? It is left to the individual to decide, for neither the skeptic nor the believer can prove to each other unequivocally whether or not the ghosts do exist.

Edinburgh's ghosts are not all ancient. Things continue to happen in places in and around the town that cannot be explained. The catalogue of reports of supernatural phenomena continues to grow. What is it all about? Is it all hysteria, sensationalism, superstitious nonsense? Is there a rational explanation for everything? The debate will probably never reach a conclusion. Meanwhile, stories of Edinburgh's ghosts will continue to keep children from sleeping soundly and make people stop in their tracks on dark nights in dim cobbled streets—is there anybody there?

Ann Street—The Return of Mr Swan

Ann Street is a particularly beautiful and desirable place to live in the heart of Georgian Edinburgh. At the end of the nineteenth century, one of the houses in the street was home to the Swan family. An uncle of the family was a great traveler, and the family was used to receiving letters from far-flung places describing his latest exploits. The traveler would take off for months at a time but would always keep in touch by mail and would appear from time to time, sometimes without warning, to draw breath between his adventures.

One evening the family was particularly surprised to see Mr Swan appear in their midst. They had expected him to be far away at sea, but they were delighted all the same. They rose to greet him as he strolled in through the front door, but before they had time to make him welcome, Mr Swan merely smiled at them, waved and disappeared. It was the oddest thing. The family was left to ponder the strange occurrence for some weeks until news finally reached them that Mr Swan had drowned when the ship in which he had been traveling to some distant place had sunk. The time of his death coincided with his mysterious appearance in the family home. His "visit" had apparently been a wish to keep in touch with his nearest and dearest in death just as he had in life.

Mr Swan still returns to his old family home in Ann Street. Far from being a malevolent figure, it is said that he is very much a friendly ghost, popping in to say hello.

Charlotte Square—A Ghostly Piano

Charlotte Square in the west end of the city is a busy place and is for the most part taken up with offices. But in amongst the hustle and bustle of city life, through the continual noise of the passing traffic, another sound can sometimes be heard—that of ghostly piano playing.

Corstorphine—The Haunted Sycamore Tree

Nothing remains of Corstorphine Castle apart from the ancient dovecot that stands near the east end of Dovecot Road in Corstorphine, a suburb on the northwest side of Edinburgh. The castle was destroyed in the eighteenth century. Beside the dovecot once stood an old, gnarled sycamore tree, the last of an avenue of trees that led westwards towards the castle. The tree, diseased and fragile, was carefully preserved as a well-loved historical landmark by the Corstorphine Trust until it finally gave way during a storm on the night of 26 December, 1998. The trunk snapped in two leaving nothing standing but a jagged stump.

The story of the Corstorphine sycamore and the White Lady who haunts it, is familiar to all in the district, young and old alike.

In the seventeenth century, when the castle of Corstorphine

was still standing, it was inhabited by the Forrester family, who owned most of the land in the surrounding area. The laird at the time, one James Forrester, was a charismatic man, whose overindulgence in alcohol and whose liking for a pretty face and curving figure were well known but, on the whole, forgiven on account of his great charm.

Laird James became embroiled in a passionate affair with a married woman, Christian Nimmo. The lovers were forced to meet in secret, which must have added both a great deal of excitement and a certain amount of tension to the liaison. One such meeting, in the shadows of the dovecot beside the sycamore tree, was destined to be their final. It began with a passionate embrace and ended in a murder.

When Christian Nimmo arrived at their appointed meeting place, Sir James was not there, but Christian knew his habits all too well and sent one of her servants to the Black Bull Inn nearby to seek him out. The laird was found in the inn, as anticipated, and he finally came to meet her by the sycamore tree. He had been drinking heavily, and Christian Nimmo, angered by his inconsiderate and objectionable behavior, began to quarrel with him. The dispute swiftly took on frightening proportions until suddenly, seized by a fit of uncontrollable rage, the lady pulled her lover's sword from its scabbard by his side and plunged it into him. She escaped from justice initially but was eventually hunted down and taken to meet her end at the hands of the executioner. Her ghost, dressed all in white, haunts the area around the dovecot still, the bloody sword in her hand giving evidence of the dreadful consequences of her temper.

Dalry—The One=Armed Ghost of John Chiesly

This ghostly figure was known as "Johnny One-Arm" to the

people around Dalry in Edinburgh. He haunted the streets of the area, scaring grown-ups and children alike, for more than three hundred years.

John Chiesly lived in the middle of the sixteenth century, an unhappily married man until he finally sought a divorce from his wife in 1688. He then became an unhappily divorced man. The Lord President of the Court of Session, Sir George Lockhart, had pronounced that John Chiesly should pay his wife a substantial sum annually in settlement. Feeling the sum awarded to be entirely unreasonable, being out of all proportion both to his wife's needs and his own means, John Chiesly decided to vent his anger upon Sir George. He followed him to church one Sunday morning and, catching up with him in Old Bank Close, he shot him. Sir George died, and the full weight of the law descended upon John Chiesly. He was tortured cruelly to establish whether he had acted alone or with the help of others. Then his right arm was cut off while he was still alive as fitting punishment for its part in the crime—his right hand had held the murder weapon. Finally, John Chiesly was taken to the gallows and hanged. His body was left hanging on the gallows as an example and a gruesome warning to all. Then someone—nobody knew who—took the body down and secreted it away. Had it been buried? Nobody could, or would, tell.

Ghostly happenings began to be reported in Dalry. Several people reported seeing the anguished figure of a man in the streets around the area. The ghost had one arm missing. It screamed. It laughed maniacally. It gave the neighboring children nightmares. The ghost appeared, again and again, over the next three hundred years.

In 1965, builders started work in a cottage in Dalry. On removing part of the floor they were surprised to find the skeleton of a man. The skeleton was cracked and broken, as one would expect the skeleton of a tortured man to be. Most significantly, however, the skeleton had only one hand. It could only be John Chiesly. The remains were removed from the house and re-interred in another place. The streets of Dalry are at peace now, for Johnny One-Arm no longer has cause to haunt them.

Edinburgh Castle—Phantom Musicians

Edinburgh Castle has seen more than its fair share of drama and tragedy over the centuries. No doubt there are more ghostly tales to be told about the fortress that stands so proudly on the rock above the city, but the two most famous stories concern a phantom piper and a (sometimes headless) drummer. Both are fitting tales to tell about Edinburgh Castle—the sound of pipes and drums is inextricably linked with the castle in modern times, for it is the venue of the world-famous Edinburgh Military Tattoo, in which massed bands from regiments all over the world thrill audiences of several hundred a night for three weeks every year.

The Phantom Piper

Edinburgh Castle has seen many alterations and additions since it first came into being as a fortified stronghold. The oldest surviving building on Castle Rock is St Margaret's Chapel, built in the twelfth century, but over the following centuries walls, ramparts, vaults, batteries and a cluster of buildings with both grand and prosaic functions were added until the whole finally came to resemble the castle as people can see it today, complete with a modern visitor center.

The story goes that in the course of some of these building works (although no one seems sure of when or for what purpose), workmen came upon the entrance to a tunnel that appeared to be leading down through Castle Rock, underneath the Royal Mile. In order to establish how long the tunnel was and where it went, a piper was dispatched to walk as far as he could, playing his pipes as he went, thereby allowing those who remained above ground to follow the sounds of his music and trace the tunnel's route.

It seemed like a good plan at the time. The piper set off, and the people above waited and listened. The sound of playing bagpipes could be heard, albeit faintly, and the sound was moving down the Royal Mile, much as everybody had expected it would. The people above ground kept listening and following the sound. Suddenly, getting towards halfway down the Royal Mile, the piping stopped. There seems to be no record of anybody having gone to look for the hapless piper; perhaps they were all too scared. Rather than take the investigations any further, it was decided to seal the tunnel once more and forget all about it. To this day, it is said, if you listen hard enough above the sounds of the traffic on the stretch of the Royal Mile that leads from Edinburgh Castle to South Bridge, you might just hear the sound of subterranean bagpipe music, for the ghost of the piper still plays in the tunnel below the street.

The phantom piper at Edinburgh Castle is not unique. Elsewhere in Scotland, according to legend, the sound of ghostly bagpipes can be heard in more than one other place, hidden below the earth. *(See* Ghostly Castles—Gight Castle, page 92.)

The Ghostly Drummer

The story of the drummer at Edinburgh Castle appears to date from the middle of the seventeenth century. Soldiers were garrisoned at the castle under the command of the governor at the time, Colonel Walter Dundas. One night the sentry on guard duty was startled by the sound of a military drum being played. On looking up, he saw a drummer marching on the battlements, beating out a warning of impending attack. The sentry fired his musket and raised the alarm. When others came to his aid, nothing could be seen or heard of the drummer, and the sentry was locked up, suspected of being under the influence of drink while on duty. On subsequent nights, however, the drummer was seen again by different sentries and was heard playing his drum by the governor of the Castle himself. The drummer was obviously a specter of some sort, but no one knew why the figure kept appearing.

Perhaps the drummer was trying to tell the occupants of the Castle something. Later that year, when the Castle was besieged by Cromwell's troops, the appearance of the ghostly drummer was perceived, with hindsight, to have been a warning of such an occurrence. To this day, there are claims that the drummer still appears from time to time, disturbing the peace of the night with the noise of his drumbeat. Some say the drummer is headless.

George Street—The Persistent Dressmaker

Edinburgh's George Street was for some years the haunt of a graceful lady dressed beautifully in old-fashioned clothes. Passers-by would often stop and stare, for she seemed quite real. Her appearances caused a great deal of consternation for a while. Who was this lady, so elegant but out-of-date? The figure would glide along the street, quite oblivious of other pedestrians. She would always head for the same shop, disappearing in the doorway.

It transpired that the ghostly lady was one Mademoiselle Jane Vernelt. The shop had once been hers—a dressmaker's business that she had been forced to give up on account of precarious mental health. She must have been sorry to leave it, for after her death her ghost kept trying to return.

Holyrood Palace—Memories of Murder

There are two well-known supernatural phenomena associated with the Palace of Holyroodhouse, which graces the foot of the Royal Mile. Both bear relation to Mary Queen of Scots.

The first concerns the Italian, David Rizzio, with whom the young queen formed a close friendship when she arrived in Scotland. Mary's new husband, Lord Darnley, did not approve of the friendship and became increasingly jealous of his wife's closeness to Rizzio. With the support of some of the most powerful of Scotland's nobility, Darnley plotted against Rizzio. One night in 1566, Darnley and some of his co-conspirators burst into Mary's private apartments, grabbed Rizzio and stabbed him brutally and repeatedly. After his death, attempts were made to clean the floor of his bloodstains, but these were unsuccessful. The stains reappeared again and again, no matter how often the floor was scrubbed. They can still, some say, be seen to this day.

Darnley, of course, met an unpleasant end himself when his house at Kirk o' Field was blown up barely a year after the murder of Rizzio. He also left his mark on the Palace of Holyroodhouse, albeit in a less colorful manner than Rizzio. In one of the rooms that Darnley frequented at Holyrood, the apartment where he entertained his visitors, strange shadows have been seen many a time by visitors and staff. It seems as if someone is still there, hovering about the room.

A Haunted Capital

Mary King's Close—Victims of the Plague

Edinburgh City Chambers, which stand on the Royal Mile, were built in the 1750s. Behind the City Chambers, the ground slopes steeply down towards The Mound and then to Princes Street. At either side of the City Chambers some closes of the Old Town still remain, their buildings clinging precariously to the steep slope. Beneath the City Chambers are the remains of another close, sixty-five yards or so of what was once a bustling, overcrowded street of traders in the early part of the seventeenth century. Hidden from the public eye for many years, the close is now a site for guided tours, which are proving to be popular with residents of the city and visitors alike.

Mary King's Close was particularly badly affected when plague hit Edinburgh in 1645. The plague was a horrifying disease. Scores of people died in the outbreak. Such was its severity that parliament moved from the capital city to Stirling. Attempts to isolate the sick and dying were largely fruitless, hygiene being poor or, some would say, non-existent. In the crammed dirty and rat-infested closes of Edinburgh the infection could spread rapidly. Desperate measures were called for to try to halt the rampaging disease, and one of these measures was to seal off Mary King's Close.

The plague passed, but the close remained sealed up. It would have remained uninhabited for ever, but some forty years later the need for accommodation in the already over-populated city center was becoming too pressing to ignore, so the city council gave its permission for the Close to be reopened. Some of the first residents were the family of Thomas Coltheart. Ignoring rumors of ghosts of the plague victims, the members of the family moved their belongings into one of the old houses, but they had hardly settled in before they found themselves regretting their decision. The atmosphere in their new home turned most unpleasant—spine-chillingly so. Then, all at once, a severed head appeared before the family, floating in mid-air. It was a grim, gray-haired, bearded old man—or at least, what was left of him.

This was the first of several apparitions. Over the coming days, the Colthearts were visited by a child's head, a severed arm and headless animals. At first, the family tried to pass these occurrences off as figments of imagination, but then stories began to circulate among other new residents to the close of strange happenings that bore a remarkable similarity to those in the Colthearts' home.

What happened after that is uncertain. Some say that the Colthearts fled in terror. Others say that they commanded the spirits to be at peace and then the family continued to live in the Close without further disturbance.

In later years, Mary King's Close was dreadfully damaged by fire. In 1753, work began on the City Chambers and the close ceased to exist. All the upper storeys and most of the buildings at ground level were demolished. All that remains is the small stretch beneath the offices above. But the ghost stories persist. Visitors and tour guides have heard strange noises, such as the noise of a small child crying. Some people have seen things. Quite a few visitors, unprompted, have spoken of seeing the figure of a little girl in one of the rooms. She is said to be small in stature, and dirty and dishevelled. Pustules, a sign of the plague, have been seen on her face. From time to time visitors who have seen the little girl or heard about her have left toys or sweets for her in a niche in the wall. As well as specific sightings such as this, there have been reports of visitors to Mary King's Close feeling "cold spots" in certain places. The specters of the past are still around.

A Haunted Capital

Number 17—The Room of Terror

Close to the Botanical Gardens, in a particularly attractive area of Edinburgh, is the site where once stood a row of houses, now demolished. One in particular, number 17, held a particularly gruesome secret.

Not long after the turn of the nineteenth century, when the house had lain empty for some years, it was bought by an enterprizing husband and wife who wanted to use it as a boarding house. But it was not long before they noticed that one of the attic rooms had a strange and unpleasant atmosphere. People were reluctant to enter the room, let alone use it. Sometimes it seemed as if there was something, or someone, in the room. On one particular occasion a young girl who had been employed to help with the housekeeping went into the attic room only to re-emerge at once, screaming hysterically. She collapsed with the shock of whatever she had seen and when revived could not be enticed to put into words what had terrified her so.

Word soon spread about the room in number 17, and students at the university began to dare each other to take up residence there. The young man who finally took up the dare was named Andrew Muir. It is said that, rather than taking on the challenge out of bravado, this particular young man was quite religious and was interested from a spiritual point of view. He approached the owners of the house and offered to spend a night in the room. Anxious to put an end to the rumors of something dreadful going on in their boarding house, the owners agreed. They gave Andrew Muir a bell, along with strict instructions to sound the alarm if he saw or heard anything out of the ordinary. Then they bade him goodnight and good luck. The other inhabitants of the house made themselves ready for bed and retired for the night, leaving Andrew Muir to keep his lonely vigil in the attic room.

They were all in bed asleep, and everything was quiet when all of a sudden they were woken by the noise of the bell and an accompanying scream of fear and horror. They all jumped from their beds and rushed upstairs to the attic to find out what had happened. When they opened the door of the attic room, a terrible sight met their eyes—Andrew Muir lay dead with the bell at his side. On his face was a look of abject terror. He had seen something so awful, it would appear, that the life had literally been frightened out of him. After that, the attic room was never used again. The house was demolished some twenty years later.

Victoria Terrace—The Sad Specter of Angus Roy

The story of Angus Roy is not one of dreadful deeds or sinister happenings. It is merely sad—the story of a man tormented and bullied to despair. Angus Roy was a sailor who lived at the beginning of the nineteenth century, serving on a ship that sailed out of the port of Leith. His sailing career was cruelly cut short by an accident from which he was lucky to have escaped with his life. He fell from the top of the ship's mast, and, although he miraculously survived, he was terribly badly injured. One leg was left virtually useless after the accident, dragging behind him as he limped along.

Angus came to live in Edinburgh's Victoria Terrace after his discharge from the merchant navy, but far from being able to live out what remained of his life in peace, he suffered continual torment at the hands of the local children. They teased and bullied him because of his disability, following him along the street, taunting him and calling him names. It was only after his death that Angus was able to exact some sort of revenge upon his tormentors. His ghost returned to haunt the area, a harmless specter but frightening enough to have the effect of making those who had mistreated him regret their behavior.

It is said that the sound of Angus Roy's damaged leg scraping along the ground behind him as he makes his way along the street is still heard from time to time around the area where he lived.

The West Bow—The Devilish Ghost of Major Weir

In the early part of the seventeenth century there lived in the West Bow of Edinburgh, along with his sister Grizel, one Major Thomas Weir. To all appearances, Major Weir was a worthy bachelor indeed—outwardly respectable, a veritable pillar of society. Deeply religious and knowledgeable about all things spiritual, he was a familiar figure at prayer meetings and gatherings, often playing a leading role. He was a large man of imposing appearance, and he was rarely seen without his "trademark," a black staff. He seemed to be so reliant upon this black staff that people began to speculate that perhaps it possessed some sort of magical or spiritual power. The speculations were dismissed as foolish rumor, idle and fanciful gossip. It served no good to speak of a pious man like Thomas Weir in such a way.

In 1670, however, Major Weir, for no reason that anyone could fathom, did something that sent waves of shock through Edinburgh and eventually sealed his own death warrant. He made a confession, one that would give credence to any malicious rumors that might have circulated about him, and much more. Accustomed to addressing religious gatherings, he stood up at one particular meeting and prepared to speak. When he did speak, it was not the prayers that they had been expecting that his audience heard. It was a catalogue of the most heinous and sinful deeds imaginable, especially offensive to those of religious leanings. Major Weir accused himself of having lived in an incestuous relationship with his sister for years. He told of sharing with his sister in knowledge and practise of witchcraft, satanic rituals and necromancy. He claimed to have consorted with the devil himself.

The first reaction of his stunned audience was to assume that the Major had taken leave of his senses. These were the ravings of a madman, surely! Doctors were consulted, priests were sought out for their advice, but Weir persisted. His stories were consistent and detailed. He could not and would not be ignored. Doctors finally pronounced Major Weir to be sane. There was no option but to believe his stories.

Major Weir and his sister were both executed for crimes of witchcraft. Major Weir was strangled and then burnt, a standard means of execution for condemned witches at the time. His black staff was burnt with him. Onlookers at the time were to report that the staff took on a life of its own when subjected to the heat of the flames—it danced and squirmed in a most alarming fashion. Grizel was hanged. As an act of final defiance, she attempted to take all her clothes off on the scaffold, prompting the hangman to act more quickly than he might have preferred.

It was not long before people had signs that Major Weir had returned to his old haunts after his execution. His house remained unoccupied for the most part of the one hundred and fifty years following his death—it had unpleasant associations. For a while, it was inhabited by a family by the name of Patullo, but they soon left, alarmed by the strange apparitions that plagued them. Empty or not, however, the house often seemed full of life—sounds of raucous merrymaking and devilish laughter were heard coming from the building. Lights were seen in the house at night, giving it an eerie glow. The sound of Grizel's spinning wheel was reported to have been heard by several people.

A Haunted Capital

The house was finally demolished in the first half of the nineteenth century, but Major Weir and his sister have never gone away. They continue to haunt the area around the West Bow, although the street as it once was, from Edinburgh Castle to Grassmarket, has long gone. The Major has been seen striding about the streets, swinging his staff as he walks. The sound of Grizel's spinning wheel can still be heard from time to time. Sometimes Major Weir is seen to ride out on a phantom black horse. And from time to time, it is said, the sound of galloping horses and clattering wheels can be heard as the devil himself comes riding in his coach for another assignation with Thomas and Grizel.

Ghostly Castles

SCOTLAND is famous the world over for its castles, fortified homes of the great (but not necessarily good) of times gone by. Castles in various states of repair can be found in all parts of the country, from the Borders to the far north. Some are still inhabited; some are looked after by the National Trust for Scotland or Historic Scotland as visitor sites of historical interest; some lie in deserted ruins, inhabited only by the spirits of the dead who haunt them. There can hardly be one of these castles that does not have at least one ghostly story to tell.

Abergeldie Castle

The earliest parts of Abergeldie Castle, which stands barely two miles from the royal family's country home at Balmoral, date from the sixteenth century. The castle has had its fair share of visiting guests over the years, including royalty. It also has an extra, uninvited "guest," known as French Kate or Kitty Rankie. She was apparently a French woman who was employed in the castle at one time. The unfortunate soul was suspected of practising black magic and was arrested and charged with witchcraft. She was confined in the castle until found guilty. Then she was taken to a neighboring hill, tied to a stake and burnt for her crimes. Her angry spirit returned to the castle after her death.

Balgonie Castle

Balgonie Castle in Fife was originally built in the fourteenth century, with additions made to the structure over the following three centuries or so. In times gone by, the castle was the seat of the Earls of Leven, but gradually it fell into disrepair in the eighteenth and nineteenth centuries.

The present owners of the castle, the family of Raymond Morris, have worked hard at restoring Balgonie for over ten years. The ghost for which Balgonie is most famous has been seen by the laird and other members of his family, and also by visitors. She is known as Green Jeannie and has been seen mostly at night, particularly in a part of the castle that was constructed at the beginning of the eighteenth century. As her name suggests, the apparition is bright green in color.

There have been other ghostly signs at Balgonie apart from Green Jeannie. Strange noises are heard from time to time, and shadowy figures have appeared, particularly in the area of the great hall of the castle.

Ballindalloch Castle

Ballindalloch Castle in Banffshire has quite a reputation for its ghosts. The castle dates from the sixteenth century and has been inhabited by the same family, the Grants and Macpherson-Grants, throughout its history. It is open to the public for some months of the year, and both the members of the family who live in the castle and members of the visiting public have testified to the presence of more than one ghost.

The Pink Tower, a bedroom in the castle, is the haunt of a beautiful lady dressed in a crinoline. Several visitors have seen her. She is a benign presence, and although those who see her might be startled initially, it soon becomes clear that the ghost means no harm.

The dining room, which was originally the great hall of the castle, has a ghost in the form of a green lady. Nobody knows who she is, but she has been seen on more than one occasion.

There is also a male ghost at Ballindalloch. He is thought to be General James Grant, a member of the family who died in 1806. He is buried close to the estate and is said to return there every night, riding a magnificent white horse. It is as if, even in death, he wishes to keep a proprietorial eye on his home and lands. His ghost also walks around the castle itself, making its way through a passage at the foot of the tower to the wine cellar, which was once upon a time the castle dungeon.

The fourth ghost associated with Ballindalloch has a sad story. Apparently, she was a family member who fell passionately in love, only to be rejected. Unable to accept that she had been spurned, she continued to write to the object of her desires, pleading for his attention. The pathetic vision of the young woman is seen from time to time crossing the old Bridge of Avon on her way to post another letter to her beloved. In more recent years, the old bridge was bypassed by a new one, and workmen engaged in the construction of the new bridge are reported to have seen the figure of the young woman several times.

Barcaldine Castle

Barcaldine Castle is one of two places haunted by a pair of Campbell brothers. Barcaldine, a stately sixteenth-century building, typically Scottish in appearance, stands in open countryside close to Loch Creran. The castle saw a brutal murder in the eighteenth century. The laird of Barcaldine was Donald Campbell, and for years he had been involved in a bitter feud with Stewart of Appin. The dispute came to an abrupt and bloody end when Stewart killed Donald Campbell with his sword.

Stewart knew that when his crime was found out, reprisals

by the Campbells would be swift, bitter and painful. In order to ensure his own safety, he sought refuge at the home of Donald Campbell's brother, Duncan, at Inverawe. The news of the killing had not yet got out, so Donald Campbell offered Stewart his hospitality when he was asked for it, according to the custom in the Highlands of Scotland.

As long as Stewart of Appin stayed in his home, Duncan Campbell was haunted by visions of his brother, who admonished him for sheltering his murderer. By the time Campbell had heard the news of his brother's death and had realized that he had been seeing his dead brother's ghost, Stewart had gone.

Donald Campbell's ghost left Inverawe—his brother Duncan's ghost frequents that building—and returned to Barcaldine Castle. It still appears there from time to time, an angry specter of a man cheated out of life and deprived of his brother's revenge by a wily Stewart.

Bedlay Castle

Bedlay Castle stands close to Glasgow, at Chryston. It was first built in the twelfth century as a palace for the bishops of Glasgow. The castle appears to have avoided notoriety until one day, around the year 1350, one Bishop Cameron had the misfortune to be found dead, floating face down in the waters of a nearby loch. The bishop, it would seem, had not gone willingly into the afterlife, for after his death he continued to appear in the castle in ghostly form.

The appearances of Bishop Cameron and the sounds that he made caused considerable torment to the inhabitants of the castle in the centuries to come, so much so that an exorcism was reported to have been attempted towards the end of the nineteenth century. It was unsuccessful.

Ghostly Scotland

In the nineteen seventies Castle Bedlay became home to an antique dealer and his family, and they claimed both to have seen the large figure of the bishop appearing before them and to have heard him pacing restlessly about in neighboring rooms.

Braemar Castle

Braemar Castle is still used as a residence by the Farquharson family who have been in possession of the castle since shortly after it was built in the first half of the seventeenth century.

The female ghost that haunts Braemar is thought to be a particularly tragic figure who lost her life through a simple misunderstanding. It is said that over two hundred years ago a young couple came to the castle to spend their wedding night.

In those days, of course, respectable young ladies were chaste and remained virgins until their wedding day. Many girls were left in a state of almost total ignorance when it came to sex. The wedding night, therefore, was likely to be approached with quite considerable apprehension, even fear, on the part of the bride. What would be expected of her? Would she make a "good" wife?

The story goes that the young bride at Braemar woke quite early on the morning after her wedding night to find that she was alone in the bed. She got up and searched the apartments surrounding the bedroom but could find no sign of her new husband. She became very distressed when she could not find him and at once jumped to the conclusion that, having found her to be an unsatisfactory bed mate the night before, her husband had left her. Overcome with shame and confusion, the distraught young woman flung herself to her death from the window of the bridal room.

Ghostly Castles

The poor girl had been sadly mistaken. Her new husband had not left her but had, instead, gone out hunting at crack of dawn while she was still sleeping.

When the bridegroom returned from his hunting trip and rode back into the castle courtyard, he was greeted with the terrible news that his beautiful young bride was dead. How he must have regretted departing without letting his sweetheart know where he was going!

The ghost of the young bride is said to return to the castle whenever newly-weds come to stay there. Whom does she wish to warn? Does she urge young brides not to jump to hasty conclusions, or does she want to remind the grooms that thoughtless behavior will only lead to heartache?

Brodie Castle

Brodie Castle in Morayshire is now in the care of the National Trust for Scotland. It has been the seat of the Brodie family for many centuries, and in 1889 the family experienced something for which no rational explanation could be found.

The castle had been rented out for a while, as the Earl of Brodie was abroad, in Switzerland. One night in September, the butler at Brodie Castle told some of the other servants that he could hear noises coming from the Earl's study. It sounded as if someone was inside. When the other servants listened, they too could hear noises—moaning sounds and what sounded like pages being turned or papers being rustled. This was very odd, as the Earl had locked his study before his departure, leaving strict instructions that no one was to enter the room in his absence. Thinking that there might be an intruder, the servants searched for a key to the room but could find none.

The next day, news reached the castle that the Earl of Brodie had died in Switzerland the previous night. It could only be assumed that the Earl's ghost had returned to his study on the night of his death, perhaps with a wish to deal with outstanding business.

Buckholme Tower

Buckholme Tower, now in ruins, stands close to the Border town of Galashiels. Three centuries ago, it was the home of a terrible and tyrannical man, Laird Pringle. He had a violent temper and a sadistic nature. So abusive was he to his wife and son that they were forced to flee from Buckholme, leaving the laird to live alone, apart from the long-suffering servants on whom he vented his spleen with startling regularity.

As well as indulging in his fondness for large quantities of drink, Laird Pringle is said to have spent much of his time hunting. It would seem that blood sports were one way he used to express the cruel side of his nature. One night, however, he was offered the chance to hunt not animals, but humans.

The 1680s were years of much bloodshed in Scotland. It was the time of the Covenanters, strong Presbyterians who wanted to worship as they pleased, contrary to the laws passed by the parliament in England. Forced to meet in secret, they were constantly being hounded by the Redcoat forces, driven out of their hiding places and punished most cruelly.

Pringle hated the Covenanters, and when he was called upon to assist a band of Redcoats intent on raiding a secret Covenanters' meeting on the moor near his home, he was delighted to help. He called his ferocious hunting hounds to heel and set off on horseback.

The Redcoats were too late. Someone must have warned the Covenanters, for their meeting had broken up and they had fled. The "hunting" expedition was not entirely fruitless, however, for in the course of their search, the troops came upon one old man and his son, hiding nearby. The old man had fallen and injured his back and had been unable to escape, so his son had stayed by his side. The pair could not deny that they were Covenanters, for to do so was to deny God.

Pringle would have killed the two of them then and there, but the officer in charge of the Redcoat troops prevented him from doing so. The captives were to face a proper trial, he insisted. Besides, they were of more use alive than dead, since with a little "persuasion" they might be induced to share some useful information with their captors. Pringle was to take them back to Buckholme Tower and hold them there to await further questioning and subsequent trial.

Pringle dragged the two men back to Buckholme and threw them into the cellar. The laird's sadism and thirst for blood were, however, stronger than any respect he might have had for the law. Later that night, his servants heard him lurching drunkenly down to the cellar. They listened with great apprehension.

Sounds of a scuffle could be heard, then crashes and thumps, roars and screams of agony. Too terrified of their master to take any action, the servants could only listen outside the door and wait. The screaming stopped. The laird stumbled out of the cellar, covered in blood and triumphant.

"Swine should be treated as swine!" he raged, shoving his men aside as he made his way unsteadily upstairs again. When he reached the entrance hall, he was met by a local woman standing at the door. She was the old man's wife and had come to beg for the release of her husband and son. Laird Pringle dragged her down to the cellar and threw open the door to reveal what was inside. There, suspended on the wall, iron hooks through their jaws just like two slaughtered pigs, were the man and the boy.

Pringle watched with obvious relish as the woman subsided into hysterical sobbing. Then, after a few moments, she composed herself and turned to face the laird. She cursed him for what he had done. Just as his hounds had hunted down the Covenanters, his awful deeds would come back like the hounds of hell and hunt him down for eternity.

For the first time in a long time, Pringle was really frightened. For the remainder of his life he was tormented by visions of ghostly hounds, their teeth bared, saliva dripping from their jaws as they moved in for the attack. After his death, people began to hear the strangest sounds at night—the baying of hounds on the hunt and the agonized screams of a man in fear for his life.

Although the rest of Buckholme Tower lies in ruins, the cellar remains. Sometimes at night, it is said, you can still hear the noise of dogs and of Laird Pringle's tormented screams.

The Castle of Mey

The Castle of Mey, Highland home of Her Royal Majesty Queen Elizabeth the Queen Mother, stands in the very far north of Scotland, a few miles from John o' Groats. The castle is haunted by a green lady who appears in a room at the top of the old tower. She is said to be the ghost of a young woman of the Sinclair family. She fell in love with a local lad, a farmworker. A lad such as this, of the humblest of origins, was considered by the girl's father to be a most undesirable suitor for his daughter. He sought to put an end to the relationship and confined his daughter to the tower until she saw sense. It is said that when the girl leaned out of the window to try to catch a glimpse of her sweetheart working in the fields in the distance, she lost her balance, toppled over and fell to her death from the tower.

Cawdor Castle

Cawdor Castle is the haunt of a female ghost—a woman with no hands. The castle stands a few miles from Nairn. It was built in 1370 and became a seat of the Campbell family around 1510–11. The ghost does not date from the early times but from the first half of the nineteenth century, not long after the head of the family became entitled to call himself Earl of Cawdor. It is thought that the ghost was once the daughter of an Earl of Cawdor who found herself smitten with a young man from a rival family. The Earl of Cawdor discovered the secret romance when he came upon the sweethearts one day in their secret meeting place. The Earl was infuriated by his daughter's treachery. He cut her hands off with his sword so that she might never embrace her lover again.

Claypotts Castle

Claypotts Castle in its present form was built at the end of the sixteenth century by John Strachan and his son Gilbert. In 1625, Claypotts passed into the hands of Sir William Graham of Claverhouse. The castle stayed in the Graham family for three generations, and in 1672 it came into the possession of John Graham of Claverhouse, Viscount Dundee, known as Bonnie Dundee. John Graham had achieved considerable notoriety for his actions against the Covenanters. Another nickname, coined no doubt by some of those who held him in particular contempt for what he had done, was Bluidy (Bloody) Clavers.

Many stories were circulated about Claverhouse, and who knows if they had any foundation in reality. It is known that although Claypotts was not his main residence, Graham did stay there from time to time. In the area surrounding Claypotts, rumors spread about his activities whilst in residence. He was said to have consorted with witches and warlocks, and wild orgies were reputed to have taken place at the castle. Some people believed that it was at Claypotts that John Graham of Claverhouse bargained with the devil for mystical powers. These powers were said to have made him, amongst other things, bullet-proof. Legend has it that at the Battle of Killiecrankie, where Graham finally met his end, he was killed not by a bullet but by a silver button from the uniform of an enemy soldier.

Years after the death of Bonnie Dundee, it is said that at Halloween Claypotts Castle was seen to glow with the lights of demonic fires and that sounds of revelry of the blackest kind could be heard.

On 29 May every year, it is said that a white lady appears at an upstairs window in Claypotts Castle. The White Lady appears to be very distressed and is waving a white handkerchief. This ghost is supposed to be Marion Ogilvy, who was the daughter of the first Lord Airlie. The story goes that she was in love with Cardinal Beaton of St Andrews. She would wait at the window for him to arrive and wave her handkerchief as a signal to him. On 29 May 1546, the lady waited in vain, for Cardinal Beaton lay in St Andrews Castle, murdered. On the anniversary of his death, every year, the White Lady resumes her vigil.

This story presents certain difficulties. The castle in its present form, and the window from which the White Lady is said to wave, would not yet have been built in 1546. Furthermore, Marion Ogilvy did not actually live at Claypotts. Her home was in Melgund Castle. Thirdly, Cardinal Beaton is not known to have had anything to do with Claypotts at all. If he ever visited the place, there seems to be no record of him having done so. So how did the story start and who is the White Lady?

Comlongon Castle

Comlongon Castle in Dumfriesshire has a green lady ghost that dates from the late sixteenth century. She is the tragic figure of Marion Carruthers, who was being coerced into marrying a man she did not love. Having taken refuge at her uncle's home at Comlongon, she finally despaired of the situation and threw herself from the tower of the castle.

Cortachy Castle

Cortachy Castle, north of Kirriemuir in Angus, is the family seat of the Ogilvy clan. To this day the castle is said to be haunted by the ghost of a drummer but only on certain ominous occasions. Whenever the drumbeat is heard, so they say, a death in the Ogilvy family is imminent.

The phantom drummer is said to be the ghost of a drummer at Cortachy who incurred the wrath of his master. There is more than one version of how this came to be so, but one story tells that the drummer failed to give warning when the castle was about to be attacked. As fitting punishment, the negligent drummer was dragged to the top of the tower and flung to his death, along with his drum. The Cortachy drummer has been heard not only at Cortachy but also elsewhere as, so it is said, when members of the family have been abroad. The sound of the phantom drumming strikes fear into the hearts of the Ogilvy family, for it can mean only one thing—tragedy is about to strike.

Craigievar Castle

Craigievar Castle is now a National Trust for Scotland property. It stands near Alford in Aberdeenshire and dates from the early seventeenth century. The castle is home to a number of ghosts, so it is said.

The Blue Room in the tower is reputedly haunted by a member of the Gordon clan who fell from the window there. He was forced to his death at sword-point by "Red" Sir John Forbes, a man of some notoriety. People have heard the footsteps of the unfortunate Gordon climbing the steps to the Blue Room, as if re-enacting the moments before his death.

One of the other ghosts at Craigievar is said to be very selective in his appearances. It is thought that he is the ghost of a musician, a fiddler who fell into the well at the castle and drowned. He is said to appear only to those who bear the name of Forbes.

Crathes Castle

Crathes Castle, the home of the Burnett family until it became a National Trust for Scotland property, can be found a few miles from the small town of Banchory in the northeast of Scotland. Earliest building work on the castle dates from the middle of the sixteenth century, with additions having been made in the early part of the seventeenth century and in the eighteenth century.

In the oldest part of the castle, the double tower, there is a room known as the Green Lady's Room because of the frequent sightings of such a phenomenon over many years. The identity of the Green Lady is uncertain, although some people believe her to have been one of the family. She has been seen both on her own and with a baby. The existence of such a woman in real time has been borne out by the fact that during restoration work in the building two skeletons were discovered, one of a woman, the other of a baby. It is thought to be most likely that the woman had become pregnant in undesirable circumstances and that someone had taken the decision that it would be most prudent to avoid embarrassment to the family and dispose of both mother and baby. In spite of her remains having been freed from their place of hiding, the Green Lady continues to haunt the tower.

Delgatie Castle

Delgatie Castle is a tower house of considerable historical interest, dating from the sixteenth century. The tower has one ghost, said to be a female with red hair, who has startled people there on several occasions, including a number of troops billeted at the castle during the Second World War.

Drumlanrig Castle

Drumlanrig Castle is a handsome edifice in Dumfriesshire, which was built in the seventeenth century for the first Duke of Queensberry, William Douglas. He himself spent very little time at the castle, but his family used the castle as a residence for more than a hundred years, after which it became the property of the Dukes of Buccleuch.

One ghost that haunts Drumlanrig Castle is that of a headless woman—not strictly headless, perhaps, for she does have a head, only it is not attached to her shoulders. She carries it about with her in her hands. It is thought that perhaps she is the ghost of Lady Anne Douglas, but how the ghost came to be decapitated is a mystery.

Ghostly Scotland

The other well-known ghost at Drumlanrig is a particularly unusual one—a yellow monkey. This creature, unattractive in appearance and disturbingly large by all accounts, can be seen in one particular room of the castle, which is given the name, in very early castle records, of the Yellow Monkey or Haunted Room. Nobody has any knowledge of where such a beast might have come from or if there ever was such an unusual pet at the castle, but over the years there have been several sightings of the hairy creature.

Dunstaffnage Castle

Dunstaffnage Castle, near Oban in Argyll, dates from the thirteenth century and is now preserved by Historic Scotland. Various ghostly figures have put in appearances here, including one of several green lady ghosts that are said to inhabit various places in Scotland. The Green Lady is thought to be a glaistig, and her appearances, always associated with poltergeist activity around the castle, are thought to be omens of notable occurrences, either good or bad.

Duntrune Castle

Duntrune Castle in Argyll stands in a spectacular setting overlooking Loch Crinan. In the seventeenth century it was a seat of the Campbell clan. Close to the beginning of the century, an Irishman, Coll Ciotach, brought his troops over to Scotland with the intent of waging war upon the Campbells, whom he hated. Unwilling to risk attacking Duntrune without prior knowledge of its defences or of the number of enemy soldiers he would have to face, he sent his piper ahead to try to gain the confidence of the Campbells and discover the information that was required. Pipers were privileged in Highland society and could be guaranteed hospitality wherever they went in return for a few good tunes. Coll's plan was therefore both devious and cunning.

The piper duly approached the castle and was admitted by the Campbells, but their suspicions were soon aroused. The piper seemed unduly curious about the place and asked too many questions. It would be wrong to kill him, for they had no proof that he was up to no good. Besides, they had offered him their hospitality. By way of compromise, they locked him in one of the tower rooms to prevent him from escaping while they decided what to do.

Not far from the castle, Coll's troops remained in hiding, waiting for the piper to return with the information that would help them to victory. But time passed and still the piper did not return. His men grew restive, and at length Coll lost patience. He decided to advance on the castle regardless. The piper, meanwhile, up in his tower room, was only too well aware of the dangers his master would be facing. The Campbell troops outnumbered Coll's forces and Duntrune was strong and well defended. He had to give warning to Coll somehow.

Very bravely, he took up his pipes and began to play an alarm. Coll's troops retreated at once, but the piper had signed his own death warrant. The Campbells had heard the sound of his pipes and realized what he was up to. They stormed up to the tower room and dragged the poor musician out. His fingers were cut from his hands and he was left to bleed to death.

The piper's remains were interred elsewhere in the castle. Years later, it is said, the fingerless skeleton was discovered and given a religious burial. In spite of the fact that the piper's body has been put properly to rest, his spirit will not let Duntrune forget the cruelty of the Campbells. The piper's ghostly playing can still be heard in the tower room, and strange occurrences, similar to the activities of a poltergeist, have been reported. They too are thought to be attributable to the spirit of Coll's brave piper.

Duntulm Castle

Duntulm Castle in the north of the island of Skye now stands in ruins, but its colorful history assures it of the presence of more than one ghost.

One of the ghosts is said to have been the reason why the castle ceased to be used for habitation in the early eighteenth century. The ghost is that of Hugh, Uisdean Gillespie Chleirich, who was the cousin of Donald Gorm Mor, chief of the MacDonalds of Sleat. Donald Gorm Mor was an unpopular and brutal chief and had his fair share of enemies. Hugh was perhaps the most deadly of these enemies and had long plotted to kill Donald Gorm Mor, one such plot being made known to Donald Gorm Mor. There are different versions of the story, so it is not clear exactly how this happened, but Donald, having been informed of his cousin's treachery, set about getting his revenge. He laid siege to Hugh's castle, hoping to starve him out. Hugh escaped, disguised as a woman, but he was soon captured by Donald Gorm Mor's men and taken to Duntulm. There he was locked (one version of the story tells that he was bricked up) in a dungeon. But the confinement of his enemy was not enough to satisfy Donald Gorm Mor's appetite for revenge. He saw to it that Hugh suffered cruelly for his treachery. Hugh's only means of survival in the dungeon were meagre rations of salt meat and salt fish. No water was given to him. Needless to say, he died a slow and painful death from dehydration. His screams were said to haunt the castle continuously after his death, causing great torment to all within.

Another ghost that haunted Duntulm was that of Margaret, a ward of the previous chief, Donald Gorm. After Donald Gorm's death, she was placed, according to his dying wishes, in the care of Donald Gorm Mor until she came of age. When she came of age, she was to marry Donald Gorm Mor or enter a convent. According to one source, Margaret was hopelessly in love with Hugh and devastated by his cruel fate at the hands of Donald Gorm Mor. According to another source, Margaret was cruelly rejected by Donald Gorm Mor, principally because she had only one eye. For whatever reasons, Margaret's life was an unhappy one. She did not marry Donald Gorm Mor and eventually entered a convent, but she died soon afterwards. Her ghost returned to Duntulm and could be heard weeping around the castle for many years after her death.

Donald Gorm Mor himself was also said to haunt Duntulm in the company of two drunken friends. The three ghostly figures proved to be quite a trial for Donald Gorm Mor's successor, his nephew, Donald Gorm Mor Og.

Two more ghosts haunted the castle—those of a tiny heir and his nursemaid. It is said that the baby fell from the nurse's arms out of a window high in the castle and onto rocks below, where he died. The baby's father, enraged with pain and grief, ordered that the nurse be tied up and set adrift in a leaking boat. The cries of the baby and his nurse can still be heard in the ruins of the castle and on the rocks where the poor infant met his death.

Dunvegan Castle

Dunvegan Castle on the Isle of Skye is famous not for haunting as such but for the precious Fairy Flag, which is kept in the castle. An extremely old, discolored and worn piece of material, it hardly resembles a flag at all, but it is said to possess remarkable supernatural power. Dunvegan is the seat of the MacLeod clan, and their attachment to the Fairy Flag stems from the ancient belief that, if the MacLeod family is ever in dire peril, the flag, if unfurled, will protect them from harm. This superstition has been given weight by the fact that on two separate occasions in history, the flag was unfurled in battle and the MacLeod clan and their soldiers were able to overcome their enemies in spite of what had seemed to be insurmountable odds.

How the flag came into the possession of the family is a matter of some debate, but one story tells of a party in the castle many years ago. The nursemaid who was left in charge of the baby of the family left the child for a few moments to watch the revelries, and while she was gone the child kicked off its covers. When the nurse returned, she found that the child had been covered up by the fairies with the Fairy Flag. When she picked up the child in its new silken cover, fairy voices were heard telling the MacLeod family that if ever the flag was unfurled in battle the enemy would see twice as many MacLeod clansmen as were actually facing them. The flag could only be used three times, for whoever tried to use it a fourth time would disappear, along with the flag.

The Fairy Flag has been used twice, and no one would want to have to use it a third and final time, but its very presence in Dunvegan is considered by many to be some sort of lucky talisman in itself.

Ethie Castle

Ethie Castle, about five miles from the town of Arbroath, is now the home of the Forsyth family. The castle as it stands today dates from the early fifteenth century, but there was undoubtedly another building on the site before the present one was constructed.

Cardinal Beaton, abbot of Arbroath in the fifteenth century, commissioned the building of the present castle, and his ghost is said to haunt the place still. He lived at Ethie for several years, and Marion Ogilvy, his mistress, also lived there.

Cardinal Beaton was a powerful figure in the Catholic church and a fierce persecutor of those of the Protestant faith. He had many enemies. His life came to a violent end in St Andrews on 29 May 1546, when he was brutally murdered by Protestant nobles in the castle there.

The ghost of Cardinal Beaton parades slowly round Ethie Castle, particularly in the area close to his bedchamber. The sound of Cardinal Beaton's footsteps is quite unmistakable— his gouty leg thumps and scrapes as it drags along the passageways behind him.

There was another ghost at Ethie Castle—that of a young child. The child could be heard crying sometimes at night. In addition to this, witnesses had heard what sounded like a wheeled toy being pulled across the floor in one particular room in the castle. Eventually, investigations were carried out to discover the source of the strange sounds. A small skeleton was discovered and, alongside it, the remains of a toy wooden cart. The skeleton was removed from the castle and given a Christian burial. The ghost of the child was no longer heard at Ethie.

Fyvie Castle

Fyvie Castle in Aberdeenshire was once the haunt of a green lady who is now, it is thought, finally at peace in the afterlife. Her appearances began sometime around 1920 after a strange and unpleasant fungal mass appeared on one of the walls in the castle's gun room. The owner of the castle, Lord Leith, brought in builders to put matters to rights, and when they removed part of the wall, they discovered a skeleton. The skeleton was removed from the area and the haunting of the Green Lady began. Anxious to put a stop to the disturbing appearances of the Green Lady, the laird insisted that the skeleton be replaced behind the wall, which was then rebuilt. This might have seemed a little bizarre, but it turned out to have the desired effect. Behind the wall was just where this mysterious phantom wanted to be, it would appear, for she stopped causing any trouble to the inhabitants of the castle from that time onwards.

Gight Castle

Gight Castle in Aberdeenshire has a story attached to it that is almost identical to the story of the ghostly piper of Edinburgh Castle. The piper is said to have entered a secret tunnel, playing his pipes, and never to have returned. Gight Castle dates from the fifteenth century, but there seems to be no record of the year, or century, in which the piper was supposed to have disappeared. As is the case with the piper in Edinburgh Castle, there is no mention of anyone having gone into the tunnel to look for the poor fellow after he disappeared! A third version of this tale is told in connection with Culross Abbey.

Glamis Castle

Glamis Castle, a monstrous edifice with looming towers and a gloomy atmosphere, looks as if it ought to be haunted, and haunted it is, perhaps more so than any other place in Scotland. It is now the family seat of the Bowes-Lyons,

Earls of Strathmore. Queen Elizabeth the Queen Mother, then Elizabeth Bowes-Lyon, lived at Glamis as a child, and in 1930, Princess Margaret, sister of Queen Elizabeth II, was born there. The castle, although peaceful now, has a colorful past and from time to time specters from that past return to haunt the living.

Both a gray lady and a white lady have been seen to wander the castle. The Gray Lady is most frequently seen around the area of the chapel and there seems to be no definite idea as to her identity. The White Lady, who appears very infrequently, is thought to be the ghost of Janet Douglas, who lived in the sixteenth century and was the wife of John, sixth Lord Glamis. John died and Janet remarried, settling with her new husband, Campbell of Skipness, at Glamis. The king at the time, James V, hated the Douglas clan, the powerful family to which Janet belonged. As an act of what only can be construed as pure obsessive hatred, James had Janet captured and imprisoned in Edinburgh Castle on charges of witchcraft and conspiracy to poison the king. Her husband and son were imprisoned along with her. After several years' imprisonment, Janet was burned at the stake on Castle Hill. Her husband died in a bungled attempt to flee from the castle, and her son, Lord Glamis, was kept imprisoned until after the death of James V.

Ghastly stories are also told of what befell the Ogilvie family at Glamis Castle in its early days. The Ogilvies were engaged in a bitter and deadly dispute with the Lindsay family, and one day found themselves having to call upon Lord Glamis for refuge. He duly let them into the castle and hid them, as they thought, safely in a secret chamber within the walls. Unfortunately, the Ogilvies had not chosen as safe a sanctuary as they had hoped. Lord Glamis had no intention of letting them out again, for, like the Lindsays, he too despised them.

His treatment of them was, whatever he might have felt for them, grossly barbaric. He locked the door of the secret chamber and turned away, never to return. The poor members of the Ogilvie family were left to starve to death and rot in their hidden location

Nothing more was known of the fate of the Ogilvies until centuries later when one Earl of Strathmore accidentally happened upon the room in which the Ogilvies had been condemned to live out their last, painful days. It is said that when the Earl opened the door and discovered the rotted, skeletal contents of the hidden chamber, he fainted with horror and disgust.

"Beardie" is another ghost of Glamis, with a story that is also linked to the existence of some sort of hidden chamber. Accounts differ as to exactly who Beardie was. Some say he was the first Lord of Glamis, others that he was in fact the Earl of Crawford. Whichever he was (and still is, by all accounts), the story goes that he was a gambling man with a violent temper. Unable to find anyone to play cards with him late one Saturday night as the sacred Sabbath approached, Beardie announced that he would quite happily play with the devil himself if challenged so to do.

Right on cue, a dark stranger appeared and offered to take Beardie on in a card game. The two men retired to a chamber to play. The servants in the castle were intrigued by the noises of shouting and swearing they could hear coming from the room—it appeared that Beardie was losing and losing badly at that. One servant, unable to contain his curiosity, put his eye to the keyhole only to jump back screaming in pain, having been blinded by a shooting dart of flame.

Beardie emerged from the chamber, raging at the interruption. When he stormed back into the room to continue the game, the stranger had disappeared.

The devil had gone, but he had taken with him the soul of Beardie, which the rash lord had gambled away. It seemed as if Beardie was condemned to play cards for eternity, for after his death, some five years later, the room was in constant turmoil with the sounds of cursing, swearing card-players. The story goes that after some years, the chamber was sealed up in an attempt to stop the activities of the phantom Beardie, but his ghost, a fearsome creature complete with straggly beard, is still said to appear in certain places in the castle from time to time and the sounds of raucous card-playing can still, on occasion, be heard.

The first black ghost in Scotland is said to live in Glamis Castle. He is said to be the spirit of a much abused servant boy and is sometimes seen sitting on a stone seat just outside the Queen Mother's sitting room. Some say the child was ordered to sit there and wait until he was told what to do next. Terrified at the thought of the consequences of disobedience, the little boy did just that, but was forgotten about and left there overnight. Being a very lowly servant, he was poorly clad, especially for the rigors of the Scottish climate, and having been left to sit in a freezing corridor for hours on end, he died from hypothermia.

Other ghosts that have been seen at Glamis Castle include the gruesome apparition of a woman with no tongue, who flits across the grounds with her mouth open and bloody; a dark figure dressed in what appears to be a military coat; and a fleeting figure who is seen in the grounds (albeit briefly, for he runs so fast), known as Jack the Runner. The woman with no tongue is thought to have been witness to some ghastly deed and to have had her tongue cut out to ensure that she kept her silence. Just who the other two might be, nobody knows.

The greatest intrigue at Glamis concerns another secret

room story and a monster story. At some time there is supposed to have existed, locked up in a secret chamber somewhere within the walls of Glamis Castle, a monster. Accounts
vary as to just who or what the monster is supposed to have
been and when it came into being, but all seem to indicate
that the monster was in fact a family member. There are
theories that the monster was in some way connected to
Patrick, third Earl of Strathmore. Those who follow this line
of thinking point to a picture of Patrick that hangs in the
castle. In the painting, at Earl Patrick's side is an armor-clad
figure of unknown identity, which looks as if its arms and
body are strangely deformed. The theory does not make
a lot of sense, for if the monster was so terrible that it had
to be kept hidden away from the outside world under lock
and key, why did the Earl of Strathmore have it included in
a painting?

Other accounts of the existence of a monster, or at least
a grossly deformed human being, suggest that the creature
might have been the first son of the eleventh Earl of Strathmore. The twelfth Earl, Thomas, was born in 1822, but records
apparently show that another son was born to the eleventh
Earl and his wife in 1821, a son who supposedly died just after
birth. The story goes that this son did not in fact die but was
so horribly deformed that the family had to keep him hidden
from public view. The child's younger brothers did not even
know of his existence until they came of age, when, as a sort of
gruesome rite of passage, they were each allowed to discover
the location of the secret room. When they had been taken
there, the awful truth was revealed to them. The secret of that
hidden chamber was never revealed to any woman apparently,
and was known only by three men at any one time. Those who
became privy to the secret were said to have been shocked to
the core—changed men from that day onwards.

Rumor has it that the monster lived until about 1921— if he was born in 1821, he reached the age of a hundred, a surprisingly ripe old age for someone to live to at the turn of the nineteenth century. If the monster was born around the time of Patrick, the third Earl, then the theory defies belief.

Tales of the existence of a secret room hidden within the walls of the castle, for whatever purpose, are quite believable, for in places the walls are as much as four metres thick. Visitors to the castle have been known to try to find the location of the room by hanging towels out of the windows of all the rooms that they could find. In theory, the one window without a towel hanging from it would be the window of the secret room.

Some say that the location of the secret room is still known and that still only three people living at any one time are privy to the secret. Whatever the contents of the secret room—monster, monstrous remains or something else—its story has attracted a great deal of interest and much speculation over the years. Visitors to the castle at various times in the past century and before have made claims that their sleep has been disturbed by the most awful sights and sounds. And to this day there is a walkway on the roof, known as the Mad Earl's Walk, which is rumored to be haunted by terrible noises. Here, it is said, the poor creature, the dreadful, hideous family secret, was taken under cover of darkness for exercise.

Hermitage Castle

Hermitage Castle, built in the mid-thirteenth century, stands in moorland south of the Border town of Hawick. Its rather bleak situation makes it a fitting site for ghostly haunts. Little remains of the building except a shell, but it does not take much imagination to conjure up pictures of all the things that might be lurking in its gloomy shadows.

Its grim history is recalled by the appearances of two spectral figures in particular. The first ghost is that of Sir Alexander Ramsay, Sheriff of Teviotdale, who, in 1342 incurred the wrath of Sir William Douglas, Knight of Liddesdale. The two had once been brothers in arms, but when King David II conferred the sheriffdom upon Ramsay, Douglas, who felt he had some claim to the title, was incensed. The unfortunate Ramsay was captured by Douglas in Hawick, taken to Hermitage and thrown into a dungeon in the castle. There he was left to starve to death. He was said to have tried to prolong his life by eating the few grains of corn that fell into the dungeon from the granary above. The sad, hungry figure of Sir Alexander Ramsay wanders around the ruins of the castle still.

The second ghost that is said to haunt Hermitage Castle is that of Lord Soulis—"Bad Lord Soulis" or "Terrible William." Lord Soulis had a ghastly reputation indeed, for it was widely believed that he practised black magic and used the dungeons of the castle to hold young children from the surrounding area captive before incorporating them into his hideous rituals and eventually murdering them. He finally faced justice at the hands of his neighbors. People from the surrounding area gathered in force and stormed the castle, taking him captive and binding him in chains. We are told that he was wrapped in lead and then thrown into a boiling cauldron to meet a horribly painful death.

Another version of the story of Terrible William says that he had entered into a pact with the devil. He traded his soul in return for a licence to live however he pleased, indulging in whatever debaucheries took his fancy. Then, as he grew older and faced up to the inevitability of his approaching death, he panicked at the thought of the fiery furnaces of hell. It was in order to protect him from this fate that he was wrapped in lead and boiled by loyal subjects. This story, however, seems even less credible than the first one.

The figure of Terrible William has been seen around the grounds of the castle, and the screams of the children whom he abused so cruelly are also heard from time to time.

Linlithgow Palace

The stately ruins of Linlithgow Palace are now a popular visitor site, protected by Historic Scotland. In days gone by, Linlithgow was a much favored royal palace. King James V of Scotland, who was born at Linlithgow in 1512, was said to have been particularly attached to the palace and he stayed there for long periods during his reign.

Linlithgow Palace is said to be haunted by the ghost of James V's wife, Mary of Guise. The ghost is seen in Queen Margaret's bower.

Littledean Tower

Littledean Tower stands close to the village of Maxton in Roxburghshire. The building dates from the fifteenth century. It has long been uninhabited, but it was at one time the stronghold of the Kerr family. One laird of Littledean, who lived in the tower in the seventeenth century, had a particularly bad reputation.

The laird was by all accounts a thoroughly unsavory character. He drank heavily, mistreated his family and servants, and took great pleasure in playing an active part in the persecution of Covenanters in the district. He had a violent temper, and it is said that on one occasion he became so angry with a stable lad who had saddled and harnessed his horse improperly that he trampled the poor lad to death.

The laird enjoyed entertaining his friends—the only people who could bear his company were those who shared his liking for excess and bad behavior—and they spent many raucous evenings drinking themselves incapable.

The laird's wife, Margaret, lived a miserable life. Her husband was undeniably cruel in his treatment of her. It seems, however, that she bore it all for the most part with remarkable dignity and stoicism. One evening, however, the laird overstepped the mark. He had, as usual, been drinking heavily with his companions, and one of them asked where Margaret was (it was her habit to keep well out of the way of her husband and his cronies at such times).

The laird dragged Margaret from her room and down to the dining hall where his visitors sat. He then proceeded to berate her and humiliate her in front of them. Margaret stood, confined by her husband's vicious grip on her arm, and suffered this treatment in silence.

At length the laird let her go, uttering as a final insult that he would rather be married to a woman from hell, for such a wife would have more warmth than the woman he had married.

It was a terrible thing to say, and Margaret finally broke her silence in response to it.

"You will live to regret these words," she said, before quietly leaving the room.

The laird's friends bade him goodnight and left Littledean, but the laird was too fired up with drink and bad temper to settle. He saddled up his horse and rode off into the darkness. After some time, he came to a cottage in a clearing in the woods. The door was open and the laird could see a woman inside, sitting at a spinning wheel. He dismounted and approached. His horse seemed strangely agitated as the laird got to the cottage door, and he had to hold its reins very firmly to prevent it from bolting. Looking into the cottage, the laird thought that he could see shadowy figures moving in the corners, but it was too dark to make out what they were. He tried to speak to the woman. She did not respond in words to his greeting. Instead, she stopped spinning and turned to face him, still holding the newly spun thread between her fingers. With a maniacal laugh, she snapped the thread in two.

The laird saw no more, for at that point his horse took such fright and pulled him away with such force that he almost had to let go of the reins. He regained control of the animal at last, mounted and rode away. When he eventually arrived back at Littledean, he still had the picture of the woman in his mind. She had been the most beautiful creature he had ever laid eyes on.

The next day he found that in spite of himself he was pre-occupied with the woman in the cottage. He set off to try to find her. He rode for most of the day, trying to find the same path through the wood that he had taken the night before, but in spite of many hours' searching he was unable to find any sign of the cottage where he had last seen the woman. He returned to Littledean, frustrated. As he approached his home, however, he caught sight of a graceful figure standing in a glade by the river—it was the very woman for whom he had been searching! She held out her arms to him in silence, and he went to her eagerly.

The laird's obsession with the woman grew. Every night at the same time, just before dark, she would appear at the same place by the river. His desire for her was so great that the laird ignored any need for caution. There, within sight of his marital home, he indulged his passion for this strange woman night after night.

It was inevitable that the affair would not remain a secret. The laird was seen with the woman and Lady Margaret was told about it. She confronted him and threw her wedding ring in his face. The laird merely turned on his heel and walked away.

Lady Margaret was ready to leave, but before she did she wanted to find out who her husband's mysterious lover was. Two men volunteered to go and search for the woman on her behalf. That evening they went to the glade by the river where the laird and the woman had been meeting, and after some time they caught sight of her. As they moved towards her stealthily, hoping to entrap her, she disappeared. A hare sped away from the place where she had been seen and ran far off into the distance.

The two men returned to Lady Margaret to find her in a state of great consternation. The laird was missing. There was little point in mounting a search at this late hour, for it was too dark. They had no choice but to wait.

It was far into the night when the laird's horse finally galloped up to the tower, carrying its master. The horse was sweating and exhausted; the laird was grim-faced and as white as a sheet. He was shaking as he told all those present what had happened to him.

He had been riding towards home when he had caught sight of a hare running alongside his horse. Before long, the hare had been joined by several others, racing along beside him, in front of him and behind him. They leaped around the feet of his horse and jumped up to saddle height. The laird had been very frightened and had tried first to spur his horse on to outrun them, then to cut them down with his sword and trample them with the horse's hooves. His efforts were in vain until his sword struck the paw of one hare, cutting it clean off. The paw had jumped in the air and landed in the his pistol holster. The pack of hares had then suddenly withdrawn.

By the time all this had happened, the laird had ridden all the way to the village of Midlem, a place notorious for witchcraft and many miles from his home. He had spurred his horse into a gallop and had neither stopped nor even slowed his pace until he reached the safety of Littledean.

"Devils," he muttered through chattering teeth. "Devils!"

When he had told his tale, the laird put his hand into the pistol holster to feel for the hare's paw. He screamed, quickly withdrawing his hand from the holster and throwing something down on the ground.

"It grabbed me!" he cried.

Lady Margaret looked down at the thing that her husband had thrown from his holster. It was not a hare's paw but the bloody severed hand of a woman!

The laird drew his sword and speared the hand. As he did so, it flexed, very much as if it were alive. The laird took it, still impaled on his sword, out of the tower and made for the river. When he reached the water's edge, he hurled the bloody hand into the river's murky depths with all his might. He was very close to the spot where he and the mysterious woman had been meeting, and when he had thrown the hand in the river, he turned around and saw her, crouching beneath a tree. She lifted her head to look at him. To his horror, the laird saw that her face had been transformed into a hideous, wizened countenance with an evil leer.

"You took my hand from me," she rasped. "Now it will be with you for ever!"

The laird returned to the tower, still shaking. He collapsed into a chair by the fireside and put his hand into his pocket. The hand was there again! He threw it from the window in disgust and stumbled up to his bedchamber, hoping to find relief in sleep. But when he got into bed, he realized that he could feel something beneath the pillow on which his head lay. Putting his hand under the pillow, he withdrew the hideous hand. By this time hysterical with fear, he threw the hand into the fire and hid himself beneath the covers.

The laird did not appear downstairs the next morning. After some time Lady Margaret sent servants up to wake him. Not a sound came from the laird's bedroom in spite of the servants' repeated knocking and calling. His door was locked, and they had to break it down to gain entry. When they finally managed to enter the room, they found the laird lying on the floor. He was dead. His face, far from appearing peaceful, had a look of unimaginable terror. His neck was bruised, and the bruises appeared to be the marks of fingers around the laird's neck. He had been strangled by the hideous hand.

Meggernie Castle

The ghost of Meggernie Castle in Perthshire seems quite unperturbed by her unusual appearance and is quite willing, it would appear, not only to appear to the living but also to flirt with them.

The room in the castle where the ghost has been witnessed is now known as the Haunted Room, and on more than one occasion, men who have been sleeping in the room have been woken by the sensation of being kissed on the cheek. Those who see the ghost are said to see either her top half or her bottom half but never both together. The ghost is believed to be that of the wife of one of the chiefs of the Menzies clan. Her husband was profoundly jealous of the attentions that she attracted from other men and was forever accusing her of being unfaithful. His jealousy boiled over into uncontrollable rage one night, and he killed her. In order to dispose of the body, he cut it in half. He buried the top half of his wife in the tower and the bottom half in the churchyard. He then went abroad and on his return claimed that his wife had been with him but had died.

It is said that the bottom half of the unfortunate woman parades around the lower floors of the castle and the grounds outside. The top half, meanwhile, stays upstairs and persists in teasing sleeping guests with ghostly kisses.

Muchalls Castle

Scotland has a rich history of smuggling. Various places along its coastline were used in days gone by for the landing and concealment of contraband. Smuggling was not an activity confined to the lower classes. People from all walks of life succumbed to the temptation of avoiding the dreaded Exciseman.

Muchalls Castle, by Stonehaven, had a tunnel that was a godsend to smugglers. It led underground from the castle to the shore and was used for storing wine and spirits and as a secret means of coming and going for all those who might need it.

The cave at the far end of the tunnel was flooded at high tide, and it was here that a young lady of the family at Muchalls met her death. She had gone down the smugglers' tunnel for an assignation with her sweetheart, who would be arriving by boat, but fell into the sea at the end of the tunnel and drowned.

The ghost of the young woman is reputed to haunt one of the rooms in the castle. Like so many female ghosts, the figure of the young woman is green in color.

Newton Castle

Newton Castle, Blairgowrie, dates from the fourteenth century and is haunted by the ghost of "Lady Jean." Her story is well known. She was Lady Jean Drummond, and she fell desperately in love with a local laird. He had dallied with her for a while but had become distracted by another woman. In order to win back the affection of her beloved, Lady Jean did her very best to make herself attractive. She dressed in finest silks and satins, wore shoes with silver buckles and adorned her braided hair with pearls and precious stones. The transformation in her appearance, however, was not enough to bring the heartless scoundrel back. She took to spending her time singing mournful songs of lost love as she sat alone in a tower of the castle.

Eventually she sought the advice of a local witch. The witch told her that her fine clothes were no good. She must dress in "the witchin' claith o' green." In order to do this, she must cut some grass from the churchyard, take a branch of a rowan tree from the gallows-knowe and bind them together with a plaited reed. Then she was to take them as darkness was falling to the Corbie Stone by the Cobble pool and sit there and wait.

This the Lady Jean did. After waiting for some time, she became aware of the sound of laughter. She could feel a strange sensation, as if something was pulling at her clothes. She fell asleep, and when she awoke at dawn she was dressed all in green.

The magic of the witch had worked, for Jean married her great love, Lord Ronald, still wearing the "witchin' claith." Her new husband was quite besotted with his bride in her strange green dress. The wedding ceremony had hardly taken place, however, than disaster struck. Lord Ronald looked at his bride and saw that something was far wrong. He took her hand in his, but it felt deathly cold. Then, to his horror, Jean let out an unearthly scream, fell to the ground and died. Her lifeless body was laid out on the bed where the wedding couple were to have consummated the marriage.

Lady Jean was buried nearby, and her gravestone is said to turn round three times each Halloween. Then the sound of her sad singing comes wafting from the tower at Newton Castle.

Sanquhar Castle

Sanquhar Castle, once home of the Crichtons of Dumfries, stands in ruins now but remains the haunt of the ghost of a man called John Wilson. John Wilson was the innocent party in a dispute that was going on in the late 1590s between Sir Thomas Kirkpatrick, John's master, and Douglas of Drumlanrig, ally of Robert Crichton, Lord of Sanquhar and Sheriff of Nithsdale. As an act of sheer spite against Wilson's master, Crichton had John Wilson locked up in jail, falsely accused of certain crimes. When Sir Thomas Kirkpatrick tried to protest Wilson's innocence, Crichton retaliated by having Wilson hanged. Wilson's ghost, groaning and rattling its chains, haunts the ruins of Sanquhar Castle as a testament of its one-time owner's barbarism and cruelty.

A second, female ghost is also said to haunt Sanquhar. She is a white lady, with long, pale tresses, quite beautiful to behold, so they say. Nobody is certain as to the identity of the White Lady, although she is possibly the ghost of Marion of Dalpeddar, who disappeared suspiciously in the 1590s and was thought perhaps to have befallen an unfortunate fate at the hands of Robert Crichton. In the 1870s, excavations around the castle uncovered the remains of a woman buried in a pit.

The skeleton still had some hair attached to the skull. The hair was long and blond. Was this the skeleton of the White Lady of Sanquhar Castle?

Spedlins Tower

Spedlins Tower in Dumfriesshire was once upon a time haunted by a particularly hungry ghost.

At the end of the seventeenth century, Spedlins was the property of Sir Alexander Jardine, brother-in-law of the first Duke of Queensberry, William Douglas.

One of the laird's tenants, a miller by the name of Dunty Porteous, fell out of favor with his master. The laird, having right of pit and gallows, apprehended Porteous and took him to Spedlins. Porteous was locked in the dungeon of the tower to await judgment and suitable punishment for his misdemeanors. It was a grim place to sit and ponder one's fate—an underground pit with no light source. The only access to the dungeon was through a trapdoor. No sooner had Dunty Porteous been put away than Sir Alexander had to leave Spedlins to attend to some business in the capital city. He would have to deal with Dunty on his return.

Unfortunately, when the laird set off for Edinburgh, he took the key of the dungeon with him. In his absence, it would appear that either Dunty was forgotten about or nobody thought to break down the door of the dungeon and come to his aid. Whatever was the case, Dunty was abandoned, with tragic consequences.

Some time later, when Sir Alexander finally returned to Spedlins and the dungeon was unlocked, Dunty was found to have died of starvation. It is said that in the agonies of his dreadful hunger, the poor prisoner had chewed at his own hands. Any regret that Sir Alexander felt for what had happened was clearly not great enough, for as soon as the spirit of Dunty Porteous was released from the confines of the dreadful dungeon it started to run riot at Spedlins.

Dunty's ghost was persistent and troublesome, running through Spedlins Tower screaming out in pain and hunger, crying for mercy and food. The spirit would give no peace to the Jardine family. Eventually, a chaplain was summoned to try to exorcise the ghost. His efforts were not entirely successful, for the ghost would not go away. Nevertheless, after a concerted effort, the minister and the family were able to confine Dunty's raging spirit to the dungeon with the help of a bible that was left at the site.

In time the binding of the bible became worn and needed to be repaired, so it was sent to Edinburgh to be rebound. No sooner had the bible left the premises than Dunty's ghost was on the loose again, tormenting the laird and his family as before. The bible had to be repaired and returned with all possible haste in order to confine the ghost once again.

The Jardine family eventually moved from Spedlins. The ghost of Dunty followed them, but the bible was moved too and Dunty remained subdued.

Tioram Castle

Tioram Castle has been uninhabited for more than two centuries, but the ruins that remain are sufficient to indicate to the visitor that it was indeed an impressive sight in its heyday, standing in spectacular surroundings, high on a rock overlooking the sea in north Argyll. It was a seat of the MacDonalds of Clanranald and had a colorful warfaring history.

The twelfth chief of Clanranald was John, who succeeded to his title in the late 1670s. He was a violent man, given to outbursts of temper with a distinctly sadistic touch, by all accounts.

It is John, rather than his ancestral home, with which this story is concerned, for it was the man rather than his castle that was haunted. Perhaps it was because of all the wrongs he had done, which was certainly what most people suspected, but the reason does not really matter. John was haunted, not by a green lady or the specter of one of the victims of his many cruelties. He was haunted by a frog—a hideous black creature of demonic proportions.

It is remarkable how close this story comes to the fairy tale of the princess and the frog. Just as the princess in the fairy tale was pursued relentlessly by her frog, so John found that he was unable to shake off his own slimy follower. If he left it locked in a room, it found its way out and appeared beside him again. If he tried to ride away, the frog would appear alongside him in the saddle. The frog was always there, whatever he was doing, whether he was asleep or awake. On one occasion, John tried to sail away from the castle, only to find the frog swimming alongside the boat. When he refused to let the frog on board, the weather turned so bad that all the people in the boat thought they might drown. John reluctantly let the frog on to the boat, whereupon, it is said, the weather turned calm once more almost instantly.

Perhaps if John had kissed the frog, as the princess in the fairy tale did, he might have found that it turned into something altogether more desirable, but he did not and his frog did not turn into anything else. The hideous creature remained with him, a constant but unwelcome companion, to the end of his days.

Other Haunted Castles

The stories of the castles in this chapter are just a taste of the hundreds of stories that the ancient fortifications of Scotland have to tell. They are some of the better known ones, but they are not necessarily the most intriguing to the eager ghost-hunter and others with interests in all things supernatural. Other castles that are said to be haunted make a long list indeed, but among them are the following:

Ardvreck Castle—the ghost of a former Lady of Ardvreck.

Balcomie Castle—the ghost of a young boy locked in a dungeon and starved to death.

Borthwick Castle—the ghost of Mary Queen of Scots and the ghost of a young girl impregnated and then murdered by Lord Borthwick.

Brodick Castle—the ghost of an unknown man and the ghost of a deer.

Buchanan Castle—anonymous groans.

Culzean Castle—a ghostly piper and a woman in a ball gown.

Duchal Castle—the ghost of an excommunicated monk.

Duns Castle—the ghost of a young soldier.

Inverary Castle—the ghost of a murdered servant boy.

Kellie Castle—the ghost of Anne Erskine, who fell from an upper storey window.

Megginch Castle—the ghosts of two chattering old ladies.

Neidpath Castle—a white lady.

Newark Castle—the ghosts of women and children slaughtered by Covenanting forces.

Skibo Castle—the ghost of a girl lured to the castle by a servant and murdered by him.

Wemyss Castle—a green lady.

Religious Haunts

RUINED cathedrals, dark corners of country churches, abbeys and priories can all quite easily take on a haunted appearance. Vaults, crypts and graveyards are full of the secrets of the dead. Hooded monks look like ghosts as they glide soundlessly along shadowy corridors. Members of the clergy, servants of God, are constantly engaged in the fight against sin, and hence the devil. It is only to be expected, therefore, that there are numerous stories of ghosts that torment members of the clergy, spirits that frequent religious meeting places and specters that lurk in sacred burial places. Some of the stories are undoubtedly fictitious. Others, however, merit closer consideration, especially when the ghost is thought to be that of a real figure in history and when the presence of a spirit has been witnessed independently by more than one person, previously unaware of its supposed existence.

Dalarossie

Sundays in most parts of Scotland in modern times are days when families can choose to do more or less as they wish. Shopping in one of the many big shopping centers that have grown up around the major towns is a popular pastime, while other people may choose to spend the day catching up on do-it-yourself activities or working in the garden. Sports centers and swimming pools are open, and there are Sunday leagues for amateur sports of various kinds. For those who wish to spend the day in a more relaxed fashion, there are plenty of restaurants, pubs and hotels around the country where a leisurely lunch and a few glasses of wine can be enjoyed.

All this is a far cry from the days when the Sabbath in Scotland was a day reserved strictly for God and for rest. There are some parts of Scotland where the Sabbath is still observed to some degree and where some of the above pastimes are frowned upon, but even in those places the restrictions upon the activities of the God-fearing are considerably fewer than in days of old.

In times gone by it was unthinkable to venture from home for any other reason than to go to church. Children were not allowed out to play and no one was supposed to work. For women, the Sabbath must have brought quite a welcome break from cooking and cleaning. Sport was taboo on the Sabbath, as were playing cards, gambling and drinking. To break the laws of the Sabbath was believed to invite all sorts of terrible retribution.

There are quite a few stories about people who break the Sabbath—cautionary tales to warn others of the consequences of succumbing to temptation. Some appear elsewhere in this book—the story of Beardie of Glamis Castle, for example, in the previous chapter, page 94), and the story of the fisherman at Kylesku in Hotels and Public Houses (page 157). This story does not concern one individual, however, but a whole team of sportsmen.

Twenty miles or so from Inverness stands the parish church of Dalarossie, and just beside the parish church is the glebe, a patch of land that was used in times gone by as an area of recreation.

The story tells us that two families, the Shaws of Strathnairn and the Mackintoshes of Strathdearn, had arranged to have a game of shinty on the glebe on Christmas Day. When the game was first suggested, the Mackintoshes willingly agreed, but then they found out that Christmas Day was to fall on the Sabbath that year and decided to call the whole thing off.

When their opponents turned up, all ready to play, they found that the Mackintoshes were not coming after all. The Shaws, however, were not quite so easily put off. There were enough people present to form two teams amongst themselves, so they divided up and played a game regardless. The game was a great success, and it was thought that no harm had come as a result of their breaking the Sabbath.

It seems they were tragically mistaken, for it is said that during the course of the following year every man who had played on that day died.

The ghostly shinty players return to Dalarossie once a year. Every Christmas, they play their game on the glebe as they did all those years ago on that fateful Sabbath.

Durness

In Durness in Sutherland a story is told of a manse that was haunted by a particularly ominous spirit.

According to the legend, the spirit first manifested itself many years ago when the minister in Durness became aware of the sound of knocking at his front door. The knocking became a regular occurrence. As the minister never heard anyone approaching the door, he was suspicious and did not answer the knocks.

After several repetitions of the strange phenomenon, the minister invited a colleague, the minister from Kinlochbervie, to call on him one night. He did not give the reason for his invitation. The minister from Kinlochbervie duly made the journey to Durness and settled down for a pleasant evening. After some time had passed, the men heard a knocking at the front door. The Durness minister asked his friend if he would answer it, and his friend obliged, having no idea that the knocking meant anything sinister.

The Kinlochbervie minister cheerfully went and opened the door, only to be faced with the fearful apparition of an old man wrapped in a shroud. Terrified, he saddled his horse at once and rode back to Kinlochbervie with all possible speed. He had not escaped the clutches of the terrible death spirit, however. It is said that barely a month later, although he was a man of robust health and only in his mid-forties, the Kinlochbervie minister died suddenly and mysteriously. The tragedy became a double one when his wife followed him to the grave very shortly afterwards.

It seems unfair that the minister from Durness should survive unscathed after such cowardly behavior on his own part, but it would appear that the deathly figure that came to his door had no sense of justice. It seemed, rather, to want to take whomever it could.

Lairg

At the end of the eighteenth century there lived in Lairg in Sutherland a mildly eccentric minister. In spite of being a humble clergyman, the Reverend Thomas Mackay is said to have dressed in much grander ecclesiastical attire. He died early in the 1800s, and the manse was thereafter occupied by ministers with more sober habits of dress.

The minister who lived in the manse in 1826 had two daughters, and it was they who saw the ghost for the first time. They heard a knock at the front door and went to answer it. When they opened the door they saw an old man standing on the doorstep, dressed in a long black robe. He said nothing but peered into the house for a few moments before turning away from the girls and walking off. The girls thought that the visitor might be looking for their father, so they ran to find him. When their father came to greet the visitor, there was no sign of the old man, either at the door or in the surrounding area. It seemed as if he had vanished completely.

When the family told some other older parishioners about their strange old visitor and described his appearance and attire, the parishioners were able to enlighten them as to their visitor's identity. It was none other than the Reverend Thomas Mackay, paying a visit to his former home.

The manse is no longer there; it fell into disrepair and became a ruin. However, the Reverend Thomas Mackay is said to pop back from time to time to visit the site where it once stood. It is said that one night his appearance stopped the activities of two poachers in the neighborhood. When they heard strange noises coming from the vicinity of the former manse they abandoned all ideas of a profitable night's work and fled.

Melrose Abbey

The ruins of Melrose Abbey are believed to be the haunt of a rather more sinister ghost than some. Several people have reported noticing a strange chill in the atmosphere near the place where a man called Michael Scott was buried in the late thirteenth century.

Michael Scott was a very intelligent man of great learning, interested in philosophy and science. During his lifetime he acquired a reputation as a practitioner of the black arts, and he was said to possess strange supernatural powers. It may have been the case that he was simply rather a scary intellectual, whose brain and knowledge seemed threatening to other less educated or intelligent people. Nonetheless, he was a man who inspired fear among many people, both in life and after death. The site of his grave in the abbey is believed to be haunted by his spirit. The sensations that are felt by those who are sensitive to such things are not pleasant ones. Many people reportedly have felt an ominous chill in the air when they have stood in the vicinity.

Stories of vampirism and other crimes, sometimes attributed to Michael Scott, sometimes to a monk who fell from grace in ancient times, are also associated with Melrose Abbey. A ghostly figure that has been reportedly seen sliding like a snake along the ground in the Abbey ruins is taken to be a manifestation of this spirit.

Iona

The tiny island of Iona off the west coast of Scotland is visited by many hundreds of people every year. It is a place of historical interest and pilgrimage, and it was here that St Columba landed from Ireland to begin his mission of spreading the word of God in Scotland in the sixth century. Kings of Scotland from ancient times are buried on Iona, and today the island is a religious center of quite considerable significance.

Iona was attacked by the Vikings on several occasions in times gone by, and the monastery of St Columba had to be restored repeatedly. The ghostly forms of Viking longboats are still said to visit the island from time to time. The ships glide into the harbor by night and eerie figures scramble ashore, re-enacting over and over again their desecration of this sacred place.

Monks have been reported as having been seen at various places on the island, especially in the area of the monastery, and the sound of their chanting has also been heard on several occasions.

Perth

In the early years of the nineteenth century, an Edinburgh priest who had moved to Perth, called Father McKay, was approached by a woman who had been troubled for some time by a conscience-stricken ghost. The problem was solved without the need for exorcism or dramatic intervention of any kind.

Anne Simpson, the woman who sought Father McKay's assistance, was not of the Catholic faith, but she had good reason for asking the help of a Catholic priest. It turned out that the ghost that had been appearing to her night after night was that of a woman whom she had known as a familiar figure around the army barracks nearby. The woman's name was Molloy, and she had worked in the barracks laundry. Mrs Molloy's ghost, when it appeared to Anne Simpson, was most persistent. Mrs Molloy owed money—three shillings and ten pence. She wanted Anne Simpson to tell a priest and ask him to set matters right.

So here was Anne Simpson, tired of constantly interrupted sleep, doing the bidding of a ghost! Lesser men might have sent the poor woman away and told her to stop talking such nonsense, but Father McKay listened to her story patiently and assured her that he would see what he could do.

He made enquiries at the barracks first of all. Sure enough, there had been a woman called Molloy working there, but she had died some time before. Had she owed any money to anybody in the barracks, the priest wanted to know. No, she had not owed any money there. The priest had to take his search a little farther afield. Visiting local traders, he found himself in the grocer's shop. When he asked about Mrs Molloy, he discovered that when she had died she was in debt to the grocer. And the amount of the debt? Three shillings and ten pence exactly.

The kindly priest settled the outstanding amount and left the shop. When he saw Anne Simpson some days later, he asked whether Mrs Molloy's ghost had appeared to her recently. He was quite relieved to hear that the ghost seemed to have gone. Obviously the spirit of Mrs Molloy felt at peace now that she had got all her affairs in order!

Rosslyn Chapel

Rosslyn Chapel lies quite close to Edinburgh, to the south of the city. Founded in 1446 by William Sinclair, Earl of Orkney, it is a popular visitor site and a place of historical, religious and architectural interest.

Historically, the chapel is the subject of much controversy. Some historians believe that the chapel had strong links in the past with the Knights Templar. Many theories have been proposed as to the supposed existence of religious relics—some believe this includes the Holy Grail—hidden within an underground vault beneath the floor of the chapel. The most recent theory at the time of writing is the most astonishing—that the chapel has buried beneath it the mummified head of Christ, which was worshipped by the Knights Templar hundreds of years ago. The trustees of the chapel are under constant pressure to carry out excavations to find out whether there is any truth in any of the many theories about its mysterious past.

Architecturally, Rosslyn is interesting for several different reasons. The interior of the chapel is unusually ornate for a Scottish church and is unique amongst its contemporaries. Scottish religious buildings of the time were characteristically very plain in design, and although Rosslyn is essentially a Gothic building, its fanciful decoration and exotic—some would say eccentric—ornament make it stand apart from all others. There is evidence to suggest that many foreign craftsmen were employed in its construction, which would account in part for some of the decorative elements that are in evidence in the building. One piece of particular merit within the chapel is a very ornate and beautifully carved pillar known as the Apprentice or Prentice Pillar. The Apprentice Pillar has a story of its own to tell. The story goes that when the chapel was being constructed a stone mason was requested to carve this pillar in the style of a particular column in Rome. The mason was finding it difficult to reproduce the desired effect using the picture he had of the column as his only source of inspiration. To prepare himself adequately for the task, he decided to travel to Rome to see the original column for himself. A journey of this sort was quite an undertaking in those days, and the mason was away for some weeks. In the absence of his master, the stonemason's apprentice, who had been left behind, decided to try to carve a pillar himself. He studied the picture that his master had been given and set to work.

When the stonemason returned from Italy, he found that the work that his apprentice had done was far superior to anything he might have been able to carve himself. In a fit of rage and jealousy, he killed his apprentice on the spot. The story of the murder is given credence by the fact that there had to be a delay between the construction of the chapel and its eventual consecration, which took place only after an Act of Reconciliation had been sought from the Archbishop of St Andrews.

The ghostly apprentice returned to haunt the chapel and the work of which he was so proud. His mournful figure has been seen standing beside his pillar and the sound of his weeping has been heard by many people who have visited the chapel over the years.

Another ghostly figure that frequents the chapel and its

surroundings is the figure of a monk clad in gray. He has appeared to visitors on quite a few occasions, both inside and outside the chapel.

St Andrews Cathedral

St Andrews Cathedral, dating from the twelfth century, lies in ruins now but was once the largest cathedral in Scotland and a powerful and influential religious center. In all, building work took almost two hundred years. The royal burgh of St Andrews, in which the cathedral stands, is a very old and beautiful university town, of great interest both to the historian and the ghost-hunter.

The cathedral has two ghosts that are particularly well known, one a woman, the other a man.

In the grounds of the cathedral at St Andrews is St Rule's Tower, a remnant of St Rule's Church, which was built before the cathedral and used to hold the relics of St Andrew. It is here that the male ghost has been seen. The tower is quite high, and the view from the top, looking over the town, is well worth seeing, so it is quite a popular visiting place. One visitor to the tower several years ago was startled by a figure in a cassock who appeared as he was climbing to the top. The tourist missed his footing on one of the steps and stumbled. Far from wishing to frighten the tourist, the cowled figure had genuinely intended to be helpful, for the tourist heard him offer to give him his arm on the way up the stairs. The tourist, swiftly recovering his balance, refused politely, and the figure stepped to one side to allow him to pass and then vanished without trace.

When the tourist came out of the tower at the end of his visit, he asked the man at the door whether anyone else had been in the tower at the same time as himself. The man at the door said that there had been no one else there, but he knew who, or what, the tourist had seen. The tourist discovered that the figure that he had seen was well known to those who knew the tower. He was a monk who would appear from time to time at St Rule's—not a malevolent spirit at all, it would seem, but a kindly ghost who liked to make sure that visitors made their way safely to the top of the spiral staircase.

The female ghost is a white lady who has been seen in the grounds of the cathedral. The ghost was observed to be wearing white gloves. Some of the sightings may well have been fanciful, perhaps fuelled by alcohol, as they were made by students returning from late-night revelries. Nevertheless, the White Lady has also been seen by more sober citizens of the town from time to time over a period of nearly two centuries.

The identity of the White Lady is not known, but it may be that her burial place is very near. In 1868, historians investigating the tower opened a sealed vault there and discovered it to be a burial place. There were six or so coffins inside it. They also found, it is claimed, the mummified body of a young woman wearing white gloves. The vault was re-sealed, but it appears that the historians had discovered part of the answer to the mysterious appearances of the White Lady of St Andrews.

Sanquhar Kirkyard

In the eighteenth and nineteenth centuries, the kirkyard at Sanquhar, in the Borders, achieved notoriety on account of the ghostly activities of a man called Abraham Crichton. Abraham Crichton died in 1745 in a particularly unpleasant manner after a colorful life.

Crichton was a wealthy man, laird of Carco and the owner of several properties in the area as well as a great deal of land.

However, much to the suspicion of various local people, he was declared bankrupt in 1741. His properties and land were sold off bit by bit, but rumors were circulated that Crichton was not in the dire straits that he would have people believe. He had, somewhere, secreted away a great deal of money. This, combined with the manner of his death, made it hardly surprising that his tortured soul would be unable to find peace.

There was a disused church in the district, which had been the kirk of a former parish, that of Kirkbride. For some years there had been a dispute as to what to do with the building. Some locals wanted to tear it down, whilst in the opinion of others such an act amounted to sacrilege. The story goes that previous attempts to demolish the church had been unsuccessful and that those who had taken part in the exercise found themselves the victims of considerable misfortune as a result. In the eyes of those who believed in such things, these happenings had been manifestations of the wrath of God.

Abraham Crichton was having none of this. He wanted the church to be brought down. He engaged a group of workmen to accompany him to the building to start demolition. They set to work, but hardly had they done so than an almighty storm blew up, preventing them from getting any work done. Forced to abandon their efforts until the next day, they all set off for home.

Whilst riding back from Kirkbride, Abraham Crichton met with disaster. A bolt of lightning caused his horse to rear up in panic and Crichton was unseated. A tumble from a horse is bad enough, but one of Crichton's feet had become wedged in the stirrup and as the horse bolted, he was dragged along in its wake. The horse galloped off at a great rate, and it did not stop, nor even slow down, until it reached Dalpeddar. When the frightened beast finally drew to a halt, its owner lay by its side, lifeless and bloody.

It seemed as if the death of Abraham Crichton was divine retribution. Not only had this man been dishonest in his financial dealings, said his critics, but he had also been guilty of sacrilege. He should never have tried to tear the church down. The locals shook their heads and tut-tutted self-righteously as preparations were made for Crichton's funeral.

They had not seen the last of Abraham Crichton, however. Not long after he was buried in the graveyard at Sanquhar, he returned in ghostly form. The ghost of Abraham Crichton caused great consternation in the district. He would pursue passers-by in the fields next to the churchyard. He would appear suddenly in the churchyard itself, frightening the life out of anyone who happened to be there. Always, he seemed to be trying to speak to those whom he followed. His hand would stretch out in entreaty, but none dared to take it. The kirkyard at Sanquhar became a place much feared in the hours of darkness. Locals would take detours in order to avoid passing close to the church as a longer walk was considered well worth the effort if it meant avoiding the ghost of Abraham Crichton. News of the haunting spread, and Sanquhar became a topic of heated debate amongst those who had any interest in matters paranormal.

At length it was decided that something had to be done, the ghost was causing too many difficulties. A minister by the name of Hunter was appointed to deal with Crichton's troublesome spirit. The bold minister took himself to the kirkyard one dark night with a bible and a sword to await an encounter with Crichton. He insisted on carrying out his vigil alone, and no one saw what came to pass in the course of the night. When morning came, however, the minister left the churchyard, tired but in confident mood. He never related precisely what happened during those long hours of darkness. He was, however, able to give his assurance that Abraham Crichton's ghost would wander no more.

The ghost was never seen after that, but, just in case, the people of Sanquhar secured his tombstone in its place over the grave with very sturdy chains.

Ghosts in the House

I T IS not only buildings of great history or particular architectural interest that feel the chill of the ghost's presence. Homes all over Scotland, both old and relatively new, are claimed to have been the site of supernatural occurrences. Some of these claims will certainly be fanciful, some will be mere sensationalism, but many are simply too strange to be ignored.

Abbotsford House, Melrose

Abbotsford House was the home of the celebrated poet and novelist Sir Walter Scott and is now a popular tourist attraction. A great deal of building work was carried out there according to Scott's own specifications, incorporating many of the features he had seen and admired in various buildings he had visited throughout Scotland during his life.

The house must have been a considerable financial burden to the novelist, especially after he suffered great losses when the publisher's firm in which he was a partner collapsed, but Scott worked at his writing with incredible industry to keep the house in his possession and to pay off his debts before his death. Before he died, Sir Walter Scott is reported to have made claims that the house was haunted, the ghost being, it was thought, that of one of the craftsmen who had worked on the building, a man named George Bullock. George Bullock had had a supervisory role in many of the building works at Abbotsford, but he died while the work was still in progress.

Since the death of Sir Walter Scott himself at Abbotsford

in 1832, there have been stories of the writer putting in an appearance from time to time in ghostly form, often in the dining room in which he spent his last days and where he eventually died.

Allanbank House, Berwickshire

Allanbank House is now no longer standing, having been destroyed in the early nineteenth century, but the ghost that once frequented the house is well remembered. She is known as "Pearlin' Jean"—the word "Pearlin'" referring to the distinct pattern of the lace that she wore on her collar and dress. She was thought to have been the lover of the first baronet of Allanbank, Robert Stuart, who lived in the seventeenth century.

According to some versions of the story, Jean was French and lived as a nun (presumably not in a closed convent) until she met Robert Stuart and became his lover. Some say that Pearlin' Jean actually returned to Scotland and to Allanbank with Stuart for a while. Whether or not this was the case, it appeared that Stuart did not see her as a suitable wife and, in time, he became engaged to another woman, leaving poor Jean in the lurch. Jean had sacrificed everything to be with Robert: her love, her respectability—virtually her life. She could not return to her former life; she had nothing more to lose.

Some versions of the story say that what happened next took place in Paris, whilst others place the incident at Allanbank itself. Wherever it happened, the consequences were tragic. Robert Stuart was driving out in his coach when the figure of Pearlin' Jean appeared in front of the carriage. She jumped up on to the carriage with the intention of confronting Robert and making him change his mind. Robert, on the other hand, was horrified to see Jean. He whipped the horses into a gallop,

causing the carriage to move forward with a great jolt. Jean
lost her grip and was thrown from her perch, falling under
the wheels of the carriage. Whether by accident or by design,
Robert saw his former sweetheart crushed to death beneath
the wheels as the horses galloped on.

It was Robert himself who first saw the ghost of Pearlin'
Jean. He was returning to Allanbank one night when he saw
her, a ghostly white figure perched at the gateway, her head
covered in blood. He was rendered speechless with fear.

Pearlin' Jean continued to shatter the peace of the house
long after her death, banging doors and clattering around
the corridors. She was still seen and heard at Allanbank long
after the death of Robert Stuart, but future inhabitants of the
house were not threatened by her presence as he had been.
She became a familiar sight and sound, regarded with something approaching affection. Visitors, however, were often
startled by her antics and her bloody appearance.

Since the destruction of the house, Pearlin' Jean seems to
have gone, but she will be long remembered.

Ballachulish House, Argyll

Ballachulish House has more than one ghost, but one particular tale informs us that a "living ghost" once made a habit
of visiting the place.

The house was at one time occupied by the family of Sir
Harold Boulton. Many years before he moved into Ballachulish House, Sir Harold had heard his mother talk of a
recurrent dream she had had of visiting a beautiful house set
amidst spectacular scenery. In her dreams she had become
acquainted with every corner of the place, much as if she had
really been there.

Several years later, Mrs Boulton, by then quite elderly,

visited Ballachulish House for the first time before her son and his family had moved in. The house was at that time owned by Lady Beresford. Mrs Boulton found to her great surprise that she already knew the house very well indeed—it was the house with which she had become intimately acquainted in her dreams.

When Mrs Boulton spoke to Lady Beresford about this, giving credence to her story with additional knowledge about structural alterations that had taken place over the years, she was pleased to see that Lady Beresford took her quite seriously. Ballachulish House had been visited several times over the years by the benign specter of a lady. Now, Lady Beresford was quite convinced that the specter was in fact the living ghost of Mrs Boulton.

Ballechin House, Perthshire

Ballechin House used to stand near Dunkeld, some miles from Perth. It was built at the beginning of the nineteenth century and was the home of the Steuart family. Strange goings-on at Ballechin House are said to have started after the death of Major Robert Steuart in 1876. The house was inherited by John Steuart, the major's nephew.

In the late 1890s the house was rented out for a period of some months. The family that had taken the lease, however, stayed no more than a matter of weeks. They left Ballechin in fear, having been tormented by a cacophony of strange sounds: bumps, rattles, thumps and knocks, doors slamming, footsteps and angry voices. They had also experienced an unnatural chill about the building.

On another occasion, a guest in the house was continuously tormented by disturbing noises. One night he reported that he had woken to hear what sounded like a dog trying to burst into his room. The house became the focus of great curiosity, and several people with an interest in psychical research visited the place or stayed there for a while over the course of time in an attempt to investigate further the cause of the strange events that were supposed to be happening there.

Ballechin was also haunted by nuns, who could be seen outside the house. John Steuart himself was witness to this sight and to the sounds of loud knocking. John was killed by a cab in London, and it is said that he was given some warning of his untimely death by the ghostly sights and sounds at Ballechin.

Blythswood Square, Glasgow

Blythswood Square in the center of Glasgow is a square of fine Georgian buildings with a mixed history. Now the site of offices of lawyers and accountants, it once had a reputation as being something of a red-light district. In years before that, it was more of a residential area and considered to be a very desirable place to live.

One particular gentleman, house-hunting in the area, came upon a house in Blythswood Square that was for sale. Upon inspecting the property, he was very impressed with it all, with the exception of the bathroom. There was something about the bathroom that gave the house a very unpleasant air, and the gentleman could not quite put his finger on what it was. The room had a cold and dreary atmosphere, but there was something else, something foreboding. The room made him shudder. Nevertheless, the thought of having a prestigious address such as this was too tempting for both the gentleman and his wife. The bathroom would surely take on a brighter atmosphere with a few coats of fresh paint and new fittings. They bought the house and moved in.

Ghosts in the House

The gentleman still felt very uneasy about using the bathroom, in spite of its bright new appearance and in spite of his family's reassurances that all was normal. He did not like to close the door when he was having a bath. His wife, however, protested at such immodest behavior. Reluctantly, the gentleman had to respect her wishes. The next time he went to take a bath, he summoned up the courage to close the door behind him.

The gentleman could see that there was no one else in the bathroom, but in spite of this he still had the distinct feeling that there was someone else there. It was uncanny. Trying to ignore his feelings of misgiving, he placed his candle at the edge of the bath, undressed and stepped into the water.

Hardly had the gentleman got into the bath, however, than he heard strange sounds coming from the fire grate. He tried to ignore them but they persisted. He got up to investigate, his heart hammering. Cautiously he stepped out of the bath. Suddenly the candle went out, and as the room was plunged into darkness, the gentleman tripped and fell to the floor. Frozen with terror, he then heard the sounds of loud splashing coming from the bath. Someone was in the bath, washing! But that was impossible—there was nobody there!

The gentleman hardly had time to ponder upon this, for after only a few seconds he heard the cupboard door behind him opening. A figure stepped out of the cupboard. The gentleman could hear the rustling of skirts and smell the cloying scent of perfume. The gentleman had no time to get out of the ghostly figure's way. A chilly foot in a high-heeled shoe stepped on his back quite carelessly as the specter of a woman, apparently oblivious of the gentleman's presence, made her way towards the bath.

The gentleman gasped and listened. Sounds of a struggle came from the bath, a violent struggle. There was much splashing and thrashing about. Then, all of a sudden, the noises stopped. The woman turned to face the gentleman, and through the darkness he saw a ghostly white face quite startling in its luminosity. The face was obviously that of a beautiful woman, but it was contorted with an expression of pure hatred.

The gentleman had seen and heard enough. He fumbled his way to the bathroom door, unlocked it and fled to the safety of his bedroom. When he told his wife what had happened, he was met with ridicule and told not to be so foolish. His fear was dismissed as mere hysteria.

Then one morning the gentleman's son went to use the bathroom and was greeted with the sight of a dead man floating in the bath water. His screams alerted the rest of the family, who came running. When they went into the bathroom they could see nothing. But when they were coming out, they were all witness to the sight of a beautiful dark-haired woman, a look of unmistakable hatred on her face, sweeping past them into the bathroom cupboard.

The family left the house—no matter how desirable the address, the spectral inhabitants made life there unbearable. Once they had found themselves a suitable, less sinister place to live, they made enquiries about the history of the house in Blythswood Square.

Their investigations were quite enlightening. Apparently the house had once been the property of a wealthy man married to a Spanish woman with a violent temper. The man had been found drowned in his bath one morning. The circumstances had been suspicious, but no foul play could be proved, and his beautiful widow left the country.

The gentleman and his family knew the terrible truth about what had happened, and the gentleman now realized that what he had experienced was the ghostly re-enactment of the whole sordid affair.

Boleskin House, Inverness=shire

Boleskin House is situated on the southeast shores of Loch Ness, close to the village of Foyers. The house dates from the second half of the eighteenth century, and its history was unremarkable until it was bought just over a century later by a man called Aleister Crowley. Had Aleister Crowley lived three hundred years before, his activities would have had to have been conducted in the utmost secrecy or he would have surely met a premature and exceedingly unpleasant end. As it was, Mr Crowley took a certain pride in the fact that he was proclaimed to be the "wickedest man in the world." He was known to practise black magic and to be obsessed with the satanic and profane. His house was the scene of drug- and alcohol-fuelled orgies, sacrifice and satanic ritual. He died in 1947. Boleskin House is said to be troubled by evil spirits and poltergeist activity, and both the house and the graveyard nearby—rumored to be connected by a secret underground tunnel—are said to be sites that witches haunt. The eerie atmosphere that surrounds the place and the knowledge of the lifestyle of its one-time occupant make this hardly surprising.

Broomhill House, Lanarkshire

The case of Broomhill House was given a great deal of publicity in the 1960s when a television documentary was made on the subject of its ghost. The house stood on a site that had been inhabited for hundreds of years, buildings of various forms having been successively built and destroyed during the course of time. The house in its final form was the home of the McNeil-Hamilton family at the turn of the century, and the last of the family to live there was Captain Henry Montgomery McNeil-Hamilton. The ghost that haunts the ruins, the Black Lady, is well known to locals in Larkhall, the area of Lanarkshire where the ruins of the house stand. The house has attracted the interest of clairvoyants and ghost-hunters alike, and much research has been carried out by psychic investigators and other interested parties to find out who the Black Lady was and why she haunts the place.

The ghost is a sad one, it would appear, and she has been seen and has been making her presence felt since quite early on in the twentieth century.

Captain Henry McNeil-Hamilton was a military man and served in South Africa during the Boer War. It is thought that the Black Lady was in fact an Indian woman who, having been taken to South Africa, found herself working for the British Army there. She was possibly brought to Scotland by McNeil-Hamilton to live as his mistress. There are stories of such a lady living at Broomhill, who seemed to disappear in mysterious circumstances, and some people believe that she may have met a violent end.

Broomhill suffered from a fire in the 1940s and was badly damaged. The McNeil-Hamilton family sold the house and land in 1954. The house, already in a desperate state, fell further into ruin and very little remains now. Nevertheless, in spite of attempts at exorcism over the years, the Black Lady is still said to be there, her appearances characterized by an overpowering feeling of melancholy and a smell of spices and perfume.

Bruntsfield, Edinburgh

There was, until the beginning of the nineteenth century, a house by Bruntsfield Links, one of great age, having been built in the fourteenth century, and of considerable elegance. In the years leading up to its eventual demolition (after which a school was built on the site), the house was inhabited by Lieutenant-General Robertson of Lawers and his staff. Not long after he had taken up residence in the house, the general received a complaint from one of his servants that he was getting very little sleep on account of a headless woman, carrying a baby, who would appear near the fireplace in his room night after night. The complainant was known to have a tendency to indulge in strong drink whenever given the opportunity, so naturally the general assumed at first that his servant was suffering from alcohol-induced delusions. As time wore on, however, the servant persisted with his complaints and eventually left the house to look for work somewhere else.

The general thereafter had the room in which the servant had slept primarily used for storage. No one went into the room at night, so no more ghosts were seen.

The story might have been completely forgotten about had it not been for the fact that the building was subjected to a demolition order some years later. When the builders began to tear the building down, they lifted the hearth in the servant's old room and found the skeletal remains of a woman and a baby.

The woman had had her head severed—a particularly brutal act of violence by any standards. The story goes that she must have been sewing when her killer took her by surprise, for scissors and a needle were found beside the bones of her hands, as if she had been holding them. Who she was and why she was killed so savagely along with her child, nobody will ever know.

Buckingham Terrace, Edinburgh

Buckingham Terrace is situated by the Dean Bridge, close to

the center of Edinburgh. It is an imposing crescent of houses, many of which are divided into elegant flats.

In the nineteenth century, the residents in one particular flat in Buckingham Terrace, the Gordon family, became aware of a sinister presence in their home shortly after moving in. The flat above had been uninhabited for some time and, apart from some pieces of furniture that were stored there, it was empty. Mrs Gordon was therefore very surprised and quite concerned when she awoke one night to hear noises coming from the room above her head. There was a great deal of banging and thumping, as if heavy objects were being moved around.

The noises were repeated the next night, and Mrs Gordon was moved to make a complaint to the landlord. No satisfactory explanation could be offered for the disturbances, however. The Gordon family were the only occupants of the building. There was little the landlord could do except suggest that perhaps Mrs Gordon's ears were deceiving her and that the noise was traveling from farther away, perhaps the adjoining building.

Mrs Gordon was adamant. The noises were coming from the upper flat, from the room directly above her bedroom.

It was not long after this that Mrs Gordon began to become aware of a distinct feeling of dread when she was in her bedroom. She woke one night feeling quite fearful. Normally a calm, rational sort of person, she was not given to experiencing such feelings. It felt to her as if something or someone was in the room, although she could see nothing. The presence—for it now seemed certain that something was there—would move past her as she lay in bed at night, then go out of her room quietly. After it had left Mrs Gordon's room, she could hear it climbing the stairs to the floor above. The sounds, quiet at first, would then build to a sudden crescendo. The banging noises that she had heard on previous occasions would start up again. Then the sounds would change in quality once more, and Mrs Gordon would hear staccato, stamping noises, as if someone was jumping up and down on the floor above her head.

There was little Mrs Gordon could do about the strange occurrences, for any suggestion she might make to the landlord that the place might be haunted would undoubtedly have been met with denial and probably derision. She had enquired of the rest of her family whether they had been disturbed by anything at night, but they had not heard a thing.

Then Mrs Gordon's daughter experienced similar occurrences. Her mother was away, and she decided to sleep in her room one night. She had barely opened the door than she felt something push past her, moving towards the stair to the upper floor. The girl, perhaps emboldened by a rush of adrenaline, charged after the "thing" as it headed for the empty flat above. At the doorway, she stopped, but she could hear that the thing had gone inside. Now, from the sounds she could hear through the door, the "thing" was moving furniture around!

Tentatively the girl tried the door and found it to be unlocked. She turned the handle, pushed the door wide open and stared into the gloom from the doorway. Inside, she could just make out a dark figure bending over the open case of a grandfather clock. Something told her that the figure was not human or, at least, not a living human.

Suddenly her courage deserted her, and she froze in terror. The figure turned towards her. She ran, as fast as her legs could carry her, back down to the safety of her own flat. When the girl told her mother about what had happened, Mrs Gordon's suspicions that the building was haunted grew even stronger.

The ghostly figure appeared once more, this time to Mrs Gordon. She was lying in her bed one night when she became aware of the (now familiar) feeling of dread again. She looked up and saw a man standing in the doorway of the bedroom. He had a sinister, distracted air about him. In his hands he held what looked like a bundle of rags.

The family had experienced quite enough. They arranged forthwith to leave the flat in Buckingham Terrace.

Once they had settled comfortably elsewhere, however, Mrs Gordon determined to see what she could find out about the history of their flat in Buckingham Terrace. Investigations revealed that she and her family were not the only ones to believe that the place was haunted. Several rumors circulated about the flat, one of which was the following, which Mrs Gordon took to be the most likely.

According to the story, a retired seaman, a former captain in the merchant navy, had lived in the Gordons' flat some time before. The man was an alcoholic and was also believed to have been mentally disturbed. There had been a family with a young baby living in the flat above at that time, and the baby, as babies do, often cried at night.

On one particular night, the baby, who had been left alone for a while, had woken and was crying. The constant noise of the crying had annoyed the seaman to such an extent that he had stormed upstairs in a drunken rage and killed the baby. In a pathetic effort to conceal his crime, he had tried to hide the baby's body in the case of a grandfather clock. Of course, the dreadful deed had soon been discovered, and the seaman was eventually committed to an asylum, where it was said that he took his own life.

This story was dreadful indeed, but it did explain to the Gordon family why the presence kept thundering upstairs and why the ghostly figure had been bent over the open case of the grandfather clock. The seaman's ghost was condemned to re-enact his ghastly deed over and over again.

Crail, Fife

In the picturesque fishing town of Crail, in the East Neuk of Fife, a row of Victorian houses stands overlooking the harbor. They were built by a wealthy man for his five daughters, all spinsters. One of these houses has for several years been the holiday home of an Edinburgh family who have spent many a blissful summer walking the seaside paths and guddling about on the beach nearby. The house is now seeing its third generation of the family approach adulthood and must have many happy memories stored within its walls. Members of the family and visitors who have stayed in the house testify to the existence of a ghost in one of the bedrooms. The ghost is not a frightening one. All that can be seen through the darkness is a pair of eyes, which appear to be those of a woman. The eyes always appear in the same corner of the room, hidden from the window by a large wardrobe and out of reach of the reflection of any mirror or other trick of the light. The woman's eyes watch silently but benevolently. Perhaps the original occupant of the house, denied for whatever reason the pleasures of marriage and family life, takes some comfort from the fact that her old home is now frequented by families and children.

Crawford Priory, Fife

In spite of the ecclesiastical sound of the name of the place, Crawford Priory has no connections with the church whatsoever. It was built as a private home in 1813 by Lady Mary Crawford. Its architecture harks back to much earlier times, inspired as it is by Gothic religious style. On a gloomy day its impressive facade looks undeniably grim; in fact, it looks as if it ought to be haunted. The imaginative visitor could quite easily conjure up a picture of sinister cowled figures moving around the grounds or the headless specter of some unfortunate figure from the past. Such a vision would certainly fit the appearance of the building but is far removed from the truth.

Crawford Priory is haunted, but the ghost is free of any malevolence or unhappy history. Lady Mary was an eccentric figure by all accounts, a determined and sometimes fierce spinster who, having indulged her fantasy in the building of Crawford Priory, chose to share her life with a menagerie of animals upon whom she doted. She kept many animals and birds, both wild and domestic, at the priory and seemed to prefer their company to that of human beings. Lady Mary demonstrated her great concern for their welfare even after her death. In her will, she left instructions regarding the euthanasia of her brother's horse, which she had been looking after. She wanted the beast to suffer as little pain and distress as possible.

Lady Mary Crawford died in 1833, and her funeral was quite an impressive affair. She is buried in the family mausoleum nearby, but her ghost remains at the priory, wandering around the grounds, beckoning her beloved creatures to come to her.

Cullen House, Banffshire

Cullen House is situated close to the fishing village of Cullen in Banffshire, on the northeast coast of Scotland. The house and its lands have been the property of the Earls of Seafield for more than two hundred years. The ghost that haunts Cullen House is thought to be that of the third Earl of Seafield, by the name of James Ogilvie. James was known to suffer from a severely disabling form of mental illness and was often seized by fits of an uncontrollable nature, during which he was said to be a danger both to himself and to others. When one of these fits was imminent, his staff, who could recognize the signs, would do their best to secure him and keep him from harm. On one occasion, however, they were unsuccessful. The "Mad Earl," as he was known, had a particularly violent attack, in the course of which there was a struggle between him and a very close friend. The friend was killed. When the Earl regained his wits and realized what he had done, he was completely overcome with despair and anguish. So distressed was he that he took his own life. His ghost is said to wander the site even now.

Dalkeith, Midlothian

An attractive old house on the edge of Dalkeith, just outside Edinburgh, was the scene of some very sinister events early in the twentieth century. On 3 February 1911, a large dinner party was held, after which several people fell dangerously ill and two lost their lives. A postmortem examination showed that they had been poisoned. The two dead men were named as John Hutchinson and Alec Clapperton. The poisoner turned out to have been John, the son of Charles Hutchinson. He fled to the Channel Islands after the incident and when finally cornered by police there, he ended his own life by taking prussic acid.

A strange presence, thought to be the ghost of Charles Hutchinson, remains very much in evidence in the house nowadays, in the room where the dinner party took place. The family who live there testify to a strange atmosphere in the room and the family dogs are reluctant to enter it.

Frendraught House, Aberdeenshire

Frendraught House, as it stands today, was constructed in the seventeenth century around a much older castle. The property stands in beautiful surroundings close to the town of Huntly and is haunted by a ghost whose story starts in 1630.

In 1630, the laird of Frendraught at the time, Sir James Crichton, killed Gordon of Rothiemay in a dispute over land. As a consequence of this, he was ordered by the Marquis of Huntly to pay compensation, or blood money, to Gordon's son and namesake.

Some time later, Crichton became involved in a feud with Leslie of Pitcaple. Fearing violence from Leslie, Crichton sought the services of the Marquis of Huntly's son, Viscount Aboyne, and the new laird of Rothiemay as part of an armed guard to protect him.

The men were lodged in the tower for the night. A terrible fire broke out and several people were killed—Viscount Aboyne, Gordon of Rothiemay, Colonel Ivat, English Will and their servants.

It was agreed that the fire had probably been started deliberately—Lady Crichton was the one upon whom most people's suspicions fell—but an official investigation that took place at Frendraught in 1631 was unsuccessful in finding enough evidence to blame any one individual, and the laird and his wife escaped any form of retribution.

The Lady of Frendraught apparently was troubled by her conscience after death, for she has returned to the scene of the crime several times since then. Her ghost, reportedly dressed in white, is traditionally never seen or heard by any laird of Frendraught, but other people, either living in the house or visiting it, have witnessed the presence of something supernatural, either seeing the figure of a lady or hearing loud sounds of raised voices and banging, which have no rational explanation.

Inverawe House, Argyll

On the road west to Oban lies Taynuilt, where Inverawe House, owned by the family Campbell, keeps its own store of ghosts.

One room in the house is home to one of the many green ladies that frequent Scotland. Green Jean's origins are a matter for some debate, but one theory as to her identity has a particularly charming story attached to it.

Green Jean is believed to have been a woman called Mary Cameron, who lived in the seventeenth century. She was betrothed to Diarmid Campbell of Inverawe. Mary's family lived in a place called Callart House and, according to the legend that is told, Mary had upset her father, who had locked her in her room for a period as punishment. She must have been locked in the room for some time, for whilst she was confined, it is said, a Spanish ship carrying the plague arrived in Loch Leven, a small sea loch on the west coast. The infection spread rapidly, and before long all in the Cameron household had succumbed save Mary.

Left alone in the strangely quiet building, she was greatly relieved to hear sounds of activity outside. She called out to ask what was happening and was distressed to find that the noises outside were those of men who had been sent to burn the house down to clear away all traces of infection. When it was discovered that there was still someone alive in the house, a message was sent to Inverawe to ask for help. Diarmid Campbell arrived and released Mary, but they were unable to find shelter anywhere nearby, so frightened were the people of catching the plague. Not even Diarmid's family would offer them shelter. Diarmid and Mary were forced to struggle for survival out in the wild for quite some time before Campbell's father was convinced that neither carried the disease and allowed them to return to Inverawe, where they married and lived happily. The ghost of Mary Cameron returns to Inverawe, the place which must hold many happy memories for her.

The ghost of Duncan Campbell, resplendent in full Highland dress, is another that is said to haunt Inverawe.

In the early 1700s, Duncan's brother, Donald, was killed by Stewart of Appin in a fight. Having ended the life of Donald Campbell, Stewart then took himself to Inverawe House where Duncan, unaware as yet of his brother's death, offered hospitality.

The night after Stewart arrived, Duncan was tormented by the bloody figure of his brother appearing at his bedside, accusing him of making his murderer welcome, but he took no action. Finally, the ghostly figure gave up, but not before telling Duncan that he would meet him at Ticonderoga.

Duncan Campbell had no idea where Ticonderoga was until some years later, when serving with the Black Watch in America, he took part in an attack on a French fortress of the same name. He died from the injuries that he sustained in the battle—the ghost of his brother had finally been avenged.

At Inverawe House his figure returns from time to time, visiting the room that has been named after the battle where he lost his life.

Learmonth Gardens, Edinburgh

Learmonth Gardens is a quiet street in the respectable district of Comely Bank in the north of Edinburgh. One of the houses has a disturbing history. In the mid-1930s, the house was occupied by a baronet, Sir Alexander Seton, and his family. The family took a trip to Egypt and brought back a souvenir that they would later regret ever having set eyes upon.

The trip to Egypt incorporated a visit to the Temple of Luxor and in spite of the fact that it was illegal to remove anything from the tombs, Lady Seton picked up a small bone as a memento and brought it back to Scotland with her. The bone was placed in a glass case in the dining room.

The family had hardly settled back into normal life when strange and disturbing things started to happen. Crashing sounds were heard and furniture was found in disarray. Ornaments were found broken in rooms that had been empty. Lady Seton fell suddenly and inexplicably ill with a mystery complaint.

Time and time again, the family was disturbed by strange occurrences for which no explanation could be found. Strangest of all was the sighting of a ghostly figure in long robes that appeared in the house to several people, residents and visitors alike. Servants of the family became unnerved and sought employment elsewhere.

At one point Sir Alexander lent the bone to a scientist friend. Strangely, the ghostly figure disappeared from Learmonth Gardens for a while, only to be seen at the home of his friend. The family could no longer ignore the fact that the bone seemed to be responsible for the troubles that had been affecting them. Such a story could not remain a secret within the family for long, of course, and the Edinburgh newspapers were soon full of the news of the "Curse of the Pharaoh," as they called it.

The bone was returned to Learmonth Gardens, and once more the furniture seemed to take on a life of its own. Sir Alexander himself became ill. Unable to withstand the strain any longer, Sir Alexander eventually surrendered the bone to a priest whom he knew. The bone was exorcised and then burnt. Thankfully, the torment came to an end when the bone was destroyed.

Leith Hall, Aberdeenshire

Leith Hall, Kennethmount, in Aberdeenshire is now a National Trust for Scotland property, but from its construction in the seventeenth century until 1945 it was owned by the Leith family. The family suffered a tragedy in 1763 when John Leith was shot by his wife, Elizabeth, during what is thought to have been a drunken argument. He died from his wounds. A ghost appeared to the people who were living in Leith Hall in the late 1960s which is thought to be that of the victim himself. Another ghost, a woman, is also believed to haunt the building. Her identity is not known.

An American writer called Elizabeth Byrd occupied part of the building with her husband, Barrie Gaunt. They both reported hearing strange noises for which they could find no obvious explanation and the sounds of footsteps and banging doors in parts of the house that they knew to be empty. Strange smells were noticed, too, similar to the scent of incense, and Byrd and her husband swore they could hear the sound of music playing and the drone of bagpipes. On one particular occasion, Barrie Gaunt saw the figure of a woman in one of the rooms they lived in. The figure was dressed in eighteenth-century clothing.

Elizabeth Byrd also reported that she found the atmosphere in the master bedroom most unsettling and that one night, as she slept in the large four-poster bed in that room, she awoke suddenly to see the figure of a man in Highland dress standing at the foot of the bed. The man's head was swathed in bandages, but from what she could see, he bore remarkable resemblance to the portrait of John Leith with which she was familiar.

Morningside, Edinburgh

Morningside is an area in the south of Edinburgh that has jokingly earned a nationwide reputation for being rather genteel and somewhat pretentious. Before Morningside grew into a suburb of the capital and acquired its "fur coat and nae breeks" reputation, it was more of a rural area. Here, in 1712, a man called Sir Thomas Elphinstone purchased a large house when he retired from colonial life.

Sir Thomas was a widower—his wife had died when she gave birth to their only son, who was now grown up and had flown the nest. Sir Thomas's life in Morningside might have been destined to be rather a lonely one were it not for the fact that he was courting a young lady and hoping to marry her. The young lady's family was in favor of the match in spite of the considerable age difference between the two parties, but the young lady, Elizabeth Pittendale, was not quite so enamored. Her heart belonged to another, an army officer called Jack Courage.

In spite of her misgivings, Elizabeth told Jack that they must end their relationship. Jack was about to be posted abroad, and the distance would help to sever the ties between the two of them. Elizabeth married Sir Thomas Elphinstone and settled in the house in Morningside.

It was a matter of months later that Sir Thomas told Elizabeth that she would be given the opportunity to meet his son, John, who was returning from military service abroad. When the young man arrived and was introduced to Elizabeth, however, she found it hard to behave as a stepmother might, for Sir Thomas's son, John, was none other than the young man she had known and loved as Jack Courage.

It was inevitable that their relationship would resume and, accordingly, that it would be discovered by Sir Thomas. They could not keep their feelings for each other a secret for long. Sir Thomas entered a room one day to find his son and his wife engaged in a passionate embrace. Filled with rage, Sir Thomas attacked his son, who fought back with all his strength. Elizabeth, distraught to see such violence, tried to intervene and was stabbed accidentally by Sir Thomas. The wound was fatal. When Sir Thomas realized what had happened, he was heartbroken. He killed himself. Husband and wife were buried together in the family vault.

John survived but left the house, renting it out to an acquaintance. The new tenant was the first to see the ghostly figure of a weeping lady walking down the corridor to one of the bedrooms. The man was not frightened by the ghost but was sad to see her in such distress. He sought the help of a medium, who told him that Elizabeth's spirit could not be at peace as long as she was buried beside her killer.

John was informed of this and at once arranged for Elizabeth's body to be moved. The ghost was never again seen in the house in Morningside. When John himself died a few years later, he was buried, according to his wishes, beside his sweetheart, Elizabeth.

New Lanark, Lanarkshire

New Lanark is a historic village at the edge of the market town of Lanark. It was built in the 1780s by the Glasgow banker and cotton merchant David Dale as a social experiment. Workers in the mills in New Lanark had better working conditions than many of their contemporaries elsewhere, and there was also provision for the education and welfare of their families. The village is now a World Heritage site.

It took thirty years for two people from New Lanark to find out that they had both had the experience of seeing the same ghost when they were children. The two were Mary Graham and her brother Alan who, when they were young, had lived with their parents in a flat above the family shop in New Lanark just after the turn of the nineteenth century.

The first to see the ghost had been Alan. The other members of the family had gone out for a while to visit his grandmother, leaving him alone in the house in bed. He had woken up feeling strangely cold and had seen the figure of a woman at his window. The woman was dressed in Highland clothes and she was knitting. She had walked towards the child and then passed him by, walking right through the closed bedroom door.

Alan had been very frightened by the experience, but his parents had told him quite firmly that it was nothing more than a dream, so no more was said about it.

Some time later, his sister Mary saw an identical figure in the flat. She was older than Alan. When she told her parents about what she had experienced, they admitted that what she had seen was probably a ghost. Mary was instructed that she was not to tell her brother, for he would be frightened and would not sleep at night. Mary's parents believed that the ghost meant no harm and probably had some connection with the shop below the flat, which had been at one time a doctor's surgery. Perhaps the woman had died as a result of, or in spite of, medical treatment she had received there. Perhaps she was the victim of something altogether more suspicious—no one could tell.

The tartan cape that the woman wore was possibly a clue as to where she came from originally. Many of the mill workers in New Lanark had come from the Highlands. Perhaps the ghost had been among those who had come to New Lanark to work.

Mary Graham did as her parents had told her—she never said a word to her brother Alan. It was only when they had both grown up that Alan spoke to her of his own encounter with the mystery woman. Finally, brother and sister discovered that they had both seen the same ghost.

Queensberry House, Edinburgh

Queensberry House, in Edinburgh's Canongate, was used in its last years as a hospital for the long-term care of the elderly and infirm. It is now demolished.

It was first built in the 1680s as a home for William Douglas, the first Duke of Queensberry. The Duke spent a great deal of time at Queensberry House, preferring life in the capital to staying at Drumlanrig Castle, his other residence.

A disturbing story about Queensberry House gave rise to reports that it was haunted.

It is said that there was one particular member of Queensberry's family who was insane. He was a powerful man and had to spend most of his life in confinement within the family home, both for his own safety and that of others.

One night, however, he was left at Queensberry House, locked in his room while the rest of the household went visiting elsewhere overnight. Only a kitchen hand remained at Queensberry House, tending to the kitchen fire.

The young lad was dozing by the fire when he was disturbed by the sound of footsteps. Rousing himself and sitting up, he was horrified to see the madman standing in the doorway of the kitchen. He had broken out of his room. The poor lad froze in terror as the madman came towards him, a maniacal gleam in his eye. The kitchen hand was young, small and slight. He was no match for his powerful opponent. Nor could he reason with his attacker—how can you reason with someone who has no grasp of reality whatsoever? He was helpless, abandoned to his fate at the hands of a lunatic.

The fate of the kitchen hand was dreadful. Terrible visions of his torment were to fill the nights of the rest of the household with terrible dreams for a long time to come. When they returned the next day to Queensberry House, the kitchen fire had gone out but the terrible smell of burning flesh filled the air. In the kitchen, they found the charred remains of the boy still tied to the spit where he had spent his last agonizing moments. He had, quite literally, been roasted alive.

The cries of the kitchen hand were to be heard in the old kitchen at Queensberry House for many years afterwards.

Other Haunted Houses

Compared to most of the buildings that have found their way into this book, one particular house in Edinburgh, being much less than a century old, is a surprisingly "young" place to find itself haunted. The house is in Stevenson Drive, on the western side of the city. The occupant, newly widowed, was stunned to see writing appearing on one of the inside walls. The man thought that perhaps his dead wife was trying to contact him from the afterlife, but as the scribblings on the wall were indecipherable, it was impossible to work out what she was trying to say, if indeed it was her work. After a short period, the writing stopped as mysteriously as it had begun, and no one was any the wiser as to who, or what, might have caused the phenomenon.

Another house in Edinburgh, in Hazeldean Terrace in the Liberton area, was the scene of vigorous activity by some sort of ghostly presence for a period of time. The activities, similar to those of a poltergeist, stopped quite suddenly after a period of three years or so.

Quite a few ghosts are said to inhabit houses in the granite city of Aberdeen in the northeast of Scotland. The shadowy figure of a young woman is said to haunt one particular house—the ghost of a young servant who was unjustly accused of theft by her employers. Driven to despair at having to live with the shame of their accusations, the young girl felt compelled to take her own life.

Another house is said to have been the "home" of quite a friendly ghost. The figure was that of a man, wearing a large hat and a cloak. Children in the family were well used to seeing him and were not afraid, but apparently when their mother caught sight of the phantom one day, she spoke to him firmly and advised him to leave as she did not want the children to be disturbed. The ghost, it would seem, took heed of her words and moved off elsewhere, for the family did not see him again. Who he was, and why he appeared, was never known.

A cottage in Fife is said to be one place where at least three ghosts share the accommodation quite harmoniously with its living occupants. It seems that when a young couple first moved into the cottage and began working on it to modernize it to their own tastes, strange poltergeist-type activities began to bother them. After a time, it would appear that ghosts and mortals have become accustomed to each other's ways, and the living occupants find it quite comforting to come home to a place that has signs of life in it, rather than a dark empty house with no one at home.

Hotels and Public Houses: Extra Guests

THE SCOTS have a reputation for their hospitality, but guests in some of the country's hotels and pubs, both old and new, might just find that they get a little more than they have paid for. Landladies who refuse to leave their territory even after death, specters of former guests with mysterious histories, anonymous presences that tease and torment the unsuspecting visitor—these are just some of the ghosts that haunt various establishments countrywide.

The following stories are just a selection of the numerous strange tales that the pubs and hotels of Scotland have to tell. The older inns in particular make many a visitor's stay all the more worthwhile when the presence of something supernatural makes itself apparent. Should you find yourself stopping for a drink or a meal in an old Scottish pub or inn, you would be well advised to inquire within whether there are any extra, non-paying guests in the place. In some places it will take several strong drinks before you can start to see things, but in others you can have the strangest experiences even if you are completely teetotal.

Port Ellen, Islay

The island of Islay, off the west coast of Scotland, is of interest both to nature lovers and whisky lovers. It is a bird-watcher's paradise and also, on account of its distilleries, a haven for the connoisseur of fine malt whisky.

One former distillery on the island, close to the town of Port Ellen, was converted many years ago for use as a hotel. The hotel is said to be haunted by the ghost of a man. Visitors to the hotel have seen the figure of a thickset man in one of the corridors. One visitor in particular claimed to have been troubled by a recurrent dream of falling from a great height while staying at the hotel.

The story that is told to explain these occurrences would be amusing were it not for the fact that it has such a tragic ending. Apparently, when the building was still in use as a distillery in the nineteenth century, an enterprizing and thirsty rogue with a taste for a good drop of malt broke in one night. He must have had a lovely time once he had found his way in.

He climbed to the second floor, found himself with a good quantity of whisky and settled down to enjoy himself. Obviously, he drank more than a drop—who wouldn't, after all, if given the chance to imbibe as freely as this?

After some time the burglar must have decided that enough was enough and he ought to be getting back home to his bed. A pleasant fog had settled around his brain by this time, however, and he was not entirely sure how to find his way out of the building. Which way had he come in? Unconcerned, he decided that he could not be bothered trying to retrace his steps and, instead, attempted to make his escape through the nearest window. Our hapless hero had forgotten, however, that he was on the second floor of the distillery. The nearest window was a long way from the ground, and he was killed by the impact of the fall.

The window from which the unfortunate burglar jumped was sealed up during the conversion work on the building, but his ghost still appears in the hotel from time to time, around the place where he met his death.

The Cross Keys Hotel, Peebles

Ye came, ye went,
But I hiv steyed
Fit three hunder years

[You came, you went
But I have remained here
For three hundred years]

Several ghosts have been seen in various places in and around the pretty town of Peebles on the River Tweed. The Cross Keys Hotel in particular has quite a reputation for having an extra guest. Perhaps "extra guest" is not such an appropriate term to use, for the ghost is that of Marion Ritchie, who was once the landlady of the inn. On hearing about the things that she gets up to, it is tempting to wonder whether Miss Ritchie resents the fact that the establishment over which she once presided is now in the hands of others. Perhaps she dislikes the modern world. Whatever motivates her ghost, she likes to cause trouble, although, so far, the trouble has not been serious. Things are moved from place to place, and crockery and glasses are broken. She makes her presence felt from time to time in various parts of the hotel, and people claim even to have heard her voice. Miss Ritchie's speciality is tampering with electrical goods, switching things on and off to cause irritation and consternation. Is this a sign of the good woman's contempt for all things modern or is she merely fascinated with the wonders of technology?

In 1975 the hotel attracted the interest of a group of investigators who brought recording equipment into the hotel to try to capture Miss Ritchie's voice on tape. They set up their machines and settled in to wait for some action. Obligingly,

Miss Ritchie made herself heard. The investigators were delighted. They had captured the voice of a ghost on tape! However, the playback was distorted and useless. They tried again but were rewarded with a soundless tape. Much the same thing happened with a third attempt, in spite of the fact that before setting up for recording, all equipment was checked meticulously and sound levels carefully set. It seemed that they had been the victims of another of Miss Ritchie's little tricks.

The Clydesdale Hotel, Lanark

Lanark is a busy market town in the south of central Scotland. The Clydesdale Hotel is an old building in the town, built around the end of the eighteenth century.

Long before the hotel was built, the site had been occupied by a Franciscan priory at some time in the fourteenth century. In the cellars of the hotel, staff have often reported feeling strange sensations, like sensing a figure passing silently by in the darkness, and hearing strange noises unrelated to the sounds of the hotel above them. The figure of a monk is also reputed to have been seen down there.

The Covenanter Hotel, Falkland

In the picturesque and historic royal burgh of Falkland in Fife stands the Covenanter Hotel, a building some three or more centuries old but internally altered considerably over the years. The hotel is the haunt of a female figure who has been seen floating around the bedrooms from time to time. No one can be certain of the identity of the woman. Some have claimed that it is the unhappy spirit of Mary Queen of Scots, who lived for a while at nearby Falkland Palace. The ghost of Mary Queen of Scots, however, is also said to haunt several other places in Scotland. Like the ghost of Bonnie Prince Charlie, Mary's spirit is one that more sites would like to lay claim to than are credible.

The Kylesku Inn, Sutherland

The Kylesku Inn is in Sutherland in the northwest of Scotland. It is situated by the bridge of the same name, just beside the old ferry berth. The story that is told in connection with the ghost that haunts the hotel has a touch of *Whisky Galore* about it. This story, however, does not end happily.

A ship was wrecked in the waters off the Minch sometime in the eighteenth century, and some of the cargo from the wreckage was eventually washed ashore. One lucky fisherman discovered a barrel of whisky that had survived a battering by the waves. Very pleased with his find, he heaved it up to the ferry house at Kylesku (now the Inn) and dragged it up to the loft to hide it.

The fisherman threw a little party that Saturday night, inviting a few of his friends up to the loft to share in his good fortune. Time passed and the gathering grew rather riotous. No one seemed to care that it was nearly midnight and the Sabbath was drawing near.

At this point, versions of the story differ. One version claims that it was the fisherman who tried to calm things down and bring an end to the celebrations, while another tells us that the fisherman's son was the one who became alarmed at the way things were turning out and tried to get his father to stop the party.

Whatever happened in fact will probably never be known for sure, but there was a struggle between the fisherman and his son. The fisherman was thrown down the ladder from the loft. His neck was broken, and he died. Before he breathed his last, however, he was heard to utter a dreadful curse upon his son. He would return to get his revenge. It is said that the fisherman's son was killed at sea not many months afterwards.

The fisherman himself, in spite of having got his revenge, still returns to the inn once in a while, appearing near the place where he fell to his death. Perhaps he is looking for one last sip of that whisky he found.

The Learmonth Hotel, Edinburgh

The Learmonth Hotel is conveniently situated for tourists in the capital city, for it is close to the west end of Princes' Street, the beautiful main route through the center of town. It is part of a stately terrace that was built in the nineteenth century. Visitors to the Learmonth Hotel are often fascinated as much by the ghost that haunts the building as they are by the many attractions that Edinburgh has to offer.

It is quite a mischievous presence, by all accounts, but seems to be harmless in spite of the bother it causes. It has a cheerful disposition, apparently, for staff and visitors to the hotel have heard the sound of its ghostly whistling in the corridors.

The spirit plays pranks on guests from time to time, on occasion locking them out of their rooms. At other times doors are found to have opened or closed themselves and doors that had been locked have been found unlocked.

The ghost in the Learmonth Hotel has other party tricks in addition to all this—tricks that are very similar to those that Marion Ritchie, the ghost of the Cross Keys Hotel in Peebles (*see* page 155) likes to play. It plays with electrical apparatus, irritating staff and guests when it switches kettles and hairdryers on and off.

The ghost's identity is not known, but its presence makes a stay at the Learmonth Hotel even more interesting.

The Moncrieffe Arms, Bridge of Earn

The Moncrieffe Arms is in Bridge of Earn, Perthshire, a few miles from the town of Perth. Many visitors to the hotel have had stories to tell of strange noises in the guest rooms. The landlord has also been witness to some curious goings-on, including something unseen apparently taking the opportunity to have a bath while the rest of the guests were out.

The landlord was walking along the corridor past the bathroom one day when he noticed that the door was closed. Through the door he could hear the sounds of someone taking a bath. The landlord was a little puzzled, for he thought that all the hotel guests were out, but he was not concerned. Perhaps he had been mistaken and someone was still there.

Moments later, however, coming back past the bathroom, the landlord found the bathroom door was open again. When he looked in through the door, he could see no sign of anyone having had a bath recently. There were no drips on the floor, no steamy atmosphere, no wet towels . . .

The mystery deepened when the landlord found out later that, as he had initially thought, none of the guests had been in the hotel at the time.

The Old Post Horn Inn, Crawford

The Old Post Horn Inn in Crawford, Lanarkshire, was originally a coaching inn on the road from south to north. The original building dates from 1744. It would come as no surprise to find that the inn was haunted by the ghosts of fallen Jacobite men, for the trees in the woods nearby were used to hang a few supporters of the Jacobite cause in the rebellion of 1745. However, the inn is not known for being haunted by any such ghosts. The ghost at the Old Post Horn is instead that of a little girl, who is heard singing and playing in the area of the dining room. She is thought to have been the young daughter of a one-time landlord of the inn. The dining room stands on the site of the old stables, and it is said that the little girl was especially fond of horses and spent a great deal of time there. She was playing outside when she died, tragically killed by a coach and horses visiting her father's establishment.

Pannanich Wells Hotel, Ballater

Ballater is a beautiful town in Deeside, a spa town frequented in Victorian times by the rich and influential, who sought benefit to their health from taking the waters there. The Pannanich Wells Hotel in the town dates from the middle of the eighteenth century and was most favorably mentioned by Her Royal Majesty Queen Victoria in the journal that she kept.

As well as having the honor of being visited by Queen Victoria, the Pannanich Wells Hotel has another claim to fame. It is the haunt of a gray lady, the ghost of an elegant young woman dressed in a gray blouse and a long gray skirt. The Gray Lady has been seen by various people both in and around the building. Sometimes the ghost cannot be seen, but instead people have heard noises such as doors opening and closing without apparent reason. The Gray Lady is not a ghost that causes great alarm, and indeed she is regarded with a certain amount of affection by those who are familiar with the hotel.

Tibbie Shiel's Inn, Peebles

In the early 1820s a young woman from the Borders by the name of Isabella Shiel found herself widowed. She was an enterprizing person, and in order to feed herself and pay the rent, she opened her cottage to passing travelers, offering food and drink and letting out one of the rooms. The cottage, situated between Moffat and Selkirk, soon became a very popular stopping-off point, for Tibbie Shiel's hospitality and cooking were fine indeed. Her visitors were not only travelers. Many famous literary figures of the time and scholars and religious men took to gathering at the inn, taking advantage of the chance to meet in convivial surroundings and to enjoy good food, fine ale and stimulating conversation. Amongst the well-known visitors to the inn were James Hogg ("the Ettrick Shepherd"), Robert Louis Stevenson and Sir Walter Scott.

Tibbie Shiel died in 1878, but the original inn, greatly extended over the years, still exists. The inn holds on to the ghost of its original landlady with a certain amount of pride, and visitors have claimed that Tibbie's presence can still be felt as she pushes through the crowd of customers on her way to warm herself at her favorite spot by the fire.

The White Dove Hotel, Aberdeen

The White Dove Hotel in Aberdeen has been demolished, but the story of its haunting is well known.

One of the guests at the hotel had fallen sick. The woman was an actress, apparently, and her name was Miss Vining. She had become quite ill shortly after her arrival at the hotel. When a doctor was called to examine her, he decided that she was suffering from a rare disease, thought to be tropical in origin. The patient's condition grew worse and was causing concern. The doctor pronounced that she required constant care, so a nurse was called in to attend to her.

The nurse noticed a strange, eerie atmosphere in the room when she arrived, but put it down to the condition of her patient and the stormy weather raging outside. Miss Vining was too ill to speak, so the nurse spent some time attending to practicalities, monitoring her patient's condition and assuring her comfort, and then settled in a chair beside the bed to wait quietly beside her, reading.

After a while something made the nurse look up. Her eyes passed over her sleeping patient and came to rest on another chair at the opposite side of the bed. There, seated quietly, was the figure of a small girl. It was hard to make out the child's features, for she was wearing a large hat. The first reaction of the nurse was to protest with the child: how and why had she come into the sickroom without permission? But as the nurse rose from her seat, the child raised a hand to motion her back. The child seemed to be possessed of some strange power, for the nurse found that she could not move any farther. The nurse then tried to turn to her patient, who was showing some signs of distress. Once again, she found she was unable to move. It was the oddest feeling. She sat back in her chair, and although she had not been feeling tired at all, she could not prevent herself from falling asleep.

When the nurse woke up, the child had gone, but Miss Vining was delirious with a raging fever and needed attention. The nurse, thankfully, was now able to rise and care for her. When morning came, the nurse told the doctor about the child who had been in the room. He gave strict instructions that Miss Vining was too ill to be visited by anyone. The following night, he said, the nurse was to lock the door behind her when she took up her post by her patient's bedside.

The nurse did as she was told. The next night she made absolutely sure that she was alone in the room with Miss Vining. Then she locked the door firmly behind her, ready to start her shift.

Miss Vining was comfortable and peaceful, so the nurse sat by her bed for a while. She nodded off for a few moments, and when she stirred she saw the little girl in the room, just as before. Once again, when she tried to shoo the child away, the little girl raised her hand and the nurse was unable to do a thing. She was virtually paralysed.

Miss Vining's condition grew markedly worse, and the nurse was distressed to see this, but the child still held her under some sort of spell. There was nothing she could do to help her patient. At length, after what seemed to be an interminable time, watching helplessly as Miss Vining tossed and moaned in her delirium, the nurse saw the child rise from her seat and make for the window.

Finding that she was free to move, the nurse made a grab for the little girl, knocking her hat from her head. To her horror, she saw that the girl's face was that of a corpse. She was an Indian child and had obviously been very beautiful, but it was clear that her throat had been cut and now her face was twisted in death. The nurse fainted.

When the nurse came round, the child had gone and Miss Vining was dead.

Afterwards, when hotel staff were packing up the belongings of the deceased, it is said that they found a photograph of a child, which the nurse identified as being the same child she had seen in ghostly form. On the back of the photograph were written these words:

Natalie. May God forgive us.

Nobody could find out any more, for after the death of Miss Vining, the little girl was never seen again.

Military Specters

OVER the centuries, the Highlands and Lowlands of Scotland have seen many a bloody battle as rival clans raged one against the other, or as Scots united against their enemies, particularly the English. It can be hard to imagine the horror of the hand-to-hand fighting of days gone by. The suffering that those many thousands who were wounded had to endure as they lay bleeding on the battlefields must have been immense. The bravery of the Scottish soldier in battle is legendary—the Scots were a nation of proud fighting men. Nevertheless, it was without doubt a test of even the bravest men's courage to have to fight for clan or country. The brutal consequences of some of these terrible struggles of ancient times can still be felt most acutely by those who are witness to the ghostly presences that hover near some of the old battlegrounds, even to this day.

Culloden, Inverness

Culloden was the battle that sounded the death knell for the Jacobite forces. Here, in 1746, they were defeated. Hopes for the return of a Stewart to the throne of Scotland were dashed once and for all. Bonnie Prince Charlie escaped from the battle by a stroke of good fortune and fled overseas. His followers were not so fortunate. The Jacobite forces had arrived at Culloden in poor condition.

After a fruitless journey down south in an attempt to muster support, they had returned to Scotland diminished in numbers and exhausted after many days of marching in atrocious conditions. They were vastly overwhelmed, both in numbers and strength, by "Butcher" Cumberland's men. The battle was a slaughter.

The specters of those who lost their lives are still in evidence on the field of Culloden, especially on the anniversary of the battle, 16 April. Marching Highlanders, bleeding men, corpses—all are said to have been seen. Noises of battle, such as clashing swords, gunfire and the cries of the wounded, are reported from time to time. One ghostly figure that has appeared is that of a tall young man dressed as a Highlander, thoroughly dejected and despairing. He has been heard to murmur what sounds to be the word "defeated."

Close to the battle site is Culloden House where Bonnie Prince Charlie reputedly slept the night before the battle. The house, which is now a hotel, still has the bed where he is supposed to have slept and a stick that is said to have belonged to him. Culloden House is one of the places where the ghost of the prince is said to have been seen, resplendent in full Highland dress.

Glencoe, Argyll

Glencoe is not so much a battle site as the scene of a slaughter. The Massacre of Glencoe is one of the most famous events in Scottish history. In February 1692, a company of soldiers of the clan Campbell took horrible and brutal action against the clan MacDonald. They did this in the most cowardly manner, accepting the hospitality of the MacDonalds, then surprising them by night and slaughtering many of them as they slept. Forty or so MacDonalds lost their lives.

Glencoe is a popular haunt for climbers, who come to challenge themselves on the surrounding mountainsides. On a fine day, the glen is spectacular to behold, a place of outstanding beauty and grandeur, but the weather, fickle and dangerous as it is in these parts, can change in moments. Then the hills and the glen can take on another profile, just as impressive but awesomely so.

The MacDonalds still haunt the glen. Various people have seen ghostly appearances that bear witness to the dreadful atrocity that was committed against them all those years ago. The anniversary of the massacre, 13 February, is the time at which the phantoms are most likely to appear. The weather is at its bleakest at this time of year and the air can turn even chillier at the sight of the still, staring figures of the MacDonalds. It will turn coldest of all for those who go by the name of Campbell.

The Hill of the Battle, Highlands

A story is told by a Scots writer of his own ghostly experiences near his home in a remote part of the Highlands.

The writer's house was in a particularly isolated spot, above a deep wooded gully through which flowed a small but rapid river. On the other side of the river was a high ridge, with small hills at its northern end. The writer had lived in the house for some time and had often been puzzled to hear what sounded like bagpipes playing in the distance. He was accustomed to the sound of the pipes and recognized the noise that he heard as being the sound of a lone piper playing two-drone pipes—the kind of pipes that had been played in Scotland some two or three centuries before. Modern pipes have a third drone and sound quite different.

The writer marvelled at how the sound of playing could travel such a distance—his house was some two miles or so from any other habitation. As he continued hearing the sound from time to time, always coming from the same direction, he took it upon himself to make some enquiries in the district to find out who the piper was. He was surprised to learn that there was no one living in the surrounding area who played the pipes. His curiosity was further aroused when he heard that the man who had lived in his house before him had also spoken of hearing the sounds of piping. Where was the sound coming from?

The writer tried to think of some logical explanation for the sounds that he was hearing. Could it be the noise of the water below his house? Or the sound of the wind in the trees? Sometimes, when he heard the pipes, he would take himself outside and walk in the direction from which the sound was coming. He would listen to the wind and the water. He traveled quite some distance, listening carefully all the time, but nothing could convince him that the noises he was hearing were made by anything other than bagpipes. It seemed that there was no explanation for the phenomenon, and the writer had no choice but to give up his investigations and simply enjoy the music whenever he was given the opportunity.

This he did, until one night early in the following year when he had gone to bed late and just dropped off to sleep. He had been for a walk earlier, enjoying the clear skies and the fresh air, and he had heard the pipes playing. But, of course, this was not unusual. He had not been long asleep when he woke to hear a tremendous racket coming from outside. It sounded, indeed, like the noise of ferocious fighting. Men's voices roared and screamed through the night air, punctuated by the sounds of clashing swords. The lone piper could not be heard this time. Instead, the writer heard the sound of several sets of pipes, rising above the sounds of battle.

The clamor outside was very frightening, but in spite of this, the writer felt obliged to investigate. Flinging on some clothes over his night attire, he descended the stairs towards the front door with a great deal of trepidation. As he reached the door, he realized that he could no longer hear the noise of fighting. The "battle," if that was what it was, appeared to have come to an end, but he could still hear a great deal of activity going on—clattering and clanking, and the sounds of marching feet.

The noise seemed to be coming from the direction of the hills at the end of the ridge, and it was getting louder all the time. He could make out the sounds of people crossing the river below the house and coming nearer. He could hear voices too—men's voices calling out in victory, or so it seemed. And still the pipes played, triumphantly.

The writer went outside and let his three dogs out of the byre. They ran towards the sounds, barking furiously, but within moments the eldest dog was back, whining and cowed. The other two dogs, who were no more than puppies, seemed to take fright and sped off, yelping, across the hillside and out of sight.

The army, by the sound of it, was still getting nearer and nearer, but the writer could see not a soul. To the eyes, the entire area all around was deserted; to the ears, on the other hand, it was teeming with warriors.

The writer stood rooted to the spot as the unseen army passed noisily right by him; pipers, soldiers—even women's voices were audible amidst the cacophony. Although it seemed as if he was right in the middle of the throng, nothing and no one touched him. The phantom army seemed to pass straight through the writer's home, oblivious of the stout stone walls that stood in its way. Gradually the sounds began to fade as the ghostly troops marched on into the distance.

The writer experienced the strange episode only once. After that, he still heard the sound of the lone piper at regular intervals while he lived in the house, but the phantom army never returned. It could have come only from a time long past. The writer tells that the hill from which the sounds of fighting came that night is called in Gaelic Mam a' Chatha, the Hill of the Battle.

Killiecrankie, Perthshire

The Battle of Killiecrankie took place in 1689 between the Jacobites and the forces of William III under the leadership of General Hugh Mackay. The site of the battle is nearly three miles northwest of Pitlochry, in Perthshire. The Jacobites were victorious, but their leader, Viscount John Graham of Claverhouse, known as Bonnie Dundee, was killed in the fray. In spite of the victorious outcome of the battle for the Jacobite forces, the death of Dundee was a tragic blow to their cause.

Nowadays there is a visitor center at the battle site, which is in the care of the National Trust for Scotland, and Killiecrankie is a popular venue for school parties on history trips and for tourists from all over the world.

Different experiences are associated with the battle site. Some people have reported seeing an eerie red glow. Some claim to have seen groups of soldiers marching as if into battle. Others have reported seeing a ghostly version of the battle itself, or at least a part of it. One particular story tells of a woman seeing the bodies of several dead English officers around her feet as she picnicked at Killiecrankie. Most of these stories come from people who have been visiting the site around the time of the anniversary of the battle, which is 27 July.

Two more stories connected with the Battle of Killiecrankie and the death of Bonnie Dundee are told in another chapter in this book, Second Sight, Prophecies and Curses (page 356).

Montrose Airfield

It is not the sound of pipes and clashing swords or the sight of Highland warriors that have earned the old airfield at Montrose a reputation as a haunted place. The several ghosts at Montrose come from an era when battle had become considerably more mechanized.

Montrose airfield was built as a base for the Royal Flying Corps (later to become the Royal Air Force) not long before the First World War. The first ghost associated with the airfield, now the site of a museum, dates from its early days in 1913, when a biplane, piloted by Lieutenant Desmond Arthur of No. 2 Squadron, Royal Flying Corps, came apart in mid-air and crashed to the ground in a field not far from the aerodrome. The ghostly figure of an airman, thought to be Desmond Arthur, has been seen several times since then. There have also been reports of a phantom biplane, seen in the skies around the airfield by other pilots in the years following the tragedy. On one occasion the ghost plane was nearly the cause of another crash. Another time a pilot witnessed the ghostly re-enactment of the terrible disaster in 1913.

In addition to the ghosts of Desmond Arthur and his biplane, there have been sightings of another ghostly airman and also of a phantom Second World War bomber in the skies above Montrose.

Nechtanesmere, Angus

The ghosts of Nechtanesmere date from very early Scottish history. The Battle of Nechtanesmere, by Dunnichen Hill in Angus, was fought in the late seventh century AD between the Northumbrians and the Picts. The Picts, led by Brude mac Bile, were victorious over the Northumbrian men of King Ecgfrith. The battle put an end to the Northumbrians' progress northwards. King Ecgfrith and most of his men were killed.

One report of haunting close to the site of the Battle of Nechtanesmere dates from 1950, when a middle-aged woman called Miss E. F. Smith had a strange experience while driving home from Brechin to Letham one night. It was January, and snow had fallen. Miss Smith's car skidded on the newly fallen snow and went off the road into a ditch. Unable to get her car back on the road without assistance, Miss Smith had no alternative but to walk the remaining seven or eight miles of her journey.

She was nearly at Letham when she caught sight of flaming torchlight in the distance. As she drew near to Dunnichen Hill, she saw men in ancient garb—brown tunics and leggings—wandering around in a field nearby. They kept their eyes to the ground, where the bodies of other men lay. The figures were oblivious of Miss Smith as they moved silently around.

It would appear that Miss Smith was witness to the ghostly figures of survivors of the Battle of Nechtanesmere searching the battlefield for their dead and dying comrades.

Dramatic Appearances

PEOPLE in the theatrical professions have a reputation for being superstitious. Many actors and actresses will freely admit to owning one or more lucky charms and following their own personal little rituals, which they believe will bring them luck during their performances. In addition to personal lucky charms and rituals, there are also theatrical superstitions that are quite well known to the public in general. For example, one should never wish performers "good luck" before they go on stage, for this is believed to have the opposite of the desired effect. Instead, a hearty "break a leg!" is thought to be a safer means of wishing a performer success.

Shakespeare's *Macbeth* has its own superstitious associations. Members of the acting profession believe that it is unlucky to call the play by name. It is referred to instead as "The Scottish Play."

In such circles, where people come together who are both collectively and individually superstitious and who are required by their profession to be imaginative and intuitive, it will hardly come as a surprise to those of a more skeptical nature that many theaters throughout Great Britain, and in Scotland in particular, are said to be haunted. Nonetheless, witnesses to the presence of some of these ghosts do not necessarily belong to the theatrical professions, and it is not easy to find alternative explanations for all the ghosts that are said to exist.

The Byre Theater, St Andrews

The Byre Theater, converted in the 1930s from a dairy, is a small but thriving establishment in the historic university town of St Andrews in Fife. Throughout the year a succession of performances are put on for audiences of all ages. The scope of productions ranges from serious works to pantomime, and most are well attended. In spite of the difficulties of the time, the theater was kept going right through the dark years of the Second World War thanks to the unstinting efforts of its director, Charles Manford.

It would appear that Charles Manford's dedication to the Byre has stayed with him after death. He seems to be reluctant to leave his beloved theater entirely in the hands of others, for although he died in 1955 his ghost still haunts backstage at the Byre. It makes its presence felt with a district chill in the air. The ghost does no harm—perhaps because the theater still flourishes.

His Majesty's Theater, Aberdeen

His Majesty's Theater was built in 1904 and has been the venue for a great variety of performances since then. In the early 1940s the theater saw tragedy when one of the stagehands working there, a man called Jake, was killed in an accident by a stage hoist.

Jake still haunts the theater, and a variety of strange happenings, from disappearing objects to shadowy appearances and strange noises, are associated with his ghost.

The Theater Royal, Edinburgh

The Theater Royal was built in 1768 on the site that is now occupied by the General Post Office, at the corner of Waterloo Place and the North Bridge in Edinburgh. The theater was in operation for less than one hundred years—it closed down in 1859—and yet even in that relatively short period it acquired a reputation for being haunted.

The stage manager of the theater lived with his family in a flat at the top of the building, above the auditorium, and they were the first to notice strange goings-on. At night, when the theater was empty and everything was locked up, the sounds of voices, footsteps and general activity could be heard from inside. It appeared that ghostly players were returning to the theater for spooky, nocturnal performances of their own.

The ghosts of the Theater Royal became quite famous around Edinburgh, but when the theater was pulled down in 1859 to make way for the new Post Office building, the ghosts seemed to vanish—perhaps to make an entrance elsewhere.

Edinburgh—Three More Ghostly Theaters

The *Royal Lyceum*, still a popular venue for theatergoers in the capital, *The Playhouse*, which is now used as a venue for rock concerts and musicals, and the *Edinburgh Festival Theater*, rescued from existence as a bingo hall and restored to theatrical glory, are all said to be haunted.

The Playhouse

The ghost in The Playhouse is known affectionately as Albert, and although nobody is certain as to who he might have been his presence manifests itself in a variety of ways. He is a mischievous ghost who plays tricks, apparently. People have felt his presence in certain "cold spots" in the theater. He has been seen, on occasion, as a figure in a gray coat.

The Royal Lyceum

The Royal Lyceum is believed to be haunted by a woman. She has been seen by performers on stage, who have spotted her figure high up in a gallery of the theater now used only for lighting.

Edinburgh Festival Theater

Staff at the Festival Theater claim to have seen the tall, dark, shadowy figure of a man on a number of occasions. There is speculation that this might be the ghost of the Great Lafayette, a magician who was killed in a fire at the theater in the days when it was known as The Empire.

The Theater Royal, Glasgow

The Theater Royal in Glasgow is home nowadays to Scottish Opera, but apparently it has another resident performer who puts in an appearance from time to time. She is known as Nora, reputedly a woman who worked as a cleaner in the theater some years ago. Some say that she desperately wanted to be an actress and sought employment in the theater, hoping that she would then get the chance to act. She eventually secured herself an audition with a director at the theater but was virtually laughed off the stage. Heartbroken, she committed suicide.

Mind How You Go

NUMEROUS and varied are the ghosts that are said to haunt Scotland's thoroughfares. It might be a city street or a country road, a dark corner in a dingy district or a sunlit path through a panoramic glen. Fields, mountains and waterways all have their spectral presences. There are ghosts on land and sea, in places of solitude and by bustling visitor centers. Ghosts appear wherever people have been and wherever they might go. Many ghosts haunt particular buildings or ruins, but others frequent areas that are not bound by walls. Mention has been made of some of these ghosts already—Major Weir, who strides out and rides in his carriage in the area of the West Bow in Edinburgh; Angus Roy, with his damaged leg scraping behind him along Victoria Terrace; the soldiers marching through the Pass of Killiecrankie. Some of the ghosts are nameless, while the identities of others are well known. But the tales of these ghosts just might make the reader stop and think wherever they go—who was here before me? What happened? Who might be watching?

Annan

The bizarre occurrences on the A75 near Annan were comparatively recent compared to many other tales of ghostly apparitions around Scotland. They took place in the 1960s. The fact that two young men were simultaneous witnesses to all that happened gives credence to the tale. Had there been only one of them to tell what happened, it is unlikely that he would have been believed. The incident was very much a "one-off" and just exactly what caused it remains a mystery. Is it possible that two people can share the same hallucination? If it was not hallucination, but a kind of haunting, why were these two men the only ones to be subjected to such a frightening experience? Or have others experienced something similar but been too frightened to tell? Is it likely to happen again?

The two young men were traveling back to Annan late at night and the road was very quiet. They were some ten or so miles from Annan when the driver noticed the figure of a woman gesticulating wildly in the beam of the car's headlights. He was just about to swerve to avoid knocking her down when she vanished. The passenger had seen the woman too.

Hardly had the old woman disappeared than the two incredulous passengers were stunned by the sight of a crowd of murky figures apparently rushing towards the car. The figures were mostly those of animals—dogs, cats, farmyard creatures, animals of all sorts, both identifiable and unfamiliar. Amongst the animals was the figure of an old man. His long white hair streamed out behind him as he ran and his mouth was wide open in a soundless scream.

The driver swerved this way and that trying to avoid the creatures in this strange parade, but before long he realized that whichever way he turned, none of the animals was touching the car. Were they figments of his imagination? One glance at his terrified passenger told him that they were not.

The next moment, the air in the car turned deathly cold. The driver could feel some unseen force taking the steering wheel, trying to wrestle it from his grip and make him lose control of the car. In spite of the chilling atmosphere, the two men felt as if they were suffocating. One of them opened a window. Searingly cold air rushed into the car, accompanied by eerie, menacing sounds of cackling and screeching.

The driver put his foot on the brakes, unable to continue any longer. Invisible sinister presences outside then began to rock the car violently back and forth—the men were thrown from side to side, backwards and forwards. Finally, unable to bear it any longer, one of them threw open the door, ready to flee. As he got to his feet outside the car, all went quiet. There was nothing to see, and all he could hear was the sound of the wind rustling gently in the trees and the rasping pant of his own panic-stricken breathing.

The experience had been so awful and so exhausting that the two young men stood outside and took some time to gather their wits before they got back into the car. The driver started the engine again. Both men were by this time desperate to get home. No sooner had they started the car than the ghostly animals reappeared, swarming round the vehicle, emitting unearthly noises. The driver grimly held on to the wheel and steered a straight path through them.

They were nearer to home now. Surely it would all end soon. It was reassuring to notice that at last there was another vehicle some distance in front of them on the road. They could see its lights glowing in the darkness, and from its size and shape it looked like a furniture van.

Some yards farther along the road, the driver realized that the van was not moving. He willed his foot to press on the brake, but in spite of himself, he pressed down hard on the accelerator instead. They were going to crash!

Unable to prevent the inevitable happening, both men waited, wide-eyed, for the moment of impact. A fraction of a second before the car hit the van, however, the van disappeared. The driver found that once again he could control his feet on the pedals. The old man, the ghostly menagerie and the van had all vanished. The road was quiet and empty, and at last everything had returned to normal.

Completely drained by the experience, the two men made for home.

Mind How You Go

Ben MacDuibh

Ben MacDuibh in the Cairngorms is a magnificent but lonely place to experience a ghost. Upper slopes of the mountain have snow on them for several months of the year and make an awesome sight, but even in summer the landscape possesses a certain power. The mountain is one of Scotland's Munros (hills over three thousand feet high) and is popular with walkers and climbers, but in spite of that it is still very isolated. It quite possible for the solitary walker to spend several hours on the mountain without coming into contact with another human being. On occasion lone walkers have found that they have company after all—not human company but that of An Fear Liath Mhor—the Big Gray Man of Ben MacDuibh.

Sights and sounds of the Big Gray Man have been reported for more than a century now by several people. The ghost is not only seen on the mountain itself but also in the surrounding area of the Cairngorms, in the Lairig Ghru and in Glen Derry, for example.

Several common elements link the stories that have been told by various witnesses. One of the first reported experiences was that of Professor Norman Collie from London. He was climbing back down from the summit in 1891 when he heard something behind him in the mist. It sounded as if something or someone was following him down the mountain, taking one step to every three or four of his. Professor Collie was unable to make out anything in particular, as visibility was very poor, but he was sufficiently frightened to take flight, risking a fall rather than be caught by his pursuer.

Other witnesses in the years that have followed have told stories that have strikingly common elements about them.

Often the first thing that the witness notices is the sound of footsteps; the footsteps are heavy and slower than those of a walker of average stature. This leads the witness to conclude that what he or she is hearing is probably a very large person. Sometimes this is all that the witness has experienced. Other witnesses, however, have also seen something—generally a very large, upright figure in the distance. People who have seen the figure and have tried to follow it have seen no trace of footprints. Descriptions of the figure vary slightly, but it is usually described as being gray, very tall, human in form, but somehow not quite right—unnatural.

In 1943 a man called Alexander Tewnion was on Ben MacDuibh. He was a naturalist with considerable experience in the mountains. As he climbed, he became aware of the sound of heavy, slow footsteps. After a while a large figure rushed at him out of the mist. Tewnion shot at the shape three times but seemed neither to hurt it nor scare it off. He turned and fled and eventually managed to shake off his sinister follower.

The figure on Ben MacDuibh, whoever or whatever it might be, certainly seems to be a malign presence and its manifestations have succeeded in inspiring great fear in even the most hardened mountaineers.

Discovery, Dundee

Discovery Point, berth of Captain Robert Scott's ship, *Discovery*, is now a tourist site of which the city of Dundee can be justifiably proud. The vessel was built in the city at the end of the nineteenth century, and it is a testament to the fine workmanship of its construction that it survived the rigors of its service as a royal research ship in the polar regions.

On the British National Antarctic Expedition in 1901, *Discovery* saw two tragic deaths among those who sailed on her. Just as the ship was leaving New Zealand, a seaman called

Charles Bonner fell to his death from the crow's nest of the vessel. The other death occurred some months later in Antarctica when another seaman was killed onshore.

It is the ghost of Charles Bonner, the first to die, that is thought by some to be the most likely cause of strange noises that haunt the vessel. The noises are heard above the officers' wardroom, just below the spot where the seaman fell to his death. Some visitors report a feeling of distinct uneasiness in the wardroom, as if there is a sinister presence there.

Some people also believe that *Discovery* is haunted by the grudge-bearing spirit of Ernest Shackleton, who embarked upon the expedition with Scott but was invalided out with illness and exhaustion. During the expedition, there had been serious personality clashes between Scott and Shackleton, and Shackleton was extremely bitter at being sent home.

Dunphail

The railway station at Dunphail is no longer in existence, but many years ago Dunphail was a stop on the old Highland Line. It was close to the station, in 1921, that the first recorded sighting of a ghost train happened. The man who saw the train was called John McDonald. The sighting took place on New Year's Eve. The time of the sighting, given the habits and traditions of the Scots, might have made people wonder whether the witness's mind was befuddled by drink, but it is reported that this was not the case and since that date, subsequent sightings have borne out John's story.

It was an alarming sight. The last train of the night had long gone, so to see one at all was a shock. But the strangest and most disturbing thing about it all was that although there were lights on in the carriages and steam billowed out of the funnel of the train, there appeared to be no passengers aboard. Nor was there any sign of a driver or engineer in the cab at the front.

The site where the railway track once was can be perilous for the innocent walker. People are reported to have been knocked flat by some immense and invisible force as they strolled along. The ghost train travels on, heedless of those who might stand in its way.

East Kilbride

East Kilbride, situated just to the southeast of Glasgow, was a pioneering new town when it first came into existence in the 1960s. But the ghost that is said to haunt the streets of East Kilbride comes from a much earlier time.

Jenny Cameron came from the Highlands and was a fervent Jacobite. She was a well-known figure who earned a certain notoriety around the time of the 1745 rebellion on account of the strength of her beliefs and her willingness to fight for them. Jenny Cameron was detested by the English, who circulated many an unpleasant story about her life and her wanton ways. These stories were probably completely unfounded, but they can neither be confirmed nor denied with any certainty.

Jenny Cameron's courage, however, was never called into question. It made her a legend among the ranks of the Jacobites, many of whom she joined in battle.

Jenny originally came from Glendessary, but when the Jacobite forces were finally crushed, she realized that she faced great danger from reprisals by the Duke of Cumberland's men and left her home behind. She moved south and settled in the countryside of East Kilbride, where, having bought a large house that she named Mount Cameron, she took in orphans of the rebellion and gave them a home. Her life thereafter was very different. No more a warrior rebel, she became a respected member of the community.

More than two centuries after her death, the area is now transformed. Housing estates have taken the place of countryside, and tarmac and concrete have replaced grass and rolling fields. Nonetheless, it seems that Jenny Cameron still feels quite at home and regularly makes her presence felt around the place where she once lived in East Kilbride. A hovering light has been seen by her grave on several occasions. Locals are well acquainted with her presence and feel quite comfortable with her.

The Flannan Isles

Lighthouses nowadays are operated automatically, but there was a time not so long ago when each of the lonely lighthouse rocks around the coast of Scotland had its light tended by a few stalwart lighthouse keepers. The job was vital to the safety of ships in the area, but it had considerable hazards. The job of a lighthouse keeper was a very lonely one and not for the faint-hearted—they could be isolated for weeks at a time.

Eilean Mor Lighthouse, off the island of Lewis in the Outer Hebrides, was manned by three people, a head keeper and two others. As they were confined for lengthy periods of time without other human company, they had to get along with each other or life could be very uncomfortable indeed.

In 1900 the head lighthouse keeper was a man called Thomas Marshall. His two crew were called James Ducat and Donald McArthur. In December 1900, their unexplained disappearance was to cause great consternation and speculation.

It was on 15 December that it first became obvious that something was wrong at the lighthouse. It was reported to the authorities that the light at Eilean Mor, which was supposed to burn constantly, had gone out. This posed a great danger to shipping in the area, and when the light had still not gone back on after a few days, a vessel was sent to the rock to investigate. A dinghy from the vessel was launched with a landing party, which tied up at the rock in an atmosphere of eerie silence. Why had no one come down to meet them?

The explanation became all too clear when the party entered the lighthouse itself. The place was absolutely empty. The lighthouse crew had gone. The landing party looked around for some explanation but could find none. There was no sign of there having been any disturbance. Everything was tidy and seemed to be in order, but the crew's outdoor gear, their oilskins and boots, were nowhere in evidence. Apart from the fact that the men had gone, the only strange thing that the landing party noticed was a piece of seaweed lying on the stairway, a kind that none of them had ever seen before.

It was unthinkable that the men in a lighthouse crew should ever abandon their posts. Why and where had they gone?

The log that was kept at the lighthouse gave strong indications that all had not been well before the men disappeared. On 12 December Thomas Marshall had written:

> Gale N by NW. Sea lashed to fury. Never seen such a storm. Waves very high. Tearing at lighthouse. Everything shipshape. James Ducat irritable.

Another entry for the same day read:

> Storm still raging, wind steady. Storm-bound. Cannot go out. Ship passing sounding foghorn. Could see lights of cabins. Ducat quiet. Donald McArthur crying.

Tension among the lighthouse crew was given further mention on 13 December:

> Storm continued through night. Wind shifted W
> by N. Ducat quiet. McArthur praying.

Marshall made another entry that day:

> Noon, gray daylight. Me, Ducat and McArthur
> prayed.

There were no entries in the log for the following day. On 15 December the final entry in the book read as follows:

> Storm ended. Sea calm. God is over all.

Several things were disturbing about the entries in the log. First of all, there were the mentions of Ducat and McArthur behaving as if something was wrong. Were they unwell or frightened? Was it just the storm or something else?

Then there was the fact that there had been no entry made for 14 December. Why was that?

Finally, the storm that was supposed to have raged around the lighthouse rock for three days seemed very unlikely as on the island of Lewis, less than twenty miles away, there had been no sign of any such storm. Had the men in the lighthouse been imagining things?

The official inquiry into the disappearance of the lighthouse crew was unable to shed further light on the incident. Nor were the three men ever found. But many people thought that they had been subjected to something supernatural. People had believed for many years that the rocky islands around the lighthouse were haunted.

Further evidence had been submitted to the inquiry that had only served to deepen the mystery. On the night of 15 December, seamen on a boat in the waters around the strangely dark lighthouse had seen another boat, manned by men dressed in storm clothing, cut across their bow. The occupants had not responded to the seamen's calls. The only thing the seamen heard in answer to their cries was the sound of the oars as they creaked in the rowlocks. Was this the last sight of the men from the lighthouse or were the figures in the rowing boat merely ghostly apparitions? The answer will probably never be known.

Loch Skene

Hogmanay by Loch Skene sees the return of the phantom coach and horses of Alexander Skene, who lived in those parts around the end of the sixteenth century and the beginning of the seventeenth.

Alexander Skene was renowned as a practitioner of the black arts; he is said to have spent some years on the continent studying black magic. His gruesome activities while at home by Loch Skene were rumored to include digging up the corpses of unbaptized babies from the nearby churchyard and feeding them to the crow that is said to have accompanied him wherever he went, perched on his shoulder. People were fearful of Alexander Skene and claimed that his imposing figure cast no shadow, even when the sun was at its brightest.

The appearances started after his death. The story tells that he tried to cross the loch on his coach and horses using his magical powers and that as he neared the other side he came across the devil. The coach then sank into the icy waters and Skene was drowned.

Mull

The island of Mull, some forty minutes by ferry from Oban on the west coast of Scotland, is popular with visiting tourists from all over the world. Some visitors to the island may find more than they expect during their stay, for they might come across the headless ghost of Ewan (Eoghan) Maclean, astride his horse as it gallops through Glen More. The story of the ghost is rather gruesome.

On the eve of a battle with the Macleans of Duart, Ewan came across a woman crouched by a stream, washing some bloodstained clothes. Ewan must have realized that this woman was a banshee (*bean shi'th*), a supernatural creature whose appearance meant imminent death. The clothes that she washed were those belonging to men who were about to die. Having seen the banshee, Ewan probably knew that his chances of surviving the battle were not good. Nevertheless, he was committed to his cause and would not shrink from it.

The battle was fierce, and in the midst of the fighting Ewan was killed. He was beheaded by a blow so swift and sure, it is said, that when his head was severed from his body, his body remained sitting upright in the saddle as his horse galloped away.

Some say that the appearance of the ghostly headless rider in Glen More foretells a death in the Maclean family.

Pitlochry

On the road leading out of Pitlochry heading northwards a grim spectral figure has been reportedly seen. People who know of the existence of the ghost are very anxious indeed to avoid it, for it as said that those who have come across it and have been touched by its cold white fingers will meet their death before long.

Sandwood Bay

Sandwood Bay is a particularly remote spot in the far north-west of Scotland, a few miles south of the lighthouse at Cape Wrath. It is a beautiful place, but few people go there as there are no roads leading to the bay; the only access is on foot or by sea.

Several sightings of the same ghost have been reported since early in the twentieth century. This ghost is not a nocturnal, diaphanous creature at all. Rather, he looks so real that some of the people who have seen him have tried to engage him in conversation. The figure is said to be that of a bearded sailor, dressed in cap, boots and dark-colored clothing, with gleaming brass buttons on his jacket.

Nobody knows who the sailor might have been, although there are theories that he might have drowned in the waters close to Sandwood Bay. He seems to patrol the bay with a proprietorial air, keeping watch on the few visitors—mostly fishermen and walkers—who come to the area. As he patrols the beach, however, the sailor leaves no trace of any footprints behind him in the sand.

Selkirk

This story, which comes from the Border town of Selkirk, tells of the strange disappearance of a cobbler. The secret of what exactly happened to him is known only to the dead.

The cobbler was called Rabbie Heckspeckle, and he was, by all accounts, a skilled and industrious craftsman, quick and nimble with his fingers, who shod many a fine gentleman around the town of Selkirk.

One particular morning, the cobbler was up before dawn, as was his habit, working on a pair of shoes, when a stranger came into the shop. It was unusual for anyone to come looking for service at such an early hour, but Rabbie Heckspeckle was a shrewd businessman and did not like to turn down any opportunity to make a little money. Accordingly, he greeted the stranger with his usual courtesy and asked how he could be of assistance. The man was looking for a new pair of shoes.

The stranger was well dressed, but he had a certain air of decay about him, and there was something in his manner that the cobbler did not particularly take to. Nevertheless, Rabbie Heckspeckle politely obliged him by showing him a few samples of his work.

The stranger pointed to one particular pair of shoes that were to his liking, and although the cobbler did not have any in the right size, he measured the stranger's feet and assured him that he would be able to make some in time for collection the next day. The stranger said that he would be picking up the shoes early, well before dawn, and the cobbler, although a little surprised, said that such an arrangement would be quite convenient. The sun had still not come up when the mysterious stranger left the cobbler's shop.

Rabbie Heckspeckle worked all day and long into the night, completing the shoes for the stranger. When he had finally finished, the shoes were as fine as any he had made. Congratulating himself on a fine job, he turned in for the night, hoping to catch a few hours of sleep before his customer returned.

It was still dark when the cobbler heard a knock on the door, waking him from his slumber. Rubbing his eyes, he pulled on some clothes and went to let his customer in. The stranger tried on the shoes with hardly a word. They fitted him beautifully, but he was far from fulsome in his praise for the good cobbler's efforts. He merely tossed a handful of silver coins at Rabbie Heckspeckle, turned round and made for the door.

The cobbler was intrigued by this eerie man. He wanted

to see where he lived. The man was certainly not a familiar figure around the streets of the town. Unable to contain his curiosity, Rabbie Heckspeckle set off to follow the stranger, keeping at a safe distance. He followed the stranger all the way to the kirkyard and watched as the somber figure made its way through the serried ranks of gravestones to the far side of the cemetery. There, before the stupefied gaze of Rabbie Heckspeckle, the stranger lay down on one of the graves and disappeared.

The cobbler rushed over to the grave site where he had seen the stranger vanish. There was no sign of digging nor of disturbance of any kind. Where had the stranger gone? Hurriedly, the cobbler left a pile of stones on top of the grave as a marker and rushed off to tell everybody about what he had just seen.

At first, nobody would believe him. The cobbler must have imagined it. The stranger probably walked out the other side of the graveyard unnoticed. The idea that he had vanished into a grave was quite preposterous, after all. But in spite of all the ridicule, the cobbler persisted with his story, and after a great debate it was agreed that the grave should be opened.

The gravediggers were summoned and the coffin was disinterred. The coffin was then opened in full view of several witnesses. Inside the coffin they found the body of a man dressed just like the stranger had been and wearing a pair of brand-new shoes. The shoes were so beautifully crafted that they could only have been made by Rabbie Heckspeckle. The townspeople had to believe his story now.

Nobody really knew what to do next. After some debate it was decided that the best thing to do was to seal the coffin again and put it back in the grave. Time would tell whether the ghostly stranger was likely to put in another appearance in the future. But before the coffin was re-interred, the cobbler reclaimed the shoes that he had made. They were a fine pair, after all, and what use could they be to a dead person?

He had made a big mistake. Next morning, before dawn, the neighbors had a rude awakening. Sounds of a terrible struggle were heard coming from Rabbie Heckspeckle's cobbler's shop. Several people, who had all been disturbed by the thumping and screaming, ran to the shop to investigate. They could find nothing except a set of footprints leading from the shop to the graveyard. The footprints led right up to the grave that had been dug up the day before.

There was nothing else for it—the grave had to be dug up once again. When the coffin was lifted out and opened, the townspeople shuddered when they saw what lay inside. The corpse, it seemed, had got his new shoes back. There they were, on his feet, just as before. Of Rabbie Heckspeckle, however, there was no sign, apart from a piece of his shirt, which the corpse held in its pallid, decaying fingers.

Rabbie Heckspeckle was never seen again. The people of Selkirk were left to wonder, with fear in their hearts, what had happened to the cobbler at the hands of the ghostly stranger.

St Boswells

The ghostly figure that once haunted the village of St Boswells in the Borders is said to have been that of a minister who murdered his housekeeper, but details of the incident are not clear. The identities of the minister and his unfortunate victim are not known—nor is it known when the murder took place. The ghost, nevertheless, is one that several people are said to have seen over a period of some twenty years at the turn of the nineteenth century.

The specter of the clergyman—tall, deathly pale and dressed

in black clothing—was seen by a pair of sisters on two occasions in the late 1800s. On each occasion, the ghost appeared very clearly, walking along the road for a moment or two. The figure was visible for minutes only. Then, quite suddenly, it seemed to disappear into thin air.

Similar sightings were made by various people over the following years, and, each time, descriptions of the figure that was seen matched. He was reported to be wearing ecclesiastical clothing—a black frock coat, gaiters and a black hat shading his eyes.

The Tay Railway Bridge

The first bridge that was built for trains to cross the River Tay was long planned. The idea was first proposed by an engineer of the Edinburgh, Perth and Dundee Railway Company in 1854. Proposal after proposal was discussed and resisted by various bodies involved until, finally, permission was obtained to build a bridge in 1870. The first stone was laid in 1871, and the bridge was completed and opened for traffic in 1878. Its life was tragically short.

On 28 December 1879, the Tay found itself in the teeth of a raging gale. By early evening, officials were in grave doubt as to whether it was safe to allow trains to cross the bridge in such conditions. A train from Edinburgh to Dundee was due to cross the bridge and arrive at seven o'clock. At the Dundee side, hopes were high that the train had been stopped before it crossed and the passengers disembarked. The minutes passed by after seven o'clock and the train did not arrive. Staff at the Tay Bridge Station, hoping that the train had never tried to cross the bridge, tried to signal to the southern side, but communication was impossible.

At length, the dreadful truth came to light. The train had

been crossing the bridge when disaster struck. The structure of the bridge had not been strong enough to withstand the stresses that the gale had caused. A portion of the bridge had collapsed and the train had gone down with it. Some seventy-nine people were thought to have lost their lives, but the figure could not be given accurately, for not all the bodies were recovered.

On the anniversary of the dreadful disaster, a ghostly train has often been seen to cross the River Tay from south to north, following the line of the doomed bridge.

Tomintoul

Not far from Tomintoul, a particularly courteous and helpful ghost has appeared to travelers in the area. She is reported to be an old lady dressed in a long plaid skirt and shawl, accompanied by a wee black dog.

In the 1960s, a young couple staying in the district on a trip that combined business with pleasure were returning to their hotel after a pleasant day's sightseeing when their car had a puncture. As they set about changing the wheel at the roadside, a little old lady approached them and asked if she could offer them any assistance. The young couple were touched by her kindness but turned down her offer politely. They had almost finished their task, and, besides, she seemed a little frail to be changing wheels. The lady bid them good evening and passed on, leaving the couple to get on with what they were doing. The job was done in a matter of minutes. They got back into the car and set off on their way once again. They fully expected to pass the old lady a short distance farther along the road and were debating whether or not to offer her a lift.

The old lady had not been walking fast, so she cannot have gone very far at all, but in spite of this, and in spite of the fact that there was nowhere else for her to have gone except open countryside, the couple saw neither hide nor hair of her or her dog for the rest of the journey. It was as if she had vanished into thin air ...

Ghosts, Assorted

T HERE are some ghost stories that do not fit quite so neatly as others into any of the previous categories. They should not be ignored, however, and hence have been given a chapter of their own.

Two Dead Pedlars

Life must have been dangerous for the original traveling salesmen. Carrying their goods and their profits around with them, they were easy prey for robbers. There are quite a few stories from various parts of Scotland that tell of poor pedlars who have come to grief at the hands of ruthless vagabonds. Sometimes something remains to make sure that the fate of the pedlars is not forgotten.

The Schoolmaster and the pedlar

In the early nineteenth century the body of a pedlar was found floating in the waters of Loch Assynt. The body had a severe wound to the head, and no one could find his pedlar's pack. Foul play was immediately suspected.

The pedlar had been a "weel-kent" figure around those parts. He made himself a fine living selling his goods around the district and was thought to have been reasonably wealthy. Robbery was therefore the most likely motive for the attack, but no one had seen or heard anything.

As no evidence had been left at the scene and there had been no witnesses to the event, it was decided to resort to the old practise of "ordeal by touch" in an attempt to identify the pedlar's killer. This practise had no basis in scientific fact but had once been widely used in Scotland as a means of eliminating suspects in cases of murder. Suspects were made to touch the body of the murder victim. When the corpse was touched by the killer, it was supposed to bleed.

All those who had been in the area at the time when the pedlar met his death were asked to touch the body, and most of them obliged. The schoolmaster in the local school, however, refused to take part in the bizarre ritual. He argued, most convincingly, that the pedlar had probably fallen into the loch and hit his head on a stone. There was no gain to be had from pandering to superstition.

The schoolmaster was an intelligent man with considerable influence in the community. It was agreed that his theory as to the likely cause of the death of the pedlar was plausible. Besides, there was no real evidence to the contrary. The case was closed, and the pedlar was buried.

Some weeks later the pedlar's brother came looking for him. When he heard the story of his brother's death he was not at all satisfied that justice had been done. If the pedlar had not been robbed and murdered, then where were his pack and the goods and money that would have been in it?

The pedlar's brother investigated the matter himself and at once began to suspect the schoolmaster. He seemed to have an awful lot of money, even for a man in his position, and his tastes were undeniably expensive.

The pedlar's brother consulted a man with second sight, and the man told him of a vision that he had had of a murder committed by the schoolmaster. This was not real evidence in itself, but the visionary was then able to tell the pedlar's brother and the police where the empty pack had been hidden.

The schoolmaster was questioned. Eventually he confessed to his crime and suffered the appropriate penalty. But the fate of the pedlar is not forgotten. The terrible deed on the shore of Loch Assynt is re-enacted in ghostly form every year. The sickening sound of a skull being cracked echoes across the water, followed by a splash and the sound of the culprit's footsteps fleeing the scene.

The Sanquhar pedlar

There was once a shepherd called Gourlay who lived near the town of Sanquhar in Dumfriesshire. He was smitten by a young woman who lived in a farmhouse a few miles away. The woman's name was Mary Graham, and she lived with her two brothers, Robert and Joseph.

One night the shepherd went to call on Mary Graham, but as he approached the farmhouse, he was alerted by the sounds of a struggle. Deciding that it was better not to risk going straight in by the front door, he crept up to a window and surreptitiously peeked inside. To his horror, he saw his sweetheart and her two brothers struggling with a man. It was hard at first to make out who the man was, but as soon as Gourlay caught a glimpse of his face, he recognized him as a pedlar who regularly plied his wares around the district. Within moments, Gourlay saw Mary Graham and her two brothers beat the poor man into submission and then strangle him.

Graham fled back home, all thoughts of romance gone. He was horrified at what he had seen—obviously the Grahams had been intent on robbing the pedlar. What were they going to do with his body? It was too terrible to contemplate. He told his mother about what had happened that night and swore her to secrecy.

The pedlar's horse was found wandering around in the woods close to the farmhouse the next day. There was no sign of the pedlar or his pack.

Gourlay stopped visiting Mary Graham. After some days

had passed, she called upon Gourlay to ask him why his courtship seemed to have ended so suddenly. Gourlay was not quick-witted enough to think of any other response—he blurted out to her that he could not contemplate a relationship with her after what he had seen her doing on that terrible night. Mary turned on her heel and left his house in a grim silence. Gourlay had signed his own death warrant.

The Graham family did not wait long before they got rid of Gourlay and his big mouth. They ambushed him on his way home a couple of days later. He managed to run away, but they chased after him. Gourlay fell into the river. He would have been swept away there and then but he managed to get a grip on a tuft of grass at the water's edge. The Grahams hurled stone after stone at him as he clung desperately to the bank. Finally, his fingers lost their grip, and he slipped back into the water and was drowned.

The Grahams thought that their secret was safe. They did not know that Gourlay had told his mother what he had seen. Shortly afterwards, Gourlay's battered body was recovered from the river, and his mother was filled with rage. Without hesitation, the old woman pointed the finger of blame at the Graham family. Unfortunately, the Grahams managed to escape into hiding and were never brought to justice.

The pedlar's body was found buried in moorland some years later. The ghost of Gourlay returned to the spot where he was killed by the Grahams to haunt the place. The cries of the poor man as he clung on to the banks of the river in the last moments of consciousness were heard in the same spot from time to time for a long time afterwards.

Spinning Jenny

A small stream near the pretty town of Ballater in Deeside

has been named "The Spinning Jenny Burn" after a very persistent and industrious little ghost that has haunted its banks for many a year. A small, bent old woman, she is seen to work away feverishly at her spinning wheel by the stream, oblivious of any mortal that might lay eyes on her. The ghost is completely harmless and has never been known to interact in any way with living people. Who she is, or why she works so hard, no one knows.

The Modernization of a Manifestation

There are quite a few stories told of ghostly vehicles that have been witnessed the width and breadth of Scotland, and some have been included elsewhere in this book. None is quite as strange, however, as the story of a ghostly vehicle that changed with the times. The story originates in the Isle of Skye, where it is said that for many years the sound of galloping hooves and the clatter of wooden cart wheels would herald the arrival of a phantom horse-driven carriage to a house in a remote part of the island.

Some time after the invention of the motor car, the occupants of the house realized that they had not heard the coach and horses for some time. Then, one night, they heard another sound. Unmistakably, it was that of a motor car. The house was in an isolated spot and vehicles were few, so when the car's engine seemed to stop, the occupants of the house looked out of the window to see who had come to call on them. There was no one and nothing to be seen. Puzzled and a little disappointed, everybody sat down again. Then a few seconds later, they heard the car engine start up again. The noise began to fade, as if the car was driving away. But no matter how hard the people in the house peered into the darkness, no one could see anything.

Motherly Love

There is nothing on earth as strong as a loving mother's instinct to protect her children. The following story tells us how that instinct can endure, even beyond the grave. The story originates in Ross-shire.

There was once a crofter and his wife who had three children. They had little money, but the children had a secure and happy family life. Their mother saw to it that her little ones were always well fed and warmly clothed. The children's needs always came first. Then, one winter, the crofter's wife suddenly fell ill and died.

The crofter struggled to keep the family going, but it was hard to manage the land and care for his children all alone. It was not long before he realized that he must find another woman to take the place of his wife and care for his home and family. He embarked upon a courtship with another local woman, and before long the two were married.

It was a classic case of the wicked stepmother. The woman was prepared to enjoy the benefits of married life, but she did not care for the children at all and treated them quite cruelly. Come winter, when the nights were long and cold, the children would lie shivering in their beds in spite of the fact that there were plenty of spare bedclothes stored in a chest in the cottage. When the children asked for more blankets, their stepmother refused.

One morning, however, the children woke to find that they were no longer cold. Their bedclothes felt heavier and they were cocooned in warmth. Someone had put extra blankets on their beds during the night. The children were delighted; their stepmother must have relented. But their stepmother had had nothing to do with it. When she woke and saw what had happened she was furious. She took the blankets from the children, stuffed them back into the chest and secured the lid with a lock.

The next morning she was enraged to find that the children had extra blankets on their beds again. The blanket chest still had its lock intact. How had the children got in? The stepmother threatened and hit the children, but they could not or would not tell her how they had got the blankets from the chest.

Night after night the same thing happened. The children would go to bed with a few meagre coverings, but by morning they were always snugly wrapped in soft woollen blankets. In spite of all the stepmother's efforts, she could not get the children to tell her how this happened. She said no more about it, but after a few days had passed she decided to stay awake through the night and watch.

The children went to bed as usual, curled up tightly against the cold. Their stepmother went through the motions of preparing for sleep, but when she lay down in her bed she kept her eyes wide open. She did not have long to wait. She had been lying in the darkness for less than an hour when she became aware of something moving by the blanket chest. She peered across the room and could just make out the figure of a woman opening the lid of the chest. The woman took out a pile of blankets and carried them over to the bed where the children lay huddled together. With great care not to wake the children, the woman covered them up with the blankets, tucking the edges round their sleeping forms. Then she kissed each child softly on the forehead. As the woman straightened, the stepmother caught a glimpse of her face. It was the children's mother. The stepmother leapt from her bed and made a grab for the woman, but she disappeared into thin air.

The stepmother left the house the next day.

A Faithful Pet

Dogs are widely thought to be sensitive to ghosts. The following story, which comes from the west coast of Scotland, tells of a dog with a particular attachment to a ghost.

An elderly crofter was heartbroken when his wife of many years died. His two sons had grown up and now had crofts of their own to manage. The old man found his widowed state particularly lonely and hard to bear. His only company at home was their dog, which his wife had been particularly fond of. The dog pined terribly after the death of its mistress and would not eat for many days afterwards. At one stage the crofter feared that the dog might die, but after some time the beast seemed to rally and returned to its former boisterous self.

The crofter would take the dog onto the hillside every day to give it some exercise. The dog was usually very obedient and stayed close to its master, but one day, some weeks after the death of the crofter's wife, the dog ran off. This was completely out of character. In spite of the crofter's whistles and calls, the dog disappeared. The crofter waited for some time but eventually returned home. Some time later the dog returned.

This was to set a pattern for the coming weeks. Mostly the dog would stay in sight of the crofter when they went out, but every few days it would take off and disappear for as long as an hour.

The old man did not have the energy to run after the dog, but one day he followed at his own pace in the direction the dog had taken. Over the brow of a small hill, he came upon an astonishing sight. There was his dog in the distance, in the company of a familiar figure—the crofter's beloved wife. The crofter stood and watched for some moments, then the figure of his wife faded to nothing. The dog, large as life, came bounding back when the crofter called to it. The two made for home, the crofter happier than he had been for a long time because of what he had seen.

The Black Dog of Tiree

Humans are not the only creatures to return in ghostly form after death. There are plenty of spectral animals to be seen around Scotland, especially dogs. The hounds that howl by the ruins of Buckholme Tower in the Borders inspire fear in those who hear them. Another phantom dog has been heard crashing against a bedroom door in Ballechin House in Perthshire. Tiree has yet another canine ghost.

Tiree is a beautiful island off the west coast of Scotland, blessed with long stretches of silver sand around its shores. On and around one such beach on the northern side of the island a ghostly dog has been seen and heard several times. The dog is large and black and usually makes itself heard first with a strange, hollow-sounding bark. It will follow people along the beach for quite some distance before it disappears into thin air.

The Ghost Elk

In *Not of This World*, Maurice Fleming cites the tale of a ghostly elk which was seen by Laurence Blair Oliphant, the Laird of Ardblair.

As a small boy, his Lordship saw, in the woods near his house, "this large, red, antlered animal, running through the trees." Because the trees were so closely planted, there was in fact not enough room for such a big beast to run like that nor, come to think of it, did he hear the thunder of hooves.

Years later, his wife reported seeing a similar creature running noiselessly through the very same stretch of woodland.

It was only later even than that that they realized the animal they had seen was an elk, which used to roam the Great Caledonian Forest, alongside the wolves and bears which are also now extinct in Scotland.

Exorcisms and Clearings

The Church and Exorcism

TO RID yourself of a ghost or malevolent spirit, many have had recourse to exorcism or clearings. Though most church ministers scoff at the idea of exorcism and houses or people being in the grip of troubled spirits, others are more open to the idea. If nothing else, they see no harm in saying prayers at a person's home if doing so will give them some comfort and reassurance.

The Reverend Charles Robertson, the minister of Canongate Kirk in Edinburgh, is one such. He shrugs off the tale, cited in Roddy Martine's *Supernatural Scotland*, detailing how he led a prayer service of commendation and blessing to rid a young family of a seemingly evil cloud that hung over the baby's cot, as "just a daft story," but it is intriguing nonetheless.

The young couple in question had an infant baby with whom they were naturally delighted. However the mother, Chrissie, became very disturbed by a small white cloud that seemed to hover over her child whenever it was left alone. Upon investigation, it seemed that the cloud was the spirit of a long-dead baby who had been born out of wedlock at a time when such occurrences meant social ostracism and often destitution, and was subsequently murdered by its frightened parents.

What the spirit wanted no-one really knew, though one ghastly conjecture was that it sought a new body to live in and Chrissie's child was the first baby it had come across.

After the Rev Robertson's little service, the cloud never again reappeared and hopefully that tragic baby's soul was thus laid to rest.

Sinister as this story sounds, Robertson believes it is important to distinguish between the idea of exorcism as a rite established to cast out demons and Satanic influences, and simple prayers to rid people of seemingly supernatural activities that trouble them, such as poltergeist-like activity, or inexplicable presences.

These latter, he says, potentially fall into the bracket of a minister's pastoral care.

The Church of Scotland seems to agree. A Deliverance Group was set up in March 2003, to consider the case for deliverance and exorcism. In December the following year, it concluded that though religious rituals could be effective in easing people's fears, an established ritual for exorcism "would do more harm than good and create unwarranted publicity and demand."

Yes, demand. It should be remembered that, following the release of the film The Exorcist, there was a wave of exorcisms and illicit rites, some conducted by ordained ministers but others conducted by occultists and fraudsters. In the UK in 1974, two Charismatic Methodist ministers were involved in a horrendous case that quite rightly made most church people want to steer clear of this kind of activity forever. They had performed an extended, rather harrowing exorcism ritual within the church walls, on a man convinced he was demonically possessed. They then left him alone, thinking he was asleep, exhausted. He woke, went home and, convinced his wife was the devil, bit off her tongue, causing her to bleed to death.

Whilst deliberating the deliverance issue, the church had been warned by mental health experts against encouraging a belief in demonic possession which they believe only further stigmatizes people with mental health problems.

Yet, according to a survey of more than 1000 church officials, including prison and hospital chaplains, more than two thirds believe "supernatural forces of evil exist today."

Exorcisms have been carried out, not just by Church of Scotland ministers but also by ministers from the Scottish Episcopal Church and the Roman Catholic Church, though it is only the latter that has a specific rite. This rite, it should be said, is one that most priests "wouldn't touch with a barge-pole" according to one Catholic commentator.

A Confused Ghost

A particularly fascinating story from the casebook of the medium Albert Best (who is discussed in The Spirit World: Communing With the Dead, page 252) is cited by Archie E Roy, professor of Astronomy at the University of Glasgow and a staunch believer in Spritualism, in his book *A Sense of Something Strange*.

The case concerns a young couple called Karen and Peter Wood, who had two young daughters and had recently moved into a brand new council house in a small town in the west of Scotland.

The disturbances began with mysterious footsteps heard in the corridor. At first, they assumed it was their three-year-old Katie, but further investigation revealed she was fast asleep in her cot almost every time. Even visitors were aware of the noise, asking Karen if there were other children staying with them.

All this was unsettling enough, but a very frightening incident one night convinced Karen that doing nothing was not an option. Having fallen asleep in front of the TV one evening—Peter was away on business—Karen woke and became immediately aware that she was not alone. Looking up, she saw the figure of a woman, dressed in black, glaring down at her from her standpoint beside the fireplace. She was not a comfortable presence and Karen turned and fled upstairs.

As if that was not enough, a while later, Katie came charging into her parents' bedroom crying that a "monster" had attacked her. They told her it was just a bad dream, but the Woods were worried.

Professor Roy was alerted to the case and he decided to enlist the services of Albert Best, whom he considered to be a very gifted psychic. On the drive there however, he told Best nothing of the circumstances of the trouble, thinking it more appropriate that his friend approach the subject with a clear mind.

Best began by wandering through the rooms of the house, finally stopping in the corridor to observe, "There are children here. They come from the other side. They like to come here. It's a good loving atmosphere so they like to come and play here."

But then he went downstairs to the living room and the first thing that caught his attention was the fireplace; the very spot where the mysterious, malignant ghost had stood. Though the house was recently built, the fireplace had been constructed, by Peter and his father-in-law, from old stones taken from the ruins of a demolished dwelling in an old street on the edge of town. And it was these stones that were, it seemed, at the heart of the problem.

Without being told, Best knew the name of the street they came from—Baird Street—and that the big stone over the fire had been the lintel of the cottage in which the ghost woman had lived. Best made contact with the spirit, and found that she was as shocked as everyone else to suddenly find herself transplanted to a new house full of noisy kids and her apparent unpleasantness had all been down to her deep confusion and sense of being invaded.

Best discovered that this poor spirit did not realize she was even dead. She apologized for the anxiety she had caused and Best assisted her in "moving on" to the other side.

Walking Into The Light

Psychics often describe this process as showing spirits, who have become temporarily trapped between this life and the next, how to "walk into the light." Once they do so, they find peace—as do the people they leave behind.

This gentle and compassionate guiding of spirits is a world away from the often violent, frequently hysterical image that most of us have of an exorcism, but experience shows that Albert Best's practise is nearer the norm when it comes to dealing with troublesome spirits trapped between heaven and earth.

Looking through the annals of supernatural Scotland, cases of exorcisms are few and far between but that is to be expected. Our modern churches are a little wary of discussing exorcism, viewing it as a rite that belongs in the Dark Ages. Nevertheless, there have been times when such services are called for.

The People Through The Wall

Lorraine Hedges, a computer programmer lived in a little town called Lilliesleaf, in the Scottish Borders. Being a very pragmatic, down-to-earth sort of person, Lorraine was extremely disconcerted to discover that she and her daughter Katherine were not alone in their own home. And that their "visitors" were varied, numerous and clearly not of this world.

Lorraine described being woken up by something or someone during the night and realizing that there were people in her bedroom, usually standing in a corner, looking at her.

At first, she took it in her stride because "they seemed a nice sort of people, there was a mother and a child and they were nice friendly people."

They only stayed for a very short time. "(Then) they would come towards me but not in a threatening way and they would fly over my head and into the walls. And this went on for ages and I kept on thinking, am I seeing things? What's going on?"

Young Katherine was haunted by spirits too. One time, she returned to her bedroom to find that some mischievous person unknown had splattered bubble bath and body spray, which had been sitting sealed on a shelf, all across her bed. All of which was very tiresome for the sleepless two but not, as yet, actually frightening.

Then things turned nasty. One night, waking as usual, Lorraine felt a presence in the room, a rather malignant presence.

"He was a really threatening man, horribly unshaven. I just got the shock of my life. I really thought it was a real person who had broken in and that my number was up. And then it came towards me and I couldn't move. He went over me and through the wall. I was absolutely petrified. It was the first time I had been frightened; up till then, I'd just accepted it."

No more. The next day, she went through her house with a Native American "Smudge Stick," reputed to have powers to ward off evil. But just to make sure, she also enlisted the services of a Church of Scotland minister, who arrived with a small group of colleagues, and sat in her living room to recite a short series of prayers.

After that, the visits ceased. Not immediately, but over the course of a few days. It was a similar story with the Woods, who had a few more noisy nights, though the noise was increasingly short-lived, and then peace.

Tolbooth Theater, Stirling

In the case of the Tolbooth Theater in Stirling, which became the locus for some pretty bizarre goings-on following renovation work, the church was by-passed in favor of a psychic who, according to the theater's Operations Assistant James Wigglesworth, "instantly pinpointed the exact spot as a place of ghostly activity."

The exact spot being what was once the condemned cell of this former prison. Employees heard what sounded like bodies being dragged across the floor of this cell, and were spooked by the sight of wine glasses flying off tables in the new restaurant and door handles moving by themselves.

Was this a case of an old building still traumatized by its violent past? Or a just a bad dose of mass hysteria amongst its employees?

Well, perhaps the fate of Allan Mair will help to answer this. Mair was a notorious murderer who was hanged outside the Tolbooth in 1843 for bludgeoning his wife to death with a stick. During the renovations, his skeleton was found in a rough wooden coffin, his boots still clearly discernable. After he was removed and given a Christian burial, the disturbances died down considerably.

Galdenoch Tower, Galloway

Galdenoch Tower dates from the sixteenth century. It was originally owned by nobility but after one hundred years or so it changed hands and became part of a farm.

The farmer's family at Galdenoch found themselves in the midst of the struggles of the Covenanters. The farmer was a staunch Presbyterian and proud to have a son who took up the cause against the Royalists.

The Covenanter forces were losing the struggle, and the son found himself on the run, hounded by Royalist troops. Taking a chance that he would find an ally therein, he knocked at the door of an isolated farm one night and asked for shelter. The owner was initially hospitable, but after some time his attitude became more menacing. When the young Covenanter decided that it would be prudent to try to leave, his host attempted to prevent his departure by force. Terrified at the prospect of being handed over to the Royalist troops, the young man fought with his captor and killed him. He then fled for his life, back to Galdenoch. No one had seen him arriving or leaving the farmhouse, so he hoped that the dreadful secret of what he had done would never be discovered.

The young man's crime did go unpunished by law, but he had not seen the end of the man whom he had killed. At Galdenoch a few nights later, the young man was roused from sleep by the ghost of his victim. The ghost made further sleep impossible for the young man by throwing objects and furniture around the room, and laughing and shrieking maniacally. The ghost then set about tormenting the rest of the family, and soon all the inhabitants of the farm spent their days in dread and their nights in fear. For weeks on end the activities of the murdered man's spirit continued relentlessly. A minister was summoned to help, and he tried to exorcise the ghost, but the ghost was having none of it. The torment went on, night after night, week after week, until, driven to distraction, the family fled.

The ghost remained at Galdenoch, and when a new family moved in it started a campaign of mischief of another sort. For most of the time it was quiet, but then, unexpectedly, it would play sudden and dangerous tricks.

The family, sitting by the fire one night, were startled into frantic activity when a peat from the fire suddenly flew out of the hearth. Within moments, one of the outbuildings in the farm was ablaze.

On another occasion the malicious ghost lifted the grandmother of the family from her chair, carried her to a nearby stream, ducked her in the freezing water, lifted her out again and left her on a nearby wall, wet, shivering and frightened half to death.

Many attempts were made with the help of various members of the clergy to rid the tower of its unwanted inhabitant, but the ghost seemed to have the measure of anyone who came. It would taunt people with its demonic voice and laugh at their feeble attempts to banish it.

Finally, one particularly determined minister came to the house. Summoning a band of followers with good, strong voices, he took on the full force of the ghost. The minister and his helpers opened their psalm books and began to sing with gusto.

The ghost was stirred into activity by the sound of the singing and, rising to the challenge, began to sing its own songs in response, louder than the minister's choir. So the minister urged his people to sing louder as well. The louder the choir sang, the louder the ghost sang, until both parties were singing at top volume.

All night the minister urged his choir on as they worked

their way through psalm after psalm. When all the psalms that they knew had been sung, they started with the first one again. The people in the choir were very tired and their voices were croaking, but still the minister urged them on, his voice rising above the others as he sought to outdo the ghost. As the first light of dawn glimmered in the distance, the ghost had to admit defeat. Finally, it had found a force stronger than it was. Its creaky voice was heard for the last time as it told the assembled crowd that it had given up.

The minister and his victorious forces, exhausted, made their way home. The ghost of Galdenoch was never seen again.

The Spirit World:
Communing with the Dead

S PIRITUALISM is the art of communing with the dead and where there are those who dismiss it as a Victorian parlor game with special effects, there are others who sincerely believe in it and who cleave to it as a comforting proof of the eternal life of the spirit.

Scotland has a long tradition of Spiritualism. Indeed, some of the most celebrated names associated with Spiritualism hail from, or lived in, Scotland—Arthur Conan Doyle, Helen Duncan, Albert Best and Gordon Smith, to name but four.

To those with faith, Spiritualism is much more than a spooky pastime; in fact, it is a religion and is recognized as such by the British government.

The Seven Principles of Spiritualism, as revealed to Emma Hardinge Britten, a Spiritualist pioneer, do not contradict a belief in a single, all-seeing God, nor the idea of a human soul being brought to account in the hereafter for conduct during Earthly life.

The principles can be summarized as follows:

1: God is the father of mankind.
2: Humanity is one family; we are all each other's sisters and brothers.
3: Communion with the spirit world is possible and desirable as spirits can offer us guidance and wisdom from the Other Side.

4: The human soul lives on after physical death.

5: We each must take personal responsibility for ourselves and our actions.

6: For our deeds on Earth, whether good or evil, we will receive compensation or retribution in the afterlife.

7: Even after death, the possibility of redemption and spiritual progress is available to every soul.

Spiritualists believe that we are surrounded by spirits, though not everyone has awareness, not even every Spiritualist. Only "sensitive," psychic people can access this parallel universe and even then, only through honing and developing their skills.

These sensitives, who become known as mediums because they serve as a channel of communication, usually discover their gift in early life, often during adolescence. They may encounter someone who has recently died, or a beloved relative, and have what appears to be a perfectly normal conversation with them.

Or, like Alannah Knight, the Edinburgh crime-writer and psychic, they may have access to the worlds beyond in a more direct way. Roddy Martine, author of *Supernatural Scotland*, recounts how the 16-year-old Alannah was visiting Holyrood Palace in Edinburgh with her parents, when she suddenly decided to leave the rather serious guided tour and take a stroll outside in the garden. This garden was beautifully ornate and bordered by unspoilt grassy aspects. Modern Edinburgh had curiously vanished. As she walked further into the garden, she came across a freshly dug grave, roughly marked as that of a D. Riccio.

It was not until 30 years later, when she next returned to the capital, that Alannah realized how odd this experience had been. Seeing the High School on Calton Hill, where before she had seen only grazing sheep and a windmill, brought it home to her that the place she had visited before had been another country—the past.

Further investigation led her to believe that she had seen Holyrood Palace as it had been four centuries previously, when Riccio, the ill-fated Italian foreign secretary to Mary, Queen of Scots, had just been brutally stabbed to death and his body flung into a rude grave in the palace grounds.

Riccio's body, according to a plaque on the wall of Canongate Kirk, was later removed from Holyrood Palace to the nearby church, though no-one has ever been able to pinpoint the exact location of his original grave.

Furthermore, old maps reveal that the layout of Holyrood's immediate environs when Mary was on the throne was, as Alannah had witnessed, an intricate set-up of walled gardens.

All very curious, unless you take on board the words of the Rev Charles Robertson, of Canongate Kirk, who asserts: "There is no now and then, only now. Time and place belong to the eternal here and now, and we dip in and out of them constantly."

Or rather, those with certain sensitivities can.

Once identified as psychic, people are encouraged to develop their skill in Spiritualist "development circles," where they receive advice and encouragement, and the chance to practise their art in a safe, non-critical environment.

Gordon Smith, also known as the Psychic Barber, lives and works in Glasgow, and was invited to join a Development Circle by several mediums who singled him out as someone possessed of a very special psychic gift.

In the course of these Circle meetings, Gordon learnt, not just how to clear his mind and, as he says in his autobiography *Spirit Messenger*, "wait for the spirit world to draw close to you and 'impress' you with the messages they wished to convey," but also to develop sufficient self-awareness to distinguish between his imagination and his "natural ability to perceive spirit people."

These days, he conducts both public meetings, at which he will convey messages to audience members, and private sittings. In both cases, he transmits messages, in his own voice, that he "hears" from the spirit world, often through the medium of his Spirit Guide. His sessions are reassuringly low-key, often notable for their humor and warmth.

Psychic Communication

Physical mediums

Not all Spiritualist mediums work in the same way. There are the so-called physical mediums, who are able not just to communicate with spirits, but make them visibly manifest. Helen Duncan, the famous war-time medium and the last woman ever to be tried under the 1735 Witchcraft Act, was a physical medium.

Testimonies to her extraordinary powers include astonishing accounts of human forms rendered visible through ectoplasm emanating from the medium's own body. People looked on in amazement as long-dead loved ones materialized before their very eyes, sometimes perfect and recognizable in every detail. One or two of these incredible events are even captured in photographs.

Clairaudience

Other mediums operate on a less spectacular level, and often through choice. Albert Best, the Belfast-born medium who made Glasgow his home but traveled the world practising his craft, is said to have told the Spirit World that he "didn't want that."

He, like many before and after him, was a clairaudient. That is, he transmitted the messages he received from the Spirit World, often not understanding the implications or content of these messages but simply passing them on to their intended recipients.

There are other variations of mediumship, such as a clairvoyant, who literally "sees" the spirits and is thus able to describe the appearance of the sender of the message. Some clients find it enormously comforting to know that a loved one who died, for example, wounded in a war or as a result of a disfiguring illness is, in death, restored to their former selves.

Clairsentients

Clairsentients actually "feel" their spirits, experiencing pain or illness just as the departed soul felt them. Horribly, they may even experience how a spirit met their physical end.

Clairomas

Clairomas, as the word suggests, experience smells associated with the communicating spirit; it may be someone's pipe tobacco, or a special perfume.

Automatic writing

Another form of psychic communication is automatic writing. In this case, the medium holds a pen and paper at the ready in order to allow the communicating spirit to convey its message through the medium's hand. The medium, driven by the spirit, scribbles fast and furious messages which, like the spoken ones, are generally only explicable to the intended recipient.

Many mediums combine a number of these elements.

Trance mediums

Finally, there are trance mediums, who appear to be taken

over by the voices of spirits which speak through them. This form of mediumship, where odd, sometimes very strange, voices emanate from an apparently sleeping person, has led some to believe that Spiritualism is, in fact, a form of demonic possession.

Skeptics

Most mediums are happy to deal with skeptics and agree that, after all, why should you believe something that you have never personally witnessed? They urge people to attend Spiritualist meetings with an open mind. However, there are a number of questions that surface again and again with regards to Spiritualism.

One that is often asked is how can a medium be sure that the spirit with whom they are communicating is not malevolent and bent on imparting destructive messages? One answer is that not every spirit is a good one. Gordon Smith relates a hilarious, though also rather sad, tale of a spirit who wished to communicate with his still living wife.

On hearing that it was her no-good husband, this Glasgow housewife responded: "If he thinks for one bloomin' minute that I have anything to say to him, he's up a bloody gum tree! The day that ratbag died was the happiest of my life!"

Needless to say, the less-than-ideal husband "scuttled (back) to his realm of guilt and remorse."

More seriously, mediums do warn amateurs to beware of evil spirits, who can be called up easily enough, through seances and ouija board sessions, but prove much harder to get rid off. Most mediums have one or more spirit guides, who are there to ensure that "lower" or malevolent spirits do not escape through the portal from the Other Side, created temporarily by the medium during a sitting or trance.

Another question—or rather accusation—that is raised by skeptics is that mediums make statements that are so general they are bound to apply to someone in a large audience. Couple this with the fact that many mediums cannot always offer a name for a spirit, and it is easy to see the comparison with daily newspaper horoscopes in which readers are given such nebulous information that practically any outcome would fit.

The case for the defence includes Albert Best, a former postman, who was able to deliver not just precise names, but addresses too.

A further charge is that mediums seed their audiences with "plants" so that, even if the real messages prove vague and unconvincing, the psychic can fall back on a couple of sure things. This, the reasoning goes, ensuring that audience members go away with the impression that the medium made meaningful contact with the "other side," even if they were not lucky enough to be recipients this time.

There is also the claim that mediums respond to verbal and non-verbal clues unwittingly given by audience members. For example, a young woman twisting a wedding ring could be a new bride experiencing marital problems. Or the medium could say he has a "Dave" and an eager audience member will supply the full name, and even betray details of the relationship with him or her.

There have been studies conducted by, amongst others, the Society for Psychical Research, which was established in 1882 by a group of Cambridge scholars, with the express purpose of investigating paranormal activities in a rigorously scientific manner.

Past presidents, including former British Prime Minister AJ Balfour, eminent physician Sir William Crookes and physiologist and Nobel Laureate Charles Richet, testify to the high status of its membership.

One such investigation, published in the Journal of the Society in January 2001 and conducted by Gary E Schwartz, Linda GS Russick, Lonnie A Nelson and Christopher Barentsen, considered the very issues just outlined.

They hoped to ascertain whether a skilled medium really could obtain accurate and replicable information from the spirit world, or whether, indeed, they relied on the information they could glean from their sitters.

Five individual mediums took part, and one subject, unknown to them all. The subject, a woman from Arizona, had experienced six significant losses within the previous decade and prior to the sittings, completed a comprehensive questionnaire detailing the circumstances and nature of her losses. After which, she met with each medium. Needless to say, the mediums were barred from conferring with each other. To eliminate the possibility of visual clues, the woman sat behind a screen during each sitting. And to eliminate the possibility of verbal clues, she was allowed to give only "yes" and "no" answers to any questions the mediums may ask of her.

Video cameras recorded each sitting and full, verbatim transcripts were made.

The results were incredible. The study showed that the mediums achieved an average accuracy of 83 per cent. The average accuracy for 68 control subjects, where chance was the only factor in play, was by contrast only 36 per cent.

In a further experiment conducted by the same team, accuracy levels were recorded at an average of 77 per cent. Leading the researchers to conclude that skilled mediums can indeed obtain accurate and replicable information from the spirit world.

Not everyone is convinced, some maintaining that other, as yet unknown, factors may be at work. And there are, unfortunately, enough fraudulent mediums at work to make anyone wary.

Whatever your view, there is no doubt that Spiritualism is alive and well in the modern world, particularly in Scotland where Spiritualist churches flourish in major conurbations and small towns alike and where new mediums, such as the now internationally-renowned Gordon Smith, keep springing up, generation after generation.

Origins of Spiritualism

As far back as 540 BC, Pythagoras was interpreting messages from the dead, assisted by his student Phlolaus. However, it took two millennia for communion with the dead to become a widely practised phenomenon.

Spiritualism exerts an ever-growing fascination in our modern world. It's a curious paradox that, the more we progress in terms of technology, science, philosophy, the more we seem drawn to the inexplicable, to the realms of intuition, other-worldliness and Spiritualism.

Perhaps then we should not be surprised that 19th-century Scotland, a nation that brought forth great inventors and thinkers, the pioneers of the Enlightenment, should also have been a nursery for the Spiritualist movement.

Certainly the Victorian era was one of unprecedented change, in which all the old certainties were being swept away by the impatient hand of modernity. Traditional systems of labor were undermined and ultimately made obsolete by the new age of machinery, long-standing communities collapsed as people migrated to the now sprawling cities in search of work, religious tenets were contradicted by scientific breakthroughs, and the ancient and comforting idea of earthly life as a precursor to a heavenly afterlife went up in smoke.

The Foxes

To those who recoiled from the new, seemingly soulless world, the strange tale of the Fox sisters must have been irresistible.

To explain a little of the origins of Spiritualism we must leave the shores of Scotland briefly to look at the events of 19th-century New York State.

Margaret and Kate Fox were two young, perfectly normal sisters, growing up in the small town of Hydesville, south of Buffalo, New York. The only extraordinary factor was that the house in which they lived was reputed to be haunted, by the spirit of a traveling salesmen who had been murdered in their cellar many years before. This latter, however, was unknown to them initially, and the town records were a little sketchy.

The girls, then aged 9 and 11 years, were constantly troubled by knocking and banging sounds during the night. So much so that, on the night of 31 March 1848, Kate attempted to communicate with the restless spirit. Urging Mr Splitfoot, as she nicknamed him, to do as she did, she clapped her hands twice. Mr Splitfoot responded with two loud raps. Establishing a system of two raps for yes and one for no, the girls were able to conduct a coherent dialogue with their guest, who told them of his history and led them to a fragment of skull and hair interred in the cellar.

The Fox girls' father called in the neighbors to testify to the veracity of these incredible events and word soon spread. Joined by their sister Leah, the Fox girls were soon embarking on Spiritualist tours, where people gathered to witness their terrifying yet intriguing dialogues with the dead, who communicated through loud raps on the table top or by manipulating objects around the room.

It began as a craze, an absolute must-see on a par with freak shows and circuses. But it grew to be much more than that. Naturally, it attracted the ire of the established churches. The Fox sisters, and those who followed in their footsteps, were subject to verbal and physical abuse and were denounced as ungodly and blasphemous.

Yet, by the close of the century, Spiritualism had elevated itself from the status of vaudeville to a serious religion with millions upon millions of followers.

Even more curiously, Margaret Fox, in later life, confessed that the events at Hydesville had all been a hoax. The knocking sounds—she now claimed—had been made by the girls themselves, who were adept at cracking their toes. The whole enterprise had started out as a prank to scare their mother and had simply got out of hand.

Defenders of the Spiritualist faith, however, point out that Margaret, by then a penniless widow and heavy drinker, was coaxed to confess by an enterprizing news reporter offering a substantial fee. And in any case, in 1891, she retracted the confession. Furthermore, how else could three unworldly young women have known about the murdered salesmen other than via a supernatural agency?

Spiritualism thrived in the teeth of its detractors and Margaret's confession, perhaps because it fulfilled a very human need—that being to communicate with the dead, and be comforted by the certain knowledge that everything did not end with the death of the body.

The Fox sisters inspired people across America, despite the disapproval of the church. Their home town, which still has a plaque proudly commemorating the events as the "first proof of the continuity of life, which was the beginning of modern Spiritualism" is a hotbed of Spiritualist activity and something of a pilgrimage destination for modern-day seekers of communion with their dead.

Ghostly Scotland

Emma Hardinge Britten and the spirit of Robert Owen

One of the many people inspired by the Foxes was the mother of English-born Emma Hardinge Britten, then living in America. Thus, when the young Emma received an inexplicable message from she knew not where informing her that the ship she was awaiting—*The Pacific*—had gone down at sea, her mother seized on it as proof of a fledgling psychic sensibility. Emma, it seems, did not need too much coaxing and was soon sufficiently skilled in the art of mediumship to give readings to the public, including some in the company of Kate Fox.

Emma is perhaps most famous for being the recipient, in 1871, of the Seven Principles, which were she received in a message from the spirit of Robert Owen (1771–1858), the great Welsh-born social reformer, best known for establishing the model village of New Lanark, in Scotland, to function along the lines of socialism. These Seven Principles became the foundation stone of the Spiritualist religion and are still adhered to today.

Owen had converted to Spiritualism late in life, following a sitting with an American medium called Mrs Hayden, who traveled to Britain in the 1840s to become the first working Spiritualist outside the United States and who was clearly a great hit. Indeed, she paved the way for Spiritualism in Europe.

Meanwhile, poor Emma Hardinge Britten found she did not have the stomach for the vilification she received at the hands of America's religious communities and eventually departed her adopted land for England, where the social atmosphere was rather more tolerant.

Her Spiritualist career thrived and, as enthusiasm for this new phenomenon spread across the English-speaking world, she embarked on lengthy tours of both Australia and New Zealand.

Her final claim to fame is that she founded the first weekly Spiritualist magazine, entitled *Two Worlds*, in 1887. The National Spiritualists Federation, Britain's first official Spiritualist organization, was established shortly afterwards, in 1890.

The Victorian Cult of Death

Britain was perhaps more open to Spiritualist ideas because of the Victorian Cult of Death. Queen Victoria, who reigned from 1837 till her death in 1901, was bereaved early in life and, many said at the time and still do today, grieved for her husband Prince Albert, who died in 1861, excessively. Retreating to her beloved Scottish idyll at Balmoral, she wore full mourning for the remaining forty years of her life and would have withdrawn from public life entirely if her Prime Minister had not warned her that such a move could imperil the standing of the monarchy in the eyes of the public.

Was she the inspiration for her era's obsession with mortality? To an extent, certainly. This imposing figure—this somber queen draped in widow's weeds—chimed with an age where, despite the dawn of major medical advances, infant mortality remained devastatingly high and life expectancy low. Death stalked everyone, even the very rich, even the queen herself, and many attendant rituals were developed during her reign.

A widow was expected to mourn her spouse for a whole year, while a mother would mourn a lost baby for nine months, followed by three months of half-mourning. The household clocks were stopped during that period, and the mirrors draped in black crepe. Amongst the wealthier classes, tombstones and mausoleums became hugely important and many of the nation's most impressive cemeteries, including the Necropolis behind Glasgow's St Mungo's Cathedral, were constructed during the Victorian era.

Death, far from being a taboo subject, became something that everybody lived with. The dear departed were remembered at every turn and from this sprang the age's fascination with post-mortem life.

Spiritualism did seem to offer something more concrete, in the form of a direct communication with the dead. The traditional image of the Victorian parlor séance, with its wildly flickering candle-flames, sinuous shadows and weird, disembodied voices may set the hairs on the back of the neck on end, but their purpose was not to scare, rather it was to reassure and bring comfort.

Spiritualism also had a social advantage over the established faiths. It was more inclusive, particularly of women, and less learned. Women, according to the beliefs of the time, were actually considered to be more conducive to the spirit world, and more likely to have psychic sensibilities.

Unsurprisingly, Spiritualism became typically known as the pastime of wealthy housewives, and the séance became a realm in which women, for once, were dominant.

An interesting footnote is that Queen Victoria is alleged to have been assisted in communicating with her much-missed husband through the agency of her trusted and loyal Scottish ghillie, John Brown. Indeed, it is said that those of Celtic blood have a natural affinity with the world beyond.

Daniel Dunlas Home

Of the early Spiritualist pioneers, the name of Daniel Dunlas Home stands out. Born in Edinburgh in 1833, this troubled young man grew up to become an internationally renowned physical medium whose demonstrations of levitation are the stuff of legend.

Home's family, like many in those days, upped sticks and

emigrated to America in 1842, in search of a better life and prospects. Things did not turn out well for them, with Home's mother dying in 1850, leaving him to the tender care of his sole remaining aunt. His mother was possessed of a certain psychic ability but Home was too young for her to have passed on her skills and knowledge by the time she died. However, it seems he inherited her sixth sense nonetheless.

As a teenager, strange, poltergeist-like activity began to occur in the house he shared with his aunt. Furniture moved of its own accord, objects flew from one side of the room to the next, and odd, inexplicable noises were heard day and night. Poltergeist activity is often associated with unhappy youngsters and Home definitely fitted into that category, but this phenomenon had another cause, as his aunt was about to discover.

She called in a priest, hoping he could exorcise the house of what she imagined to be some kind of demon. Instead he surprised her by deducing that the source of the problem was the boy's psychic abilities and that the solution was to control and develop his skills.

She must have taken his advice because, by the time he reached young adulthood, Home was an established medium on the Spiritualist circuit. He traveled throughout the United States, holding séances at which tables would shake, vibrate and even lift off the floor and spirits would send long, complex messages through a code of sharp raps. Even more astounding were the hands that would miraculously materialize in mid-air and set about penning messages on the sheets of notepaper that were always available, and the musical instruments that would suddenly appear and play themselves. In 1852, he pulled off the feat of actually levitating himself.

No wonder Home's appearances prompted eager queues

round the block. And no wonder he aroused the suspicion of skeptics, eager to prove him a fraud.

In 1855, Home returned to Britain, where he gave fantastic demonstrations of levitation and psychic communication at sittings in London, including with the first of his calling, Kate Fox.

Home was a trance medium which meant that, upon commencing a sitting, he would fall into a somnambulistic state, from which he could only be roused very slowly. Whilst in one of these trances, on December 13, 1868, he performed his most famous demonstration of levitation. He was holding a sitting in London, in the top floor room of a patron's house. He entered his trance as usual and shortly afterwards, to the amazement of his onlookers, rose up bodily from his chair and sailed elegantly out of the open window. Outside, he hovered over the quiet, suburban street for some minutes before flying back through the window from whence he had come and returning to his seat.

It need hardly be said that this event caused a sensation amongst the chattering classes of London and made the opponents of Spiritualism even more determined to unmask him as the charlatan they believed he surely was.

Step forward Sir William Crookes, an esteemed doctor and president of the aforementioned Society for Psychical Research. He approached his subject with the objectivity of the scientist and conducted a series of rigorous tests to ascertain, once and for all, the integrity of Daniel Dunlas Home. He found no evidence whatever of fakery or illusion and could only conclude that Home was either a man way ahead of his time in terms of trickery, or he was for real.

However, to this day there remain those who regard Home as a conman of the first order, pointing to his early retirement at the age of 40 as indicative of the fact that only a young man could pull off such convincing stunts.

That said, even Harry Houdini, an arch-skeptic with, nevertheless, a long-standing fascination with Spiritualism, could never replicate Home's incredible levitations and moving furniture spectacles.

This flying Scotsman died in 1886, of tuberculosis.

Arthur Conan Doyle

Arthur Conan Doyle was born in Edinburgh in 1859 and is perhaps best known as the creator of the fictional detective Sherlock Holmes. But Sir Arthur, as he became after serving in the Boer War of 1899–1902, is also famous for being one of the great champions of Spiritualism. To many he is regarded as something akin to the St Paul of the Spiritualist movement.

Such was his faith in the endurance of the human spirit after death, and his enthusiasm for a religion that incorporated actual communication with these departed spirits, that he forfeited much of his credibility in the eyes of his peers and contemporaries. To Conan Doyle this did not matter, Spiritualism was a faith that endured to the very end and brought him great peace and comfort.

He had a difficult start in life. Though born of moderately wealthy parents, his civil servant father suffered from epilepsy and increasingly acute alcoholism. His mother Mary, however, was his guiding light. A great storyteller, he recalled her voice "sinking to a horror-stricken whisper" as she neared the conclusion of one of her captivating stories. To the young Arthur, stories were a vital diversion from the otherwise chaotic character of his early home life.

He was sent to a Jesuit school as a youngster and quickly came to hate its brutal regime. He later lost his religious conviction, declaring himself an agnostic. Such was his integrity that, as a young adult struggling to get a start in the medical profession, he refused to enlist the help of his father's friends because these were Roman Catholic church connections and he felt it would be wrong to exploit them. This robustness of character was one of Conan Doyle's outstanding features.

Upon leaving Stonyhurst College which, if nothing else, furnished him with a fruitful panoply of characters which were later incorporated into his works of fiction, Conan Doyle entered the School of Medicine at Edinburgh University.

His early career as a doctor took place aboard various ships and in the towns of Plymouth and Portsmouth. However, he was also pursuing a parallel career as a writer and in 1887 and to enormous acclaim, published his first Sherlock Holmes story, A Study In Scarlet. In 1891, he was sufficiently successful to take the plunge into a full-time writing career and by the 1920s, he was one of the most celebrated and highly paid novelists of his period.

But this hard-earned literary life was to be rudely inter-rupted, causing Conan Doyle to change direction once again. First came the Boer War. He was 40 and therefore too old to enlist but this did not deter Conan Doyle from assisting in a cause in which he believed deeply. He volunteered to work in a field hospital, where he witnessed appalling suffering and death. In his memoir, The Great Boer War, he described see-ing more people die of typhoid as a result of the hopelessly inadequate hygiene than of war wounds. The sight of so much waste, so much death, affected him deeply.

In 1906, his first wife Louisa died. Then, the greatest blow of all: his son Kingsley, whose birth in 1892 he had described as "the chief event" of he and Louisa's life, died of pneumonia during the First World War.

Conan Doyle also lost his brother, two brothers-in-law and two nephews to this dreadful conflict.

It was these terrible experiences that undoubtedly sowed

the seeds of Conan Doyle's subsequent devotion to Spiritualism.

The First World War

Interest in Spiritualism had peaked in the mid-19th century, when it counted as many as 11 million devotees worldwide. But by the dawn of the 20th century, its popularity was already fading as the upper and middle classes found other amusements, and the half-lit world of the séance began to seem hopelessly Victorian and old-fashioned.

The fact that the Spiritualist movement was disastrously disorganized and factionalized, and that the Spiritualist circuit was awash with fraudsters charging extortionate fees and offering feats that would not have been out of place in a Music Hall performance further accounts for the movement's rapid decline.

But the First World War changed all that, and prompted a huge revival of Spiritualism, particularly amongst the working classes.

The War to End All Wars, as it was briefly known, broke out in 1914 and quickly became a world-scale conflict and arguably the most brutal mankind had ever seen. Never had so many soldiers been called up, from all across the class spectrum, nor so many slaughtered in action, many would say needlessly and as a result of poor direction on the part of the officers. "Lions led by donkeys" is how the spectacle of brave young foot soldiers being sent to their deaths by ignorant upper-class officers was later to be described.

Over nine million were killed on the battlefield in the course of this four-year war, and as many again died as a result of genocide, starvation and bombing raids.

Hundreds upon thousands of women were left widowed, with young children to raise alone, as whole generations were wiped out at a stroke. Small villages were left with no young men at all, farms struggled on without sons, industry without male apprentices. People lost count of the dead; it was on an unimaginable scale.

Thus it seems natural that these suddenly bereft, desperately grieving people would seek means of saying goodbye to the loved ones so rudely snatched away from them, and Spiritualism offered a route. The séance and sitting flourished during and after the War years, as mediumship again went into ascendancy.

One of the primary attractions that Spiritualism held for Conan Doyle was that, if it was true, then it meant his beloved son existed somewhere still.

From skeptic to believer

Conan Doyle's interest in Spiritualism dated as far back as 1881, when he was prevailed upon to attend a lecture on the subject. He went on to describe this event in an article for *The Light*, a leading Spiritualist periodical. However, at that time, his feet were firmly planted in the skeptics camp.

Later, when he was working in Southsea, he attended a series of séances at the home of a General Drayson, a teacher at the nearby Greenwich Naval College and one of Conan Doyle's patients. The medium in attendance was a railway signalman with, it appears, remarkable powers of physical mediumship. Tables trembled, objects flew, weird creatures materialized in mid-air. It was, frankly, all too much for the young, pragmatic Edinburgh doctor, who left with the distinct impression that someone was having a joke at his expense.

Nevertheless, the experience kindled his interest in the supernatural.

In the February of 1889, Conan Doyle, who was nothing if not possessed of a thirsty mind, attended a lecture on mesmerism, given by a Professor Milo de Meyer, who attempted to mesmerize, amongst others, Conan Doyle, unsuccessfully as it happened.

These were exciting times for students of the human mind. Sigmund Freud had discovered the subconscious, the arts of hypnosis and mesmerism were being utilized in the pursuit of further discoveries and mental illness was being re-evaluated in the light of modern medical knowledge.

In 1894, having joined the esteemed Society for Psychical Research some years before, Conan Doyle, alongside Dr Sydney Scott and Frank Podmore, took part in his first psychic investigation.

A Colonel Elmore, living in Dorset, had reported a disturbing case to the society. His wife and daughter, he said, had been hearing mysterious noises during the night, including a rather chilling moaning call and the sound of chains being dragged along the floor by person or persons unknown. Not only that but the family dog now refused to enter certain rooms and most of the domestic staff had taken fright and left.

Suitably intrigued, the three-man team despatched to Dorset, where they spent a night attempting to record the "fearsome noise" that ensued and to trace its source. It was certainly a hair-raising experience but their experiments were inconclusive. Conan Doyle, however, was convinced that something untoward and possibly supernatural had occurred.

This gut feeling was compounded when, many years later, the long-deceased body of a ten-year-old was unearthed in the garden. The record does not show whether the Elmore hauntings ceased upon this discovery, but Conan Doyle was certain that it was the source of the disturbances.

Conan Doyle was also involved in further investigations, a series of which convinced him that telepathy existed between sympathetic souls. Ever studious, he continued to study the phenomenon of Spiritualism, finally hitting upon a book called *Human Personality and its Survival of Bodily Death*, written by the Cambridge Classics scholar and founder member of the Society for Psychical Research, Frederick WH Meyer. This profound work greatly influenced Conan Doyle's thinking and is still a literary touchstone of the Spiritualist movement.

Several mediums are said to have received messages from the irrepressible Meyer from beyond the grave, often relating to intellectual matters such as those outlined in his signature work.

The death of his son accelerated Conan Doyle's examination and, a year later, he was rewarded when a Welsh medium brought forth a message from the young man. It was a profoundly moving and welcome experience and Conan Doyle believed firmly that it had been Kingsley's voice he heard, speaking of "concerns unknown to the medium." Another time, he encountered his long lost mother Mary, and one of his nephews, who materialized before his eyes "as plainly as I ever saw them in my life!" thanks to the efforts of a physical medium.

Skeptics, however, maintained that these were the distortions of a grief-stricken mind. In short, that Conan Doyle saw what he craved to see and nothing more.

In 1917, after much careful consideration, Conan Doyle went public about his belief in Spiritualism, addressing a lecture to the London Spiritual Alliance in October of that year. This speech went on to form the basis of his book The New Revelation, published a year later, when he and his second wife embarked upon a world tour of lectures, encompassing Canada, Australia and New Zealand.

This public statement of belief was the scandal of its day,

and caused many to think the poor man had gone mad. But even the most cynical concluded that, whatever the truth of the matter, Conan Doyle was sincere in his beliefs. Harry Price, one of the great investigators into psychic phenomena, who made it his business to unmask fakers and fraudsters—and a very profitable business it was too—said of Conan Doyle: "His extreme credulity ... was the despair of his colleagues."

Doyle and the Cottingley fairies

This queasiness in the face of Conan Doyle's convictions was exacerbated by the case of the Cottingley Fairies. In 1920, Conan Doyle was fascinated to hear of a series of photographic images taken by two young women, living in Cottingley, Yorkshire, apparently of fairies at the bottom of their garden. Elsie Wright, 16, and her school friend Frances Griffiths, 10, had taken a number of photographs of what appeared to be perfect little fairies, complete with diaphonous wings and tiny, doll-life features. Indeed, they so resembled the Victorian picture-book version of ladylike fairies, as opposed to the traditional Celtic image of rough, hairy folk with dark powers, that Conan Doyle should have known better.

Alas, he did not, and went so far as to publish an article in *The Strand* magazine describing the images as unquestionably authentic. Kodak film laboratories were not so sure. Though they confirmed that the images were neither double exposures nor had the negatives been tampered with, they were also able to confirm that the "special effects" could be reproduced with ease.

It seems that these two English girls had pulled a stunt that rapidly got out of hand. Sixty years later, they confessed, though their handiwork had long since been exposed as fakery. Something of which most onlookers had not really needed convincing.

Houdini

That same year, Conan Doyle met the master illusionist Harry Houdini who, as previously mentioned, had a huge, if arms-length, interest in Spiritualism. Following the death of his mother, Mme Weiss, to whom some say he was unnaturally close, Houdini was pitched into a welter of grief, from which he never truly recovered. In the immediate wake of her passing, he sought out medium after medium, hoping to make contact with her. Instead he discovered, to his great horror, that most of the mediums he encountered were crude tricksters, more practised in the art of exploiting people's grief than communing with the dear departed. That set him off on another mission—to debunk Spiritualism once and for all.

Surprisingly then, Houdini and Conan Doyle became great friends. Houdini was greatly appreciative of Doyle's open, honest and earnest personality, describing him as at least "one intelligent person" associated with this damnable art. He asked Conan Doyle to prove that Spiritualism was for real and the great writer naturally accepted the challenge.

Thus, in 1922, they met up in Atlantic City along with their wives. Conan Doyle's second wife, Jean was a psychic herself, transmitting messages from the other side through automatic or "inspired" writing. She served as the medium at the ensuing séance, during which she contacted Houdini's mother, passing on her messages to her son in written English.

Houdini was unimpressed. For a start, Mme Weiss could not speak English, conversing in her native Hungarian right up until her dying day. Furthermore, she failed to mention to the medium that this particular day was her birthday; something that would never have slipped her mind during her lifetime!

Lady Jean attempted to dismiss these concerns, arguing that the messages of spirits are always transmitted in a language that the medium understands and that Mme Weiss would have little truck with birthdays now she was on the other side. This only incensed Houdini, who left the meeting deeply troubled.

The Conan Doyle–Houdini friendship was subsequently strained to breaking point when the former attacked the latter in the press, accusing him of actually being a medium himself, hence his zeal to debunk Spiritualism. Doyle explained that Houdini did not perform amazing feats of human endeavor but simply achieved his escapes through "dematerializing" in one place and rematerializing in another.

Houdini responded angrily, saying Conan Doyle was "senile" and continued in his crusade against what he considered dark arts indeed, culminating in the publication, in 1924, of A Magician Amongst the Spiritualists, in which he exposed many of the prominent mediums of his day.

For his part, Conan Doyle was unshaken in his beliefs. He died in 1930 of heart disease, writing on the eve of his passing: "The reader will judge that I have had many adventures. The greatest and most glorious of all awaits me now."

Helen Duncan, "Hellish Nell"

If Arthur Conan Doyle was the St Paul of the Spiritualist movement, then Helen Duncan was the St Joan, in that she suffered deeply for her art and died a premature and pitiful death.

Born in the small, picturesque village of Callander, near Loch Lomond, in Scotland, Helen Duncan was to become one of the most famous physical mediums in history and was the last woman ever to be tried, and convicted, under the Witchcraft Act of 1735.

Her life began simply enough. She was born on November

25, 1897, the daughter of a slate-maker and builder and the fourth of eight children. During her rather frugal childhood, she had a number of clairvoyant experiences, which her mother warned her not to speak about in public. Helen, whose tomboy behavior had earned her the nickname Hellish Nell, brought further disgrace to her family when, at the age of 16, she fell pregnant without a husband in sight. She was thus banished from her small town home to Dundee, where she worked in one of the city's many jute mills and lived in a women's hostel. After a period in a sanitorium, where she was treated for tuberculosis, she worked as an auxiliary at Dundee Royal Infirmary, working predominantly in the psychiatric wing.

It was in Dundee that she met her future husband Henry, who had been invalided out of the army with rheumatic fever, an ailment that set the precedent for his future, chronic ill health. Like Helen, Henry was a "sensitive" with a profound and intellectual interest in Spiritualism. Because of his ill health, he was often unable to work. Instead, he devoted much of his time to reading Spiritualist literature and using his accumulated knowledge to assist his wife in developing her skill.

Though there was little time for that. Times were very tough for this young couple, Helen endured no less than twelve pregnancies, of which only six children survived. She worked for a time in a local bleach factory, an awful, health-impairing way to make a living, while working as a medium in the evenings.

From the start then, we can see that mediumship was a way of earning money for Duncan; a fact that caused many to be suspicious of her, not least because, the more spectacular her sittings, the more she coined it in.

However it should be noted that, if raising the dead was

lucrative, then so too was debunking the art of Spiritualism. Not all of Duncan's critics had the intregrity of Harry Houdini; some were just out for a good story to sell to the popular press for a fat fee. Unsurprisingly, the hard-working Helen was often incensed by her detractors, and would physically lash out at loud-mouthed skeptics who attended her sittings.

What should be remembered is that, like most of her clientele, Helen Duncan was a bitterly poor woman who struggled to survive, aided only to a small extent by her husband, due to his general unfitness for work. Dumpy, poorly-dressed and matter-of-fact, she was like thousands of working class women, many of whom were left widowed by the war and thrown on their own resources, and this was at a time when women were paid substantially less than men for the same labor.

Her mediumship offered solace in these bleak lives, a glimpse not only of peace to come in the hereafter but a chance to speak to those who had passed over and to bask for a while in the past. Thus what has been described as her somewhat mercenary approach to Spiritualism—she expected to be paid, and decently—was not frowned upon by the majority of her patrons. A woman had to make a living, after all.

Can the camera lie?

Her mediumship was also, without doubt, a performance in itself. Once immersed in a trance state, ectoplasm would begin to emanate from her body, sometimes from her nostrils, sometimes her mouth. On one occasion, according to a witness, it actually seemed to "spurt from the nipples of her breasts." This curious material, never satisfactorily analysed, would coagulate in mid-air, finally resolving into the figure of a spirit from the other side.

One photograph, alleged to have been taken at a Helen Duncan séance, shows the spirit form of an elderly man, rendered visible by ectoplasm, which gives the appearance of his being draped in a thick white sheet. Though his body is pretty much entirely concealed, the details of his face are remarkably rendered.

This eerie figure seems to emanate from the side of the medium's head, to which it is connected by a kind of ectoplasmic umbilical cord.

Speaking many years later at Helen Duncan's trial, Hannen Swaffer, a renowned Fleet Street journalist of his day and the founder of the Spiritualist weekly *Psychic News*, declared that anyone who mistook ectoplasm for butter muslin, a common charge, "would be a child. Under a red light in a séance room it would look yellow or pink whilst these spirit forms all displayed a white appearance."

The photographic evidence, such as it is, seems to bear Swaffer's assertion out, revealing spirits of a ghastly white pallor.

Duncan was assisted in her remarkable work by her spirit guide, a rather snooty, elegant gentleman called Albert who nonetheless channelled a considerable array of other-wordly guests her way.

In demand

Word soon spread regarding this remarkable woman, and it was not long before people across the country were clamoring to see her. During the 1930s and 40s, she began touring the country, hosting public meetings at Spiritualist churches, village halls and private houses. As the Second World War began to ratchet up horrendous numbers of casualties, so the demand for a contact with the recently departed increased. At this time, estimates suggest there were upward of a million active Spiritualists in Britain alone, over a thousand Spiritualist churches and several thousand home circles, the latter being the smaller-scale, more domestic setting for a séance.

Wherever she went, Helen Duncan did not disappoint—the dead rose up before the living as if by magic, imparting messages so detailed and accurate that onlookers could only gasp. How, they wondered, could this ordinary looking, middle-aged Scottish housewife be capable of such amazing feats?

A widower called Vincent Woodcock attended one of Duncan's sittings, along with his sister-in-law, and was converted to Spiritualism by what he witnessed. Helen Duncan did not merely pass on a message from Woodcock's dead wife, she caused her to materialize in their midst in a wave of ectoplasm. This phantom then took off her wedding ring and placed it on her sister's finger, saying: "It is my wish that this takes place for the sake of my little girl."

All of which was music to the ears of Woodcock and his sister-in-law, who subsequently married, returning years later to another Helen Duncan séance. The dead wife obligingly reappeared, this time to bestow her blessings on the new union.

Woodcock was one of the many grateful clients who testified in Duncan's favor at her trial, held at the Old Bailey in London in 1944. But more of that later.

Major JH Webster MBE, in his book *Voices of the Past*, recounts two incredible materializations at the hands of Helen Duncan.

In 1942, during the summer, the Scottish medium held a séance in Manchester at which a Mr Ramsden, a Squadron Leader in the RAF, was in attendance. Though a keen student of Spiritualism, he was yet to be fully persuaded as to its authenticity.

The séance began as normal, with prayers and a hymn or two. The curtains were then drawn and Duncan descended into a trance. Within minutes, ectoplasm began to emerge from her body, forming an eerily opaque, moon-colored cloud in mid-air. Gradually, the refined features of Albert, her spirit guide, began to distinguish themselves.

He addressed himself, without ceremony or hesitation, to the startled Mr Ramsden, who had booked himself in under a false name. Albert, it seems, was not fooled for a minute and announced that there was a woman waiting in the spiritual wings who was desperately impatient to meet with him again.

This woman transpired to be Mr Ramsden's mother, who soon afterwards appeared, as if in the flesh. Rather tongue-tied at first, she confessed that, "I have been waiting for this moment for years, and now I am here I feel too excited to know what to say."

Nevertheless, she did relate enough private family information to convince her son that what he was witnessing was more than a mere figment of his imagination.

Perhaps more startling still is the epilogue to this little story. In conversation with him afterwards, Helen Duncan revealed to Mr Ramsden that she never saw the spirit forms herself, indeed had never seen a spirit form in her life. "I am sure that if I did then I would die of fright," she told him.

At a subsequent séance, in March 1943, Duncan accurately transmitted messages to what was a very international audience in a variety of languages of which she had no previous knowledge. Duncan had barely attended school, and gone to work very hard and very early; how could she therefore have a working knowledge, all of a sudden, of Afrikaans, a Bolivian Spanish dialect, Polish and Dutch?

At this same sitting, Duncan also brought forth the spirit form of a recently killed New Zealander pilot. His Wing Commander, a guest of Mr Ramsden, could only gasp his astonishment.

Bill Watson, the deceased airman, went on to describe the

nature of his death, pinpointing the cause to his inability to use his escape hatch. His Commander, suddenly regaining control of himself, demanded to know more and Watson was only too happy to oblige. His technical knowledge, the listeners insisted, far surpassed anything that Helen Duncan could have picked up.

In fact, it is claimed that this Wing Commander later instigated a programme of modifications to the model of aircraft used by the tragic airman. And along the lines suggested by Mr Watson's ghostly debriefing.

A challenge

Mediumship was an insecure profession. Even someone of Helen Duncan's fame was subject to fashionable changes of heart, and thus she took up every paying opportunity that presented itself. Like Arthur Conan Doyle before her, she presented herself at the London Spiritualist Alliance, though she shied away from intellectualizing her work, preferring the direct approach of actual mediumship.

She also, and perhaps unwisely, took up the challenge laid down by Harry Price, the arch-skeptic, and former member of the Society for Psychical Research. He left this organization to form his own, the National Laboratory of Psychical Research.

Malcolm Gaskill, in his book *Hellish Nell: Last of Britain's Witches*, describes the intrusive manner in which Price set about Helen Duncan. First, two doctors were enlisted to conduct a physical examination, to determine whether she secreted objects or materials about her person. To all intents and purposes, it was as humiliating and invasive as the kind of strip-search conducted in prisons to ensure inmates are not carrying illegal drugs.

Next, she was rudely awoken from a trance by someone shouting in her face. Meanwhile the ecotoplasm that was beginning to emanate from her person was snatched for analysis.

This analysis revealed Duncan's ectoplasm to be composed primarily of egg-white and woodpulp while a series of X-rays revealed her incredible ability to swallow and regurgitate, at will, the materials required for her performances. Harry Price thus concluded that Duncan was "one of the cleverest frauds in the history of Spiritualism."

The records of the Helen Duncan séances conducted at the National Laboratory of Psychic Research, with observations by a number of leading academics, were published by Harry Price in 1931 in a single volume, entitled *Regurgitation and the Duncan Mediumship*.

Duncan was deeply shaken both by Price's rough conduct and his damning conclusions. Yet the Spiritualist movement was unshaken in its faith in her and the work continued.

A hugely popular magician of the day, Will Goldston, insisted that the effects produced at a Helen Duncan séance were not replicable, even by a man of his considerable skills. Such tributes gave Duncan heart.

Alec Harris, a notable Welsh medium, was convinced of the truth of Spiritualism, despite a very orthodox, Christian upbringing in the Rhondda Valley, by a visit to one of Duncan's séances. His sister Connie had recently died and he was both gratified and deeply shaken when she appeared to him as if from nowhere.

Connie not only greeted and reassured him, she also urged her brother to recognize his psychic abilities and to develop and use them. Which he most certainly did, going on to become one of the most successful mediums of his day.

Everything changes

But the event that was to turn Duncan's life upside down

took place in Portsmouth, in 1941, though it was at a later séance in 1944 that the full force of the law began to bear down upon her.

The town was home to Britain's naval fleet and, as such, a target for the German Luftwaffe. Thus we can be assured that the war was very much on the minds of everyone who attended Helen Duncan's séance on the night of the 19th January 1944. Well, perhaps not everyone. In the midst of the credulous audience sat a police officer in plain clothes, there on a twelve-and-a-half shilling ticket, purchased for him by a naval officer called Lieutenant R Worth, who believed Duncan to be of the lowest order of common trickster.

What caused his ire? Possibly that, in 1941, Duncan had called forth the spirit of a young sailor who explained to his attendant mother that he had been killed when his ship, HMS Barham, went down on November 25, 1941. This was a profound shock to the mother and, as news of this ghastly revelation got out, came as something of a rude surprise to the Admiralty too, who were yet to release details of the sinking of the warship. Could Duncan, some wondered, be a spy? Suffice it to say that Duncan's activities were of enough concern to attract the attention of MI5, who were instrumental in building the case against her.

Doubtless a strong dose of wartime hysteria infected proceedings because, in all likelihood, Duncan's mediumship was not half as accurate as people were later lead to believe. It is not beyond the realms of possibility that an anxious mother named the ship and that, when Duncan produced the son's name, they both put two and two together and made four. A warship sinking in wartime is hardly an unwarranted guess. And almost certainly, the story grew arms and legs in the telling.

In one version, by way of an example, the dead sailor

appears wearing a cap on which is clearly brandished the legend, HMS Barham. Not only that, but we hear that Helen Duncan's subsequent arrest was on the express orders of none other than Winston Churchill, the very man who later branded the whole business of the trial absurd.

Whatever happened exactly, the events of January 1941 ensured that Duncan's activities were closely monitored thereafter, concluding with this fateful night in 1944.

As was often the case, in the course of the sitting, ectoplasm began to emanate from Duncan. In appearance, it looked like a large, floating white sheet. The police officer, assuming that that is exactly what it was, jumped up from his chair and grabbed at it, causing it to vanish into thin air. Or rather, as her supporters maintained, to snap back into her body, an action that happened much too fast and caused her body to be scarred with nasty friction burns.

A fingertip search of the room, conducted immediately afterwards, uncovered neither a white sheet nor any other incriminating or even suspicious paraphernalia. Indeed, it was customary for Duncan, prior to every sitting, to allow herself to be thoroughly strip-searched, in an ante-room attended by women only, in order to throw off the oft-heard accusation that she concealed objects and material about her person to assist in her performances.

But back to the fateful night of 1944; after failing to grab hold of the ectoplasm, the officer then roused Helen Duncan abruptly from her trance, a move that her friends claimed did her irreparable damage as mediums should always be allowed to emerge from their trances in their own time. Finally, she was arrested, as were three of her sitters, presumed by the officer to be "plants" seeded into the audience to enhance the fraud.

Portsmouth Magistrates Court subsequently charged all four under the Vagrancy Act. Had they been convicted of this charge, they would each have incurred a five-shilling fine. Despite the relatively minor nature of the charge against her, Duncan was refused bail and sent down to Holloway, the notoriously unpleasant women's prison in London.

Whilst there on remand, Duncan learnt that the charge against her had been upgraded to one of Conspiracy which, during times of war, carried with it the death penalty. This charge was later amended to one of Witchcraft as per the 1735 act. Under this ancient law, considered by most practising legal people to be all but obsolete, she was charged on the grounds that it was unlawful to "exercise or use human conjuration that through the agency of Helen Duncan, spirits of deceased dead persons should appear to be present."

She was also accused of Larceny, "by falsely pretending she was in a position to bring about the appearances of the spirits of deceased persons."

The Spiritualist community, both in Scotland and throughout the world, were up in arms about these charges and a defence fund was quickly established in order to underwrite the traveling expenses of witnesses to her sterling character from all corners of the globe.

The Law Societies of both Scotland and England declared the trial a travesty of justice. They were not alone in their outrage. On hearing of the case, wartime Prime Minister Winston Churchill, who had an interest in Spiritualism himself, wrote to Herbert Morrison at the Home Office demanding: "Let me have a report on why the Witchcraft Act, 1735, was used in a modern Court of Justice. What was the cost of this trial to the State, observing that witnesses were brought from Portsmouth and maintained here in this crowded London, for a fortnight, and the Recorder kept busy with all this obsolete tomfoolery, to the detriment of necessary work in the Courts?"

All this notwithstanding, the trial went ahead, lasting seven days in all and feeding the insatiable tabloid press with lurid story after lurid story.

Amongst those who flocked to testify on Duncan's behalf was Kathleen McNeill, a Glasgow housewife, who told the court how her sister had materialized at a séance. Given that she had died only hours previously it was inconceivable, said McNeill, that Helen Duncan had any foreknowledge. Only her spirit guide Albert could have imparted such information.

Alfred Dodd, an academic and the author of a number of learned works on Shakespeare's sonnets, described how he was brought face to face with his deceased grandfather through the agency of Ms Duncan. This ancient, portly gentleman appeared, as he had in life, wearing a smoking cap from which his familiar donkey fringe protruded. After conversing with his grandson some moments, he turned to Alfred's friend Tom, who was sitting beside him, and said: "Look into my face and into my eyes. Ask Alfred to show you my portrait. It is the same man."

James Herries, a journalist on the respected broadsheet *The Scotsman*, and a Justice of the Peace into the bargain, related how Duncan called forth the spirit of the late lamented Arthur Conan Doyle.

They may as well have saved their breath because Helen Duncan was convicted under the ludicrous charges and sent down.

Duncan's defence team had urged her to demonstrate her powers before the Court but the Court refused to allow this. The latter wanted her to testify, a request she refused on the grounds that the alleged incidents took place while she was in a state of deep trance. This meant that she would, could, have no recollection of them.

The judge, after a weekend of deliberation, declared that the Court's business was not to ascertain whether "genuine manifestations of this kind are possible" but rather, to determine whether the accused had acted dishonestly. The Court, he said, had concluded that she had, and he handed down a ten-month sentence.

Helen Duncan is said to have wept bitter tears on hearing this, declaring: "I never hee'd so mony lies in a' my life."

She served rather less than the prescribed ten months, but emerged from prison shaken by the experience and with her health, never good in the first place, severely impaired.

During her time in prison, Duncan's supporters attempted an appeal, but it was thrown out by the House of Lords. It was clear that the British establishment was thoroughly embarrassed by the whole sorry force.

Duncan's supporters also clamored for a change in the law and got that at least. In 1951, the 1735 Witchcraft Act was finally removed from the statute books and replaced by the Fraudulent Mediums Act. This law, in contrast to its quasi-medieval predecessor, was contemptuous rather than fearful of the supernatural. It equated mediumship with showbusiness and concerned itself solely with whether or not money changed hands. If it was done for free, it was deemed harmless entertainment.

Meanwhile, on the inside, Duncan continued to work as a medium, with the warders and prisoners comprising her new clientele. One apocryphal story is that Winston Churchill himself visited her in Holloway, apparently to seek out her services. This, however, receives no confirmation from official sources. In fact, his outrage with regards to the trial appears to be his only contact point with the life and times of Helen Duncan.

Upon her release, and despite previously insisting that she

would not, Duncan resumed her Spiritualist career, though on a much lesser scale than before. The lurid publicity of the trial, coupled with the stain of incarceration, had tarnished her image in the eyes of the public. Not only that, but her psychic abilities appeared to be evaporating to the extent that the official Spiritualist body, the National Union of Spiritualists, eventually revoked her license.

Though she continued to scrape a halfway decent living, Duncan was still subject to police raids, including one in Nottingham in 1956. Such was the shock she received on this occasion that she died five weeks later, aged only 59, after an exhausting lifetime of hard graft and endless, often vicious criticism.

But the story does not quite end there. Helen Duncan remains a revered figure within the Spiritualist community, and is regarded by many as a martyr to the cause. She had made a number of notable appearances at modern séances, including one in which materialized before her daughter Gina, through the agency of the medium Rita Goold.

Should we really be surprised to hear that this extraordinary Scottish housewife, breadwinner and mother should still be making appearances at séances, albeit from the other side?

Albert Best

Albert Best was born in Belfast, on 2nd December 1917, though he spent the majority of his later life in Glasgow. An intensely private individual, he was widowed young and subsequently lived alone. However, through his mediumship, he reached out to thousands of people, and his contribution to the world of Spiritualism is considerable.

Best was brought up by a woman who was not his grandmother but did go by the name of Mrs Best, his mother having died when he was still a boy. It was a rather austere and not particularly happy childhood, by all accounts though, Albert did have one thing in common with his elderly guardian: a psychic gift.

As with most mediums, Albert's first encounter with the other side occurred when he was very young and it left him baffled. Aged seven, he met a man brandishing a lamp on the stairs. Curiously, he had string tied round each knee. Naturally alarmed, Albert rushed to point the figure out to Mrs Best, who responded by telling him he was seeing things. However, as soon as she thought he was out of earshot, she addressed the mysterious figure as "Father," urging him to go away as he was "frightening the boy."

A natural talent

It was a few years before Albert began to get to grips with his unusual talent. Rosalind Cattanach, a friend of Best's and one of the few people to have gathered much in the way of biographical detail regarding the famous medium, recounts how, during his teens, he got talking to a window cleaner who invited him to attend his local Spiritualist church. Which Best did, only to be told by the attendant medium that, one day, he would don an army uniform and travel to Africa. For a working-class lad from Belfast, this was the equivalent of being told he would don a spacesuit and travel to the moon; he left distinctly underwhelmed, though he never forgot her words.

During this period, Albert was experiencing a deeply disturbing phenomenon. He kept hearing a voice, which seemed to emanate from within his own head. This voice gave him advice and made suggestions as to what he should do next. He was troubled by it, as you can imagine. Perhaps he feared he was going mad, or developing some sort of split personality.

Yet the voice itself, far from sounding evil or demented, was very reassuring. Still, he was terrified that other people could hear it and he would take himself off into the country on his days off—by then he was employed at a ropeworks, having left school at 14—so that he could commune with the voice without having to worry about being overheard.

A few years later, the mystery of the voice was solved for him. It seems to be the case with Spiritualism that it takes one to know one, and it was not until Best attended a Spiritualist church in Chichester that he encountered a medium who told him she could see lights all around him; a clear indication of strong psychic powers.

He went on to join a development circle, alongside his old friend the window cleaner.

Development circles

Development circles have been described as the "backbone of the Spiritualist movement" and anyone who is serious about developing their psychic skills is advised to attend a circle or seek out a sympathetic medium who can guide them.

The Spiritualist National Union is a good first port of call and most would-be psychics are encouraged to attend Spiritualist services for at least six months before even thinking about attending a development circle.

There are, of course, more secular versions, often called home circles, but novices should check out the credentials of the presiding medium first as, sadly, psychic charlatans did not die out with the Second World War.

Development circles are less religious in character than Spiritualist services. The group usually sits in a circle so that, physically, everyone is on an equal basis, and the session begins with a hymn or a meditation or even just an informal chat. The idea is that everyone feels relaxed and at home before the business of contacting the dead gets underway. Anyone who wishes to is encouraged to speak up if he or she detects a spirit presence or has a message to impart, but there is no pressure as every individual's psychic ability develops at a different pace.

These kinds of gatherings, overseen by a skilled and experienced psychic, are an essential first step for a medium as it allows the novice to ask questions about the various forms of mediumship and the terminology used, and to ask for tips on technique and talk though any personal experiences.

Many mediums hail from families where psychic abilities are commonplace and oft-discussed. These people can come to a development circle with a certain amount of confidence and foreknowledge. Others, like Albert Best, come to Spiritualism with very little experience of mediumship and may well be a little wary, even a little scared, of the whole subject. A strong, supportive development circle is therefore invaluable and it is not unusual to move from one to another, as Best apparently did, looking for the "right fit."

Developing a psychic gift requires a deal of patience. Even unusually gifted people like Best can take years to polish up their craft to the extent that they can serve their church and host public meetings. Some develop only so far, using their gift solely for private purposes.

This long apprenticeship is necessary to ensure that the new medium has confidence and consistency of approach and is able to distinguish between and accurately read even the most difficult of spirits.

Initially, mediums must learn how to clear their minds and use their senses to their utmost. Expecting phantoms and Native American spirit guides on the first night is not only unrealistic, it can lead to false imaginings and interfere with the real process of development.

One Glasgow Spiritualist to whomI spoke describes it as trying to achieve something akin to the Buddhist concept of contemplation.

"The human mind is a noisy place," he says, "only once it is free of all thoughts and expectations can the spirit world make contact and expect to be heard."

The presence of an experienced medium is very important at the development stage because novices cannot always be sure that the spirits they draw are necessarily benign ones. A good guide can ensure that anything untoward is dealt with decisively.

Being a successful medium requires study, self-awareness and commitment. Not unlike any religion, when you come to think of it.

The Second World War

When the second world war broke out, Best, then aged 22, signed up to the Inniskillen Fusiliers. The seemingly crazy prophecy made by the medium at his first Spiritualist meeting came true in 1940, when he was dispatched, wearing British Army uniform, to Algiers, in North Africa. It was a horrendous and dangerous campaign and whilst out there, a disturbing memory surfaced in Best's mind.

His real grandmother, whom he met only once, when he was in his teens, had said to him: "You'll be a widower before you are twenty-four. I haven't seen you all my life, but I'll be with you in Goubellet."

Goubellet Plain is in the north of Algiers, near the border of Tunis. Best's batallion was charged with the duty of clearing it in preparation for an Allied advance. It was a lethal job and Best, along with a number of his comrades, was left for dead, having been picked off by German soldiers looking down at them from a high ridge of land. Lying wounded, and perhaps ready to throw in the towel, Best heard a voice urging him to stand up and walk. Eventually he heeded it and was captured and taken to a prisoner-of-war camp.

Perhaps it was the same voice that had talked him through his lonely adolescence? Certainly it was one he trusted, even though it led him into the nightmarish experience of a wartime prison camp. That said, perhaps his guiding spirit knew he would survive this ordeal and go on to perform important work.

Best eventually returned home on a hospital ship, only to receive the most dreadful news of his life. During the blitz on Belfast, his young wife Rose and their three infant children had been killed outright. He did recover physically from his injuries, going on to serve his country again in Italy where he received further wounds, but he never recovered emotionally from the loss of his family.

This deep grief, which he carried with him all his life, was reflected in the enormous compassion he offered everyone who approached him for help. He knew only too well the bitter taste of sudden loss and the frustration of never having had the chance to say goodbye. Best was not alone in this of course. All across the world, in America, France, Germany, Britain, were people agonizing over the deaths of their loved ones in war, and Spiritualism was enjoying a sudden surge in popularity, as the story of Helen Duncan testifies.

A friendly medium

However, it was a few years before Best took up work as a medium. In the interim, he left Belfast and settled in Scotland, where he took up a job as a postman; a calling that would stand him in good stead in the future. Best was not one of those mediums who uttered vague names and descriptions whilst glancing wildly round the room hoping someone would help him out. By contrast, he did not just get the names of his spirit visitors absolutely right, he was often able to fill in details as to exactly where they lived, right down to the house number. Once a postman ...

Best was a member of a number of development circles during the late 1940s and early 50s. It was during this period that the spirit world seemed to offer him the possibility of becoming a physical medium, though the story he told his friend Laurence Goss is anything but inspiring.

Best was sitting in a chair having a rest when, suddenly opening his eyes, he saw that ectoplasm was seeping from his eyes, mouth and nostrils and forming a cloud in the mid-air. Addressing the spirit world, he said firmly, "No, no, I don't want this" and the weird substance vanished. That, it seems, was the beginning and end of his career as a physical medium.

Instead, like most modern mediums, Best heard the voices of his spirit visitors and passed them on to his earthly ones in his own voice. Sittings with him were friendly, down-to-earth affairs, with none of the dramatics associated with the likes of Helen Duncan. Perhaps that is why people from all across the world sought him out. Best traveled extensively, to Australia, India, even South Africa and counted amongst his clients members of royal families and celebrities. People trusted him and that trust was merited because, whatever secrets Best knew, he took them with him to the grave.

A typical example of his work is that cited by Agnes Kemp Miller, a lifelong devotee of Spiritualism. In an article submitted to the *Ghost Club of Britain* newsletter, Summer 2002, she relates how she was often visited by what she describes as "ghostly presences," from early childhood onwards. She came to realize in time that these spirits were nothing to be afraid of, that they were visitors from the spirit world and intended her no harm. Her accounts of visitations are vivid and often humorous.

But one experience really stuck in her mind. Waking up during the night, she beheld a little boy, about four or five years old, gazing up at her from his perch at the side of her bed.

"He had nice blonde hair and I noticed his bright red jumper. When I put out my hands and asked him what his name was, he giggled childishly and vanished."

The mystery of this little one's identity was resolved by Albert Best, whom Agnes sought out for a private sitting some time afterwards.

Best made contact with Agnes's husband, who had died a few years previously. He informed her that the little boy she saw was her grandson Stephen, whom he had just met on the other side. Stephen had died while still a toddler, and was now growing up in the spirit world. At the time of this sitting, he was four years old, according to Agnes's husband.

Spiritual healing

Best's work was not restricted to passing on messages from the other side. He was also a renowned spiritual healer, and worked for many years at Thornhill, a non-denominational healing center in the Southside of Glasgow, established by a wealthy businessman who had retired early following a heart attack in 1959.

Just as mediums depend on their spirit guides, so Best the healer relied on the services of his spirit helpers, Dr Wong, Ally and Hans. These helpers provided spiritual support and guidance and sometimes even supplied messages from well-wishers on the other side who wished to reassure the patient.

Best healed by placing his hands on a patient's body, never seeming to penetrate the flesh. It may have been unremarkable to watch, but some of his results were astounding.

Rosalind Cattanach's tribute to Albert Best, entitled *Best of Both Worlds*, relates the story of Morag and James Darroch, of Greenock, whose daughter Janice greatly benefited from her consultations with the Spiritualist healer, beginning in February 1969.

At nine months, she was "literally wasting away. She had no control or power in any of her muscles, and in effect couldn't even suck a bottle." Even the medical specialists were in despair, so the Darrochs took their daughter home, with the object of at least ensuring she was comfortable and in the company of those who loved her.

It is not clear how much faith these two understandably anxious parents had in Spiritualism, but they had nothing to lose after all, and so they called on Albert Best.

Upon meeting the ailing infant and her parents, Best asked James to hold the baby and as he did so, he felt "a very strong heat going through my body and presumably being transmitted to the baby." Whatever was happening, it felt very peaceful and positive.

Afterwards, Best instructed them to feed Janice. They did, without hope initially, and were astonished to see her suck on her bottle with an unprecedented vigor.

Though Janice never thrived, she had a genetic disorder that caused her to be chronically debilitated, her parents are convinced she lived a much longer and happier life than would ever have been possible without the intervention of Best. They had not expected their little daughter to live beyond infancy; in fact, she lived a relatively full and enjoyable life, dying finally in 1991 at the age of 22.

"They've come. You will have to let me go"

But what of Best's own tragic circumstances? He told a reporter for the *Psychic News*, in January 1972, that he had never attempted to contact the long lost Rose himself because, simply, "I don't wish to."

However, he did meet her once, through the agency of a medium called Alec Martin, of Ayr, at a Home Circle meeting. Martin was a physical medium and brought forth the fully materialized form, not just of Rose, but of her and Albert's three children too. Best embraced them joyously but, as far as all the accounts go, that was the only time he met her again this side of the grave.

Best died on 12th April, 1996, having slipped into a coma over a week before. However, he did wake up just before he died, to see his friends, including the Glasgow medium Gordon Smith, standing round him. Smith, who was greatly inspired by Best and enjoyed a close friendship with him, gradually became aware of another, spiritual presence at Best's bedside but could see no-one else standing there. But when Best, speaking barely above a whisper, announced that "My wife is here and the children," Smith felt he could "see" a slim young woman with long, reddish-brown hair and a slowly beaming smile.

"They've come. You will have to let me go," were Best's final words on earth.

Though Best was a delightful man to meet, the *Psychic News* reporter was frustrated by the medium's reticence. This trait never deserted him. Years later, he only agreed to Rosalind Cattanach's biography of him if she kept the personal details to a minimum! Perhaps he will be more forthcoming from the other side?

Ghostly Scotland

Gordon Smith

Glasgow born and bred, Gordon Smith is known as the Psychic Barber because he combines a career as a hairdresser with that of a practising medium, is author of two books, *Spirit Messenger* and *The Unbelievable Truth* and is a resident spiritualist medium on UK Living TV's popular *Most Haunted* show. He is hailed as "Britain's most accurate medium," counts Professor Archie Roy of Glasgow University, former professional footballer Ally McCoist and British soap actress Michelle Collins amongst his fans and has a diary booked up months in advance with engagements across the world.

Unlike Albert Best, who served as something of a mentor to this rising talent, Smith is very upfront and at home with the media. Though he would never spill the beans on the experiences of private individuals, he is eager to spread the word about Spiritualist mediumship and to persuade people that there is life after physical death.

Seventh son of a seventh son

Gordon Smith was born the seventh son of a seventh son. To the superstitious, this fact alone already marked him out as someone who would develop supernatural powers. But it was not until adulthood, by which time he was well established in a regular, strictly non-psychic profession, that he was to fully realize those gifts.

However, one incident in childhood should, perhaps, have tipped the young Gordon off.

Interestingly, it happened following a quite serious childhood illness. Some speculate that a close call with death, whether brought about though illness, or working with ailing and dying people, for instance in a hospital, or being around the dead, as during a war, can trigger a powerful reaction in "sensitive" people. Maybe it was Smith's rheumatic fever, so severe it required a spell in hospital, that prompted what came next.

It happened during his period of convalescence, when he was playing in the garden, his pals and brothers having gone back to school for the afternoon. Into his line of vision sauntered a familiar figure, that of Ummy, a local tic-tac man and a firm favorite with the neighborhood children. Ummy, when he had had a good day at the race track, was in the habit of passing a few pennies their way, and throwing in a few songs and jokes just for good measure.

The only thing odd about Ummy this day was that he was singing a song about being buried in Dalbeth; a song that did not spring from his usual repertoire. Ummy then bid Gordon goodbye and began walking backwards, waving as he went.

The young boy told his mother, who went rather pale and insisted it was all in his mind. Why? Because, as Gordon was soon to learn, Ummy had been dead for a week and laid to rest in, you guessed it, Dalbeth.

However, Smith was unrattled by this encounter. His meeting with the spirit form of Ummy had been a pleasant experience, had seemed utterly natural; there was nothing to be afraid of.

Though his grandmother had reputedly been a woman of psychic powers, Smith's immediate family were not particularly keen to encourage this latent gift of his. Though he had a number of curious brushes with the other side during his young life, all talk of psychic ability was pushed into the background and he left school and entered the world of work with the kind of expectations you would expect of a young man of his age. Starting out as a barber, Smith hoped one day to run his own hairdressing salon and own a big, swanky house in the suburbs. The spirit world, however, appeared to have a quite different career plan mapped out for him.

Gordon Smith, in *Spirit Messenger*, while acknowledging that his parents were less than enthused about his youthful abilities as a psychic, pays homage to them for their hard-working, kind and loving attitude to life—an attitude he has clearly adopted and which has stood him in very good stead throughout his career.

For those with a gift there appears little danger of a psychic ability being snuffed out by a lack of parental encouragement. People with psychic abilities, even those from the most skeptical of families, always seem to get a call from the other side at some point in their adult lives.

As Gordon Smith says: "If the spirit world wants you to work for it, it will make sure you are in the right place at the right time. The chance will never go past you."

Finding Spiritualism

It was not until Smith was 25 that he was forcibly reminded of his strange childhood experiences. Waking up one morning, Wednesday March 9, 1987, to be precise, he saw the figure of Brian Peebles, the brother of his hairdresser colleague Christine. By the time Smith was fully awake, Brian had vanished and he concluded it was all just a figment of his half-waking consciousness.

It was no such thing. As Smith heard on the radio an hour or so later, Brian had been killed in a domestic fire leaving his sister absolutely devastated.

Of course, Smith wanted to do all he could to console and help Christine but he admits he was a shade reluctant when she asked him to accompany her to a Spiritualist service at the Glasgow Association of Spiritualists. He felt it was too soon after Brian's death and that meddling with the dead would only rub salt into already raw wounds. But they went anyway, on Christine's insistence.

The service was touching and Christine was rewarded with a message, conveyed via the Edinburgh medium Mary Duffy, from her late mother. Duffy added that the best man to help Christine through this was a Glasgow medium called Albert Best, whom she did eventually seek out, four years later, and who helped her make contact with her much mourned brother.

Another important thing happened at the Glasgow Association séance. Duffy paused to remark, to Smith, that his psychic grandmother was present, and like Alec Harris, the Welsh medium many years before, who encountered his late sister Connie at a séance, was reminded of his gift and told that, one day, he would get around to using it.

Smith took heed and began attending a Development Circle at the Spiritualist church in West Princes Street, in Glasgow's West End. Smith was fortunate because this Circle suited him to a T and he attended for eight years, during which time he went from being a rather baffled, often amused and frequently over-earnest rookie to a true professional with the common touch.

One important lesson he learnt was that you can, in fact, learn too much. Intellectualizing the art of mediumship is fine for academics and those, like Helen Duncan's husband Henry, who are fascinated by the gift but do not possess it themselves, but can serve to severely clutter the mind of the practising medium, often to the detriment of their psychic work.

One of Smith's mentors told him to slow down, and let his natural development take its course. And "all of a sudden, spiritual development became fun. Because I stopped trying to be a medium, my natural gift began to resurface."

While it seems that each medium has his or her own way of doing things, that is not quite the whole picture. Most experience the spirit world in a number of different ways, and not always consistently. Albert Best, for instance, usually "heard" his spirits, but the story he told his friend Leonard Goss alerts us to the fact that he had the capability of being a physical medium, though he chose to reject that path.

Gordon Smith often "hears" his spirits, making him a clairaudient. But sometimes he doesn't. Sometimes he "sees" them (clairvoyant) as well, and sometimes he neither sees nor hears them but clearly "senses" them (clairsentient).

Smith puts these differences down to the personality of the spirit form, equating those whose presence is felt rather than heard with quiet, rather reticent personalities who nonetheless want to come forward and make contact with a living friend or loved one. Others, by contrast, are noisy and lively, as they often proved to have been in life.

One young man, Alan, whom Smith contacted on behalf of his mother, had a gregarious personality and that came through to the medium, loud and clear. He rarely got through a sitting without laughing a few times.

The public awaits

Smith's first public demonstration of mediumship occurred four years after he joined the development circle, and quite by accident. Though, he recalls, he did get a slight forewarning. Driving to the Spiritualist service that night, he felt what he describes as an inexplicable upset in his stomach. "It was the same type of sensation that I got just before a psychic experience or premonition."

Pity he hadn't put money on it because, when he got to the church, the booked-in medium had failed to show up and there was no-one else capable of taking the service other than Smith.

Though he was petrified, he found that, once up on stage, his nerves vanished and the spirits were willing. Which just goes to show what any medium worth their salt will tell you; you cannot commune with the spirits through sheer effort of will, it is a question of letting them come to you.

As time went on, Smith became a hugely popular personality on the Spiritualist circuit perhaps because, like Best before him, he works hard to keep the atmosphere light and to reassure those who may be a little spooked by their first encounter with the spirit world.

However, he did find that being psychically sensitive has the potential to affect, to their detriment, other facets of your life. It is quite understandable that, when a medium's faculties are heightened to the extent they need to be to communicate with the dead, those same faculties run the risk of being overwhelmed by ordinary life. Smith certainly found this to be the case. "Everything in your life becomes exaggerated; you begin to see molehills as mountains."

To counter this effect, he has since learnt to take himself off and do wilfully ordinary tasks, such as walking the dog and washing the car, to "ground himself" again.

Another thing he has to guard against, Smith says, it taking his work home with him. If he doesn't "switch off," he could be subject to voices from the other side at any time of the day or night.

"My private life is my private life, and I enjoy some space away from my work at the end of the day. Otherwise, I'd never get any peace!"

Gordon Smith does not prepare for his Spiritualist demonstrations as the best preparation is a clear mind. One meeting, held at a popular Glasgow Spiritualist church, was recorded for a Radio Netherlands broadcast, an indication of how widespread acclaim for Smith has grown.

This was a very successful night, Smith having made contact with five different spirit contacts by the time he got round to

Malcolm, a reticent young man sitting huddled near the back and quite obviously trying to avoid being noticed.

Malcolm had attended reluctantly and only at the behest of his sister-in-law who had insisted that his mother, recently deceased, was trying to make contact with him. That, she said, was why the electrics in the house kept going awry; his mother was trying to get his attention!

He was unconvinced and simply sat there, waiting for the ghastly proceedings to be over.

But then Smith's gaze fell upon him. Pointing to "the man with his arms folded, you sir," Smith told Malcolm that "I have a woman with me who is not long in the spirit world."

Malcolm flushed darkly but was genuinely astounded to hear Smith relate details about his mother, and him, that he could not possibly have gleaned from any other source.

Smith concluded with some pretty astonishing proof. He said: "She's been interfering with the electrics in the house. That's just to tell you that she's there with you!"

Sadly, the documentary-maker did not follow up the story to discover whether Malcolm's flickering lights returned to normal thereafter but it is quite clear that, on this occasion, Smith's detailed accuracy thoroughly convinced one very determined skeptic.

A tragic accident

Though he loves to inject a bit of humor into proceedings, some of Smith's experiences have been truly heart-breaking.

One time, a woman called Lee Bright came to him for a private sitting at the well-known Spiritualist church in Glasgow's Berkeley Street. She was grieving for her younger son Alan, who had been killed in a road accident at the age of 28 years.

As is the case with many bereaved mothers, mixed in with her sorrow were flecks of guilt. She felt that, as Alan's mother, she should somehow have always been able to prevent any harm coming to him. Knowing that these guilty pangs were irrational did not help any.

At the sitting, Gordon made an instant connection with Alan and was able to reassure Mrs Bright that it was truly her son's messages that he was conveying. How? Because Gordon was able to relate details, both of the accident and of subsequent activity in the Bright household that proved, to Mrs Bright's mind, that Alan was not only speaking to her, but watching over her. Alan "knew" that his parents had been going through the spare room in their house, which Smith described accurately and in detail, to look through insurance papers, and that they had opened up his wallet to find his credit card, as they had been asked to do.

"This was important to me because both Iain (her older son) and Alan knew they could leave wallets or even letters and diaries lying around and I would not look at them. I have a great belief in one's right to privacy."

At each subsequent sitting, Mrs Bright left with the impression that she had "spent time in Alan's company" as Smith related family legends and in-jokes that only her son could have told him. Surely.

Well, Iain wasn't so sure, but he was persuaded to attend a sitting with his mum and Gordon Smith. That sitting convinced him that life after death was for real, and a considerable weight was taken off his shoulders.

Talking to the dead, and the living

As mentioned earlier, Smith is no stranger to media coverage, though he bristles when approached by reporters who have already made up their minds about Spiritualism and mediumship before they have so much as said a single word to him.

This was not the case with regards to *Talking To The Dead*, a balanced BBC series examining the phenomena of the afterlife and communication beyond the grave.

As part of the programme, Smith was filmed holding a sitting with a middle-aged couple, Greta and Andrew, who had lost their son in tragic circumstances.

Unbeknownst to Smith, Greta had actually already had contact with her dead son, through the agency of two different mediums, but on each occasion had left wanting more. She felt that the messages she had so far received were insubstantial and not enough to set her mind at rest.

A grief counsellor, contributing to the programme, warned that Greta would never achieve closure nor come to terms with her loss so long as she believed it was still possible to talk to her son. Greta obviously felt differently; she felt that if she could only be reassured that he was at peace, she could let go.

Smith did make contact with her son and the information he related appeared to be very accurate indeed. He knew not only the boy's full name—and this despite being given no details about the couple, nor asking for any—and occupation, but also a host of little facts and anecdotes that only a family member could have imparted to him. Finally, it seemed that Greta was satisfied and ready to move on.

These stories bring home the point that mediums most often deal with people who are in great emotional pain and therefore intensely vulnerable. Opponents of Spiritualism and psychic work in general often point to this as the springboard for their objections. Harry Houdini, for example, believed that mediums were like vultures, preying on the needy and exploiting people's distress.

Supporters of Spiritualism and many "agnostics" counter-argue that mediums, like priests and ministers, provide comfort when it is needed most and far from exploiting people, offer a valuable service.

Though mediums appear to be focussed on the dead, their real concern is with the living people that are left behind. As Gordon Smith told Greta, "You have a life after death and you've got to build on that."

He also makes a point of not charging for private sittings or for the mediumship demonstrations he gives at Spiritualist church services. Though he does charge a fee for major public demonstrations, that money is donated to charity. Perhaps the idea of charging for his services is something he finds distasteful, or perhaps he is just taking a leaf out of the great levitator Daniel Dunlas Home's book, who made it a point of principle not to charge for his services either.

Whatever his reasons, Gordon Smith relies on his hairdressing and the proceeds from his two books to get by. His dream of a buying a big suburban house has, apparently, had to be put on hold as the demands of mediumship, particularly when you are as popular as Smith, are incompatible with the extra hours you need to put in to reach the top of the hairdressing profession.

A challenge

Like many mediums, Gordon Smith is adamant he has nothing to hide and when challenged to prove that he is really doing what he says he is, he usually accepts. So when he was asked, in 1994, to give a demonstration of his powers before an audience comprising members of the Scottish Society for Psychical Research, he agreed with no hesitation. Archie E Roy, Professor of Astronomy at the University of Glasgow and a keen student of Spiritualism, was to host the event, with Tricia Robertson, a statistician from the Society in attendance.

He was naturally a little anxious that the spirits might not show. Sometimes they do that, he says. In which cases, he is always frank and honest with his clients; it's that or make something up as he goes along, which he says he would never do. When he draws a blank, he suggests that his client either come back at a later date, because possibly it was the wrong time, too soon maybe, for this particular spirit to speak, or find another medium, who may be more successful in this individual case.

Smith hoped he would not have to convey such a message to the Society members, who were packing out a specially reserved hall at the university on the night in question. The night was a great success though Smith admits he can remember little detail of the actual messages conveyed. This has echoes with Helen Duncan's strange comment to the formerly skeptical Mr Ramsden, to whom she admitted that she had never herself seen the materializations she conjured out of the air. Though Smith is not a trance medium, in that he does not descend into an altered, somnambulistic state before commencing his dialogue with the dead, he is still a channel for communication rather than the source of it.

At a subsequent meeting with the Society for Psychical Research, Smith was challenged by an audience member who asked him did he not just pick up clues from the way a person behaved, coupling it with information gleaned through telepathy? Smith stated emphatically that he did not, citing research by such eminent bodies as the Society for Psychical Research based in England, whose rigorous study of mediumship is detailed elsewhere in this book. Smith himself has been the subject of a study, conducted by PRISM, the acronym standing for Psychical Research Involving Selected Mediums, which is cited in Tricia Robertson's book *The Truth is in Here*.

The aim of the study was to test the theory that mediums

make such general statements that someone, somewhere is going to be able to salvage a comprehensible message out of it, just as a vague horoscope can be stretched to fit anyone's day.

The study was to be conducted using statistical methods, this being Robertson's field of expertise after all. The experiments, which included such rigorous techniques as double-blind testing, requiring the mediums and recipients to sit in separate rooms to rule out the possibility of verbal and non-verbal glues being given, were conducted over a period of four years.

The results were quite astonishing, especially those produced from Gordon Smith, whose average accuracy rate was 98 per cent, quite the highest of all the mediums tested.

Professor Roy said afterwards: "There is no doubt from the work we have done that mediums can obtain information using more than the five normal senses.

"The results so far have been assessed with hard mathematics and statistics. We believe that we have disproved the ideas that all mediums are able to do is make general statements."

Indeed, even opponents to Spiritualism and mediumship admitted, upon closer inspection, that the methodology used in this study were scientifically sound.

Speaking to a newspaper reporter, Gordon Smith said: "A lot of scientists would argue that I am downloading the information from somewhere and I wouldn't argue with that. There's not always a spirit contact. If you were very emotional you'd give off a lot of feeling and I would be able to pick up the fact that you were going through a crisis time."

But that would not be enough to generate messages, accurate ones, from the other side and in any case, "with a lot the work I've done with Archie Roy I can't even see the audience so I can't fall back on body language."

Revival, and a Down=to=earth Approach for the 21st Century

In the century and a half since Spiritualism was established on any kind of organized basis, its public image has altered dramatically. The days of phantasmagoric materializations, levitations through open windows and darkly-clad dowagers holding hands in dimly-lit drawing rooms are long gone. These days, a Spiritualist gathering is a breezy, daytime affair with mediums who are matter-of-fact and often gifted with a sense of humor.

The mysterious, amateur dramatics overtones may have gone, but it seems the popular fascination has not.

In recent years, Spiritualism in Scotland has enjoyed a real revival, with attendances at Spiritualist churches and home circles rocketing for the first time since the Second World War.

The Spiritualist National Union now has in the region of 20,000 members in the UK, with three times that number estimated to be regularly attending Britain's 300+ Spiritualist churches.

Why now? World events like the attacks on the World Trade Center on September 11, 2001, the conflicts in Afghanistan and Iraq, and the rising death toll through drugs, AIDS and cancers will have heightened people's sense of their own mortality. Plus, says John Weir, Scottish SNU chairman, modern people are seeking alternatives to the established churches which often struggle to make sense of a rapidly changing world.

He notes: "There has certainly been an upsurge in interest (in Spiritualism). Young people particularly are looking for something different that is not being given to them elsewhere. Spiritualism is answering a need in the community."

In answer to the skeptics, he says: "The only person who

can really know if it is genuine is the one who gets a message, and when that happens it is certainly a wonderful experience and it can be really uplifting for someone going through grief. People are mostly in need of comfort."

And no-one is going to argue with that. However, there is the danger of exploitative mediums, who prey on people's grief. The Fraudulent Mediums Act would not exist if these people did not. To avoid them, genuine mediums offer a few tips. First of all, if you can find one, approach a medium who doesn't make money from what they do, or at least choose one who comes recommended by a credible organization, such as the SNU. Secondly, be aware of what you hope to achieve. If it is to say goodbye to someone, fine, but don't keep returning, opening up those channels of communication again and again. If you do, you risk never finding the closure you are looking for.

Take it from Gordon Smith, who says: "Consulting a medium should be a spur to allow someone to draw a line under a separation and get on with life. For that reason I rarely give anyone more than one sitting."

Earth Energies

ONE of the features that attracts so many people to Scotland is its palpable sense of history. Not just the history of clans and kings and bloody border feuds, but also that of ancient times, of druids and wandering Celtic tribes. A history marked by standing stones and ancient burial sites, but whose inner secrets remain tantalizingly beyond our reach.

Despite enormous research, we still know very little about our ancient ancestors, their origins, belief systems and ways of life.

But modern-day investigators believe they have tapped into a least one of the mysteries of our pre-Christian forebears: their knowledge and exploitation of earth energies, those little-understood power currents that criss-cross the landscape, meeting at points that anecdotal evidence suggests are particularly auspicious for rituals, magic and paranormal activity. These points are often notable for their powerful electromagnetic fields, and include standing stone circles, cairns, fairy glens and places that were later adopted by Christians as their own, such as the island of Iona.

Investigators of ley lines often find that, as they attempt to link up one ancient site with another using straight lines, they encounter other curious features along the way. One example, discovered by author and ley line authority David R Cowan, being the "Praying Hands of Mary," a prominent split rock in Glen Lyon on a key point of a ley line that ultimately connects an ancient stone circle at Fortingall, the Croftmoraig Stone Circle in Tayside and Meggernie Castle, famously haunted by the ghost of a half woman, finally finding its source in Staffa, a volcanic island with magical associations linking it, under the sea, to Skye and the Giant's Causeway in Northern Ireland.

For many years, however, study into this area was written off by the scientific community as the pursuit of cranks. But these days, the study of ley lines has gained a newfound respectability as the correlation between electromagnetic fields, some man-made, others not, and human health has become a hot topic for scientific research.

Which suggests that the ancients may well have known what they were about after all, and that it is to our detriment that much of their wisdom has been lost over the centuries.

Ley lines

Ley lines are straight tracks or paths which connect ancient and sacred sites. It makes sense that ancient nomadic tribes created these to navigate their way across often treacherous country and straight lines represent the quickest, and therefore often safest, routes.

Ley lines only really became a subject of widespread interest relatively recently, thanks to a retired antiquarian called Alfred Watkins, who got to grips with the subject in the 1920s.

In 1925, he published The Old Straight Track, in which he expounded his theory of ley lines, claiming they were created in accordance with the positions of the sun and moon at various times of the year, particularly the solstices of midwinter and midsummer. He believed that prehistoric ley hunters explored the countryside, seeking spots where earth energies were at their most powerful, the information then being used to pinpoint ideal locations for burial and worship sites.

Though Watkins concentrated on the ley lines of England, subsequent studies have revealed that Scotland is criss-crossed by similar straight tracks. Notable is the one that runs from the ancient city of Stirling to the mystical island of Iona. The latter part of this route actually coincides with the Old Straight Track, a road used by the monks making their way to the ancient island abbey.

However, the earlier part of this track traverses rather less congenial terrain, including the summit of The Cobbler, a notorious mountain in winter, and several major water sources. Thus, unless our ancestors were able to fly, we can only conclude that not all ley lines were transport routes. Perhaps, when thinking in terms of human movement, we should view ley lines as navigational devices, a way of staying on course when maps and navigational instruments were primitive and dangers, from wild animals, weather and hunger, were many.

But ley lines are not just roads. They were, it is claimed, created in order to concentrate and redirect earth energies, to the advantage of those who knew how to use them. Some believe that the points at which ley lines cross have a profound effect on the consciousness of those who gather there, causing an uplifting, even euphoric feeling.

How do they work?

Though we can posit quite credible-sounding theories relating to ley lines' navigational purpose, we really have to rely on guesswork when it comes to their mystical purpose.

One theory has it that ley lines connect ancient power sources and indeed, these tracks often seem to begin, end or cross at such intriguing locations as Maeshowe, the prehistoric burial chambers in Orkney, and Rosslyn Chapel, connected to Glastonbury by a major ley line and widely hailed as the final location of the Holy Grail.

Standing stones and other megalithic structures are said to emit what is called Telluric energy.

Geologists have studied, not ley lines as such, but geological faults which, as it happens, often coincide with ley lines, the most famous example being the Highland Boundary Fault Line.

Geologists believe that the energy created at such places is a spin torsion field, caused by the rotation of the sun and moon interacting with that of the earth.

Another theory is that ley lines were created in order to channel energy to burial grounds. For the Celts, it seems that life was viewed not as finite and linear but as infinite, existing on a sort of endless loop or wheel. The dead went onto another life and it was the duty of the living to ensure they got there, presumably by placing their earthly remains in spots where supernatural energy appeared strongest and which perhaps served as a link between the here and the hereafter.

Rosslyn Chapel

Rosslyn Chapel, which lies to the south of Edinburgh, is believed to sit where two ley lines cross and indeed, even to this day, it is believed to be a source of tremendous supernatural power. Some even posit the theory that it serves as a kind of portal to another world.

The gothic church was begun in 1445 by Sir William Sinclair, one of the once powerful Knights Templar who fought in the Crusades. He personally oversaw the design of the intricate carvings that were created to form what has been called a "book in stone."

Many believe these carvings contain a code that once cracked could unlock the secrets hidden by the Knights Templar more than five centuries ago.

These secrets, some say, include the whereabouts of the

treasures they took from the Jerusalem Temple as they fled the Romans, these treasures including the cup of the Holy Grail and even the mummified head of Christ.

The chapel, which in detail is extraordinarily ornate for its period of construction, is privately owned and the owners have been under intense pressure to allow excavations. So far, they have resisted, perhaps to preserve the mystery, or perhaps because they fear upsetting such ancient secrets.

However, ground-breaking radar revealed, in recent years, the presence of an astonishing structure beneath the chapel—a massive subterranean chamber. Not only did this deep vault dwarf the chapel above but it appeared to have no discernable entrance or exit.

Theories relating to this include one suggesting that the chapel is a kind of spaceship, built on the spot where another one landed in ancient times.

One expert on the chapel and a grand master of the Knights Templar to boot, John Ritchie, is skeptical of the spacecraft theory but believes Rosslyn is more than a repository of looted holy relics. Pointing to the Apprentice Pillar, created by an apprentice who was then murdered by his jealous master-mason (mentioned on page 119), he describes its carvings as representing the Norse Tree of Life, around which vines twine.

"They are in the shape of the double helix, what we now know represents DNA. I believe the chapel itself is the Holy Grail in that it contains the knowledge of life itself, and the rebirth of life."

Certainly Rosslyn, in accordance with much ley line theory, has had its fair share of hauntings, not least by the spirit of the unfortunate apprentice, who returns to weep beside his beautiful handiwork.

Iona

Iona, situated off the West coast of Scotland, near the much larger and more populous island of Mull, is a tiny island with a seemingly disproportionate and international reputation for being sacred.

It is an undeniably beautiful place, but what drew Columba, traditionally regarded as the founder of Scottish Christianity, to this relatively inhospitable, infertile outcrop in AD 563?

One possibility is that he knew of it by reputation, and was keen to make his mark on a fledgling Christian community that had already established itself there.

This community was known as the Culdees, who were druids who had converted to Christianity prior to Columba's arrival. Indeed, Iona had previously been known as an important druidical center, its ancient Gaelic name being Innis nan Druidhnean (lit. island of the druids).

But what drew them to Iona?

Perhaps it was the earth energy that many claim derives from the ancient rock strata on which the island stands. Did it exude a sacred energy that the early Christians, still so intrinsically linked to the mystical druids, could feel and use to enhance their spiritual practises?

Perhaps Iona was influenced by the proximity of Staffa, built of ancient basalt rock, and said by many to tangibly exude earth energy?

Another intriguing possibility is that Columba sought out this island specifically because it was credited with having been visited by Jesus. This is not a particularly unusual story; many ancient sites lay claim to visits by the Son of God, but what gives this one a little sparkle of rarity is that a nearby island is called Eilean Isa, which is Gaelic for the Island of Jesus. (For ghostly apparitions on Iona, *see also* page 117.)

The Electric Brae

The Electric Brae is to be found on the A719 between Dunure and Croy Bay in Ayrshire. It is a very intriguing physical phenomenon in that, if you put the car brakes on whilst traveling uphill, your vehicle will nonetheless continue to roll slowly upwards.

For years, people believed this was caused by an ancient earth energy, an electromagnetic field contained within the hillside.

However, this attractive idea has been disproved. The Electric Brae is in fact an optical illusion, created by the configuration of the land on either side of the road, which makes what is in fact a downward slope appear to be heading uphill.

Schiehallion

The word Schiehallion is believed to mean either "The Fairy Mountain of the Caledonians" or the "Holy Hill." Gazing up at it from the best vantage point, the north shore of Loch Rannoch, it is certainly an impressive site, seeming to rise and rise from a quite bleak landscape to form a long ridge ending in a sharp peak.

The physical appearance of a geographical feature should never be underestimated, as this is often key to its mystical significance. Think of a mountain like Uluru, formerly known as Ayers Rock, in the Australian outback. Just looking at it gives you a sense of how powerful and magical, how awe-inspiring it must have seemed to the ancient peoples who lived around it. As cases of fake holy relics—where objects later discovered to have no relation to saints or Christ nonetheless have miraculous events attributed to them—sometimes prove, the power of an object may be all in the human mind. Not that that need be a drawback; the human mind is a hugely powerful instrument.

Not only is Schiehallion impressive to look at but, situated as it is almost in the very center of Scotland, the views from the summit are incredible, stretching on a clear day as far south as Edinburgh and far north as the Highlands.

Schiehallion is said to house a magic cave, from which those who enter have never returned. Not even, alas, to pinpoint its location on an Ordnance Survey map. The mountain also plays host to a magic well, situated on its Eastern foothills, where local girls gather on the first day of May to dance and drink for good health and fortune in the coming year.

Because it is at the center of Scotland, and in the path of its major ley lines, this mountain has long been associated with earth energies. Interestingly, it was the location of the first ever measurement of the mass of the earth, conducted by the then Astronomer Royal Nevil Maskelyne. Schiehallion's great mass, enhanced by its uniquely conical shape, caused the pendulum used by this pioneering scientist to swing away from the vertical.

Maeshowe, Orkney

The low grassy mounds that house the chambered burial cairns at Maeshowe, on Orkney, were built by the islands' neolithic inhabitants untold centuries ago. If, as archeologists suspect, they are of ages with the West coast settlement of Skara Brae, then these cairns may date back as far as 3000 BC.

Visitor numbers are high throughout the year, but the winter solstice on December 22 is said to be the best time to see Maeshowe. This is because the passage running through the main chamber faces South West—that is, directly towards the setting sun at midwinter. Understandably, many believe it was constructed thus deliberately, and that this site was instrinsic to ancient sacred rites centerd around what the Celts called the "death of the sun" on the shortest day of the year.

As with many Celtic burial sites, Maeshowe was likely to have been more than simply a repository for the dead. Celtic life, after all, was very much bound up with Celtic death.

For a long period, these cairns were feared because people thought they were the dwellings of fairy folk. They therefore left them undisturbed. Perhaps this was a clever little cooked-up legend, designed to worry strangers and keep them away from this sacred site.

The cairns may also have served the purpose of earmarking land for certain tribes, as noone would take over territory that they could clearly see was guarded by the spirits of the dead.

Dowsing and Divining

Detecting the presence of earth energies is called divining, or dowsing. There is as yet no technology that can measure earth energies, so dowsers rely on their own human senses, including intuition, and a forked stick in the case of divining for water.

As previously mentioned, areas where earth energies are strong emit telluric energy which, say dowsers, give those who stand there any length of time a sensation akin to hyperactivity; a physical buzzing through the nervous system which can be highly energizing or deeply disturbing, depending on whether the energy feels positive or negative.

Alongside points where earth energies are strong are often to be found deep water sources. During the 1930s, a water diviner called Reginald Allender Smith discovered that many ancient sites, such as stone circles, coincided with primary (deep) water sources. This proved to be a major breakthrough for the study of earth energies as it suggested that our ancient ancestors had an intrinsic knowledge of the earth, which they came about without the aid of sophisticated instruments.

If discovering earth energy points gives a diviner a buzzing, enlivening sensation, then discovering primary water sources triggers a quite different, calming sensation. Added to this is a slight tension in the muscles, which is what causes the forked stick, the divining rod, to quiver.

Water diviners have worked in commerical fields for decades, assisting in the discovery of wells and oil sources, which suggests they must be doing something right.

We know that ancient sites often have powerful electromagnetic fields, and that these affect human health and even behavior, so it seems no great leap to believe that earth energies can be detected through human agency alone.

Ley Lines and UFOs

During the 1960s, the first connection was made between UFO sightings and the location of major ley lines. In 1936, Dion Fortune, in her book *The Goat-Foot God*, had suggested that ley lines exuded an energy that not only affected people on earth but also reached out into the wider universe.

In the ensuing decades, others went on to develop this idea of a cosmic force that attracted UFOs, perhaps even helped them navigate across the surface of the Earth, and many UFO sightings have been recorded in areas associated with ley lines.

In 1969, John Mitchell, in The View Over Atlantis, posited a possible connection between cosmic harmonies, mathematical principles and earth energies, arguing that ancient man understood the need to balance his endeavor with the forces of nature. This system is known as geomancy, or the "science of wind and water," and is not dissimilar in principle to the Chinese system of Feng Shui, which seeks to create and channel positive energy through balance and harmony.

Mitchell believed that these forces were at work in the construction of such sacred sites as Stonehenge and the Pyramids—structures which, in their complexity and sheer scale, continue to baffle modern engineers. And which, according to modern ley hunters, are built on important ley line intersections and which some have even suggested operate as portals to other dimensions.

Paul Devereux, a ley line investigator writing in the 1990s, was one such. He believed that sacred sites were erected in order to intensify energy at key points, to create "gateways through which contact with spirits could be achieved." (*Places of Power*, 1990)

To ancient man, the world of spirit may have had similarities with modern-day concepts of extra-terrestrial life; many people believe that extra-terrestrial or alien life forms monitor our activities just as our ancestors once believed the gods did.

There is also a school of thought that aliens offer us salvation, if only we had the sense to understand their message. Others believe they pose a threat, and have predatory designs both on the human race and on the planet itself.

Scottish sightings and the Falkirk Triangle

Scotland is particularly rich in stories of UFO sightings. To the extent that a survey, published in 2002, found that four times as many UFOs were spotted over Scotland every year as France or Italy, the second and third most popular locations respectively.

Caledonian sightings include a giant orb seen hovering, early one morning, over the placid waters of Loch Linnhe in the 1980s and bright orange lights darting across the skies above Cumbernauld during the 1970s.

One area that regularly clocks up more sightings than anywhere else is Bonnybridge, near Falkirk, in central Scotland. It has become so renowned amongst UFOlogists—that is, those who study UFOs—that it is now internationally referred to as the "Falkirk Triangle."

Disappointingly for ley lines enthusiasts however, is the fact that Bonnybridge is not one of the places singled out as a major ley line intersection.

The Bonnybridge phenomena began back in 1979, when a forestry worker called Bob Taylor claimed to have encountered three spherical, hovering objects in the middle of the woods.

It happened on the night of 9th November, when Taylor, walking through forest just off the M8 motorway, emerged into a clearing where he beheld a giant sphere, about 20 feet across, made of a dark metallic material.

As he looked on, two smaller, spiked spheres dropped from the main one and rolled towards him. Attaching themselves to his trouser legs, they drew him towards the main sphere, where he was assaulted by an acrid stench that made him choke and finally lose consciousness. When he awoke, he found himself alone and unable to speak. He staggered home, where his wife called the police.

Though his tale was incredible, they investigated because he a man of previously reliable character, and found strange marks, like ladders, on the ground where Taylor said he had seen the spheres. Ultimately however the trail went cold, though the case remains open.

One theory is that something startled Taylor, prompting an epileptic fit. However, he had never experienced epilepsy either before or since.

Was this then a close encounter of the third kind? Taylor will not be drawn either way, but many UFOlogists believe it is the only explanation and it remains one of the most puzzling cases in the annals of Scottish UFO studies.

Another Bonnybridge name associated with UFO sightings is Craig Malcolm, who has collated video footage of weird sightings over a six year period.

This filmic record includes footage of light balls bouncing along the skyline and a wingless jet which sent a "a black reek belching out the back of it as it soared off."

Malcolm's story begins in 1991, when his brother appeared at his door, ashen and breathless, saying he had been chased by "something." Initially skeptical, the two brothers went out and saw what Craig can only describe as "a figure of eight rotating through the sky. There was no sound; just pulsating lights coming off it. We videoed it and when we played it back, we noticed smaller objects coming off it and flying off in opposite directions."

Since then, he has witnessed 180 unexplained phenomena and amassed 13 hours of footage, which he dispatched to the Search for Extra-terrestrial Intelligence Institute in America for analysis.

"It came back that 95 per cent was UFOs and 5 per cent was aircraft."

Some say that Malcolm's undeniably eerie footage is due to Bonnybridge's close proximity with a gas-flaring terminal and three airports.

He believes there is an earth-bound explanation too; that the lights and objects that litter the sky may be linked to covert military activity.

One time, for example, he and his father were "chased" by two balls of light that came at them on the road home one night. They dashed into their car and drove off, stopping only to ask two men in a red BMW, parked in a nearby lay-by, if they had seen anything.

They had not and "they didn't want to talk to us. The next day the police came to my work —I'd been in a company vehicle the night before—and asked why I'd been on that road. By the end of the week, I'd lost my job."

Malcolm adds that he knows it is a cliché to "blame the government"—"but I worked for the Ministry of Defence ... and had my eyes opened. I drove senior staff to and from military establishments all over the place—there's a lot more out there than people believe."

Not everyone is convinced by Malcolm's ideas. Some insist that the mysterious lights and objects associated with UFO sightings are caused either by natural phenomena, such as ball lightning or sun spots, or flying debris from broken up satellites.

Nevertheless, there are over 300 reported UFO sightings a year in Bonnybridge, though what draws them here, to this quite unremarkable town which has neither wide open spaces nor ancient sites to recommend it, remains a puzzle.

Even the UFOlogists are stumped. Ron Halliday, who has written two books on UFOs, believes Bonnybridge may serve as a portal to another dimension but has, as yet, no proof to back this idea up.

Meantime, visitors from across Europe and even the USA flock to this area of Scotland, hoping to experience something of its other-worldly magic.

Supernatural Creatures

S COTLAND was and is a nation of storytellers and wild geographical features, from sudden mountains to untamed wilderness to hidden lochins and secret caves. Given these factors, it is perhaps little wonder that Scotland is also home to a huge array of supernatural creatures, from the monster who haunts the depths of Loch Ness to the wailing banshee-like women who stalk the lone traveler.

It is highly unlikely that these creatures existed, though there are theories as to how the legends came about. Selkies, for example, were believed to be seals who could take on the form of a man. But many now speculate that it is seals' natural, almost human expressions that gave rise to this myth. It also served as a way of explaining the terrible toll that the sea exacted on coastal communities dependent on fishing.

Furthermore, there was surely something comforting in the notion that seals and mermaids had a human connection and were capable of forming relationships with ordinary men and women as it meant they would protect us on the high seas, guiding us safely into harbor.

Similarly, the legends pertaining to giants were probably created as a means of understanding why the landscape, with its sharp mountains and scatterings of boulders, came about. Geology was centuries hence and so the idea of a long gone race of giants flinging rocks about as they fought with each other was a means of making sense of the inexplicable.

Add to that that a society always needs heroes, preferably legendary ones capable of mighty feats, and you can see why

Scotland, like so many nations, loves its giants and man-eating monsters.

These stories were passed down through the generations by word of mouth, and were informed by stories brought by contact, through war, trade and migration, with other nations, such as Norway and Ireland.

The tales of the Fians, a mythical race of Irish heroes, crossed the Irish Sea and found a second home in Scotland while the selkie, the kelpie and the mermaid, a stock feature of our national tales, are shared between Scotland, Ireland and Scandanavia and have provided material for some of our favorite ballads as well as stories.

The oral tradition was dominant in Gaelic-speaking communities right up until the 19th century and, as these things go, it is inevitable that the tales became ever more fanciful in the telling.

Many relate to the sea, that ocean of uncertainty of which people lived in fear and to which countless superstitions attach themselves.

Others serve to explain the landscape or warn people of the ways of the fairy-folk.

And many relate to death, featuring eerie figures who warn of imminent doom or presage fearful events.

Tales of the Sea

Throughout history, many of the people of Scotland have made their living from the sea. The waters around the coast of Scotland can be treacherous and the weather harsh and unpredictable, and none are more aware of the dangers that they face than those who sail these waters. Given the many hazards of their occupation, it is not surprising that Scottish fisherfolk and sailors have always been superstitious. It is a trait that they share with seafaring people all over the world. The legends about the mysteries that lie beneath the seas around the globe have many features in common, and it is not only in Scotland that tales of man's encounters with creatures of the deep are told. There are two broad categories of creature that feature in these stories. The first category includes a variety of harmful creatures, some monstrous, that put the lives of seafarers in peril by causing storms, sinking ships, blowing vessels off course, and so on. The second category, to which mermaids and seal people belong, are creatures which have been said not only to interact with human beings, but from time to time, to have interbred with them.

Sea monsters feature in legends the world over. They are blamed for missing ships, unexpected storms and mysterious drownings. Some can emerge from their watery lair and cause devastation on land.

Many people will think of the mermaid as a fabulous creature formed by the imagination of Hans Anderson, whose story of the Little Mermaid is widely known. But in times gone by, mermaids were believed to be real. With a human head and torso and a fish tail, mer-people, and in particular mermaids, were allegedly sighted at various coastal sites around Scotland on numerous occasions over many years. In Scandinavia, belief in mermaids took hold a very long time ago, and in Scotland too, stories of the mer-folk date back over centuries. Many a fisherman has allegedly fallen for the charms of one of these fabulous creatures and few of their stories have happy endings.

The seal-folk, silkies or selkies as they are known in Scotland, resemble ordinary seals while in the water and change into human form when they come ashore and shed their skins. It was widely believed, not only in Scotland but also in Ireland and Scandinavia that seals were in fact humans, who had been put under a spell. Most of the time, it was said, these people were condemned to live as seals, but from time to time they could change back into human form. In Scotland and in Ireland, the seal people were believed to have the power of changing into human form when they came onto land and shed their skins. If their skins were stolen from them, they could not return to the sea but had to live as humans. Many children were allegedly born out of unions between humans and seal folk, and the people of the Clan MacCodrum of the Outer Hebrides were said to have been descended from a seal-woman who married an islander. The Shetland and Orkney Isles are a particularly rich source of selkie legends. The story of the crofter and the seal-woman is of uncertain origin and has a number of slightly different versions. One version of the story comes from Shetland, another from Orkney. Other versions place the story on the Scottish mainland, or on other islands. As so often happens with tales of this sort, it has also blended with mermaid legend and very similar stories are told of a fisherman and a mermaid. Wherever the tale was first told, and whether it was first the story of mermaids or a seal folk, it has found a place in the imaginations of all those who have ever believed in these fabulous creatures.

The crofter and the seal=woman

There was once a young crofter who had a patch of land by the sea, where he eked out a meagre living, growing a few basic food crops. He had a small boat and used this to supplement his income, setting crab and lobster pots on the seabed along the shoreline when the weather permitted, and selling his catch locally.

One evening, as the crofter was walking by the shore towards the cove where he kept his boat tied up on the beach, he heard the sound of women's laughter coming from behind a rocky outcrop close to the water's edge. The crofter moved closer, his instincts telling him he should not make a sound that might disturb the revellers. He peered over the top of the rocks and saw a group of beautiful women with long, silken hair, dancing on a small stretch of sand at the water's edge. The crofter suspected at once that these must be seal-women, and, sure enough, his suspicions were confirmed when he saw that laid out on the rocks behind the dancing figures, were the magical skins which they had shed when they came ashore.

The sun began to go down, but the women danced on, unaware of their silent watcher. The crofter was transfixed. There was one among them who had caught his eye, and he could not take his gaze from her. Her eyes were as black as night and her hair fell about her shoulders in a shimmering curtain of gold. Her skin glowed, an opalescent white tinged with pink by the rosy light of sunset. She was the most beautiful thing he had ever seen.

The tide was coming in and bit by bit, the water was creeping further up the sand. The seal-women stopped dancing and moved towards the rocks, ready to gather up their skins and return to the sea. Last to come was the one who had stolen the heart of the crofter. One by one, the beautiful creatures grasped their skins and slipped them onto their bodies, pulling the silver-gray cowls over their heads. But just as the last one was reaching out for hers, the crofter jumped from his hiding place and took a hold of it. He could not bear to see her change back into a seal and disappear. When the seal-woman's companions saw what had happened, they knew they could do nothing to help her. With a cry of despair, they slipped back into the sea and disappeared. A few moments later, the head of a bull seal broke the surface. The poor creature stared helplessly towards shore, with anguish in its eyes. It was the husband of the seal-woman.

The seal-woman begged the crofter to give her back her skin, and let her return to her home and her family, but the crofter's passion made him selfish. He could not bring himself to do as she wished. He asked her to become his wife. He swore that he would make her happy in a new life with him on land and that he would care for her as long as he lived. The seal-woman was trapped. She had no choice but to agree, and so the crofter led her back to his cottage. He tried to soothe her with kind words and promises, but still he could not set her free, and clutched the sealskin tight against his chest to keep it safe from her. He waited until late at night when she had finally fallen asleep, then he took the skin and wrapped it carefully in blankets. He placed the bundle in a wooden box, and hid it in beneath some straw in the darkest corner of the byre, where he knew she would never find it.

Years passed. The crofter was blissfully happy with his beautiful wife. They had seven healthy children and life was good. The crofter worked hard to support his family, and although they were not rich, they had everything they needed. The seal-woman was a good wife and mother, and turned the crofter's house into a warm and loving home. The crofter loved her more than he could ever say, and she, for her part, was very fond of him, but in spite of all her husband's kindness and the great love she had for her children, she could never forget the place she had come from. She had once been completely happy, and nothing that the crofter could say or do would ever compensate her for her loss. Sometimes, late at night, when the family was asleep, she slipped away from the cottage and tiptoed to the water's edge. She would stand there for most of the night, staring out to sea, remembering her lost kinfolk and hoping for a glimpse of their heads bobbing up and down in the moonlit waters. Somewhere out there, waiting for her, was her first husband, a selkie just like she, and her heart was still with him.

One day, when the crofter was out working in the fields, the seal-woman was in the cottage preparing food when the youngest child came running in, carrying something in his arms. He had found the wooden box that had been hidden so long ago in the corner of the byre. With a child's natural curiosity, he had opened it and discovered the sealskin concealed inside. The boy knew nothing about his mother's past. He only wanted to ask her what it was he had found, that felt so soft and warm, and had the fresh, salty smell of the sea in its silvery hairs. The seal-woman gently took it from him, her eyes filling with tears.

When the crofter came home that night, the cottage was strangely quiet. The children were all fast asleep in their beds, and a pot of soup bubbled gently on the fire, but his wife was not there to greet him, and there was nothing to indicate where she might have gone. A sudden fear gripped the crofter's heart and he ran out to the byre. When he found the wooden box open and its contents gone, he thought his heart would break. The seal-woman had gone back to her own folk, and to the husband she had before him.

In time the crofter found another wife, a good, kind woman who loved him dearly and cared for his children as if they were her own. He was content with his lot. But sometimes, late at night, just as the seal-woman had done before him, he would slip away on his own and stand at the water's edge, staring out to sea, straining his eyes for one last glimpse of his first and only true love.

The mermaid's revenge

There are almost as many Scottish stories told about merfolk as there are about selkies, for people were equally fascinated with these creatures that were half human and half fish. Mermen and mermaids were believed to be able to shed their fish tails when they came onto dry land, just as selkies could shed their skins.

But while the stories of the selkie people almost exclusively conjure up an image of a gentle creature which could be surprisingly forgiving to man in spite of his cruelty, some of the tales of the mer-people show mermaids in a less kindly light. A mermaid could make a man fall in love with her, but she could also lure him to his death. And woe betide the human who crossed a mermaid, as the following story illustrates.

There was once a merchant who lived by the sea, in a grand house overlooking a sandy cove. At the edge of the cove there was a large, black rock. This rock had been worn so smooth by the waves that its surface gleamed, and the top of it was so comfortably rounded that it looked just like a plump, well-feathered cushion. It was the favorite seat of a mermaid. Every night she came to the cove and sat upon the rock, stretching out her tail over the polished stone so that it shimmered in the moonlight. Then she began to sing. The merchant and his wife were sound sleepers and although they heard the eerie sound of the mermaid's singing from time to time, it did not disturb them unduly. They were used to it. But when the merchant's wife gave birth to her first child, everything changed.

The baby seemed contented enough during the day, but every night, after darkness had fallen, he would grow fretful and begin to cry. Once he started, nothing would console him, and the nursemaid who cared for him became exhausted with the effort of trying to soothe his tears. The baby's crying disturbed his mother as well, preventing her from sleeping. She took turns with the nursemaid, walking up and down the nursery floor with her son in her arms as she tried in vain to rock him to sleep. One night as she was doing this, the child paused in his crying to draw breath for a few seconds. There was silence in the nursery, but outside, the merchant's wife could hear the sound of the mermaid singing in the darkness, and she realized that it was the singing that was upsetting her son. It was only at night that the child cried, and it was only at night that the mermaid sang.

The next night, a servant from the house was sent to speak to the mermaid, to ask her to stop her singing, or to move away. The request was politely made, but rudely refused. There was a note of defiance in the songs that the mermaid sang that night, and the sound could be clearly heard in every room of the merchant's house. And so it went on. Several times, the mermaid was begged to stop her singing, but every time she was approached, her response was to sing all the louder. And the louder she sang, the louder the baby cried.

The merchant's wife reached the end of her tether. She called her male servants together and told them to go down to the shore with hammers and pickaxes, to smash the mermaid's rock to pieces. The men did as she had asked, and by the end of the day, there was nothing left of the rock but a heap of small, black, jagged stones. Now, perhaps, the mermaid would accept defeat gracefully and find another place to sing her strange songs.

But when the mermaid reached shore that evening and saw what had been done, not a thought of defeat crossed her mind. She was beside herself with rage that her beautiful singing stone had been destroyed, and she was determined to get her revenge. She lifted her voice to a pitch that it had never reached before, and screamed out a curse that was carried by the wind coming in from the sea, right to the ears of the merchant's wife. The mermaid's words struck horror into the hearts of all those who heard them. The venom and strength in her tone were terrible to hear, as she shrieked that tragedy would descend upon the household, and that the merchant's family line would die out. Upstairs in the nursery, the force of the sound began to rock the baby's cradle back and forth, back and forth, with increasing violence. When mermaid's last, terrible song was over, the merchant's wife hurried upstairs to attend to her child. She found him lying dead beneath his upturned cradle. Just as the mermaid had predicted, there were no more children, and the merchant died without an heir to succeed him.

The Blue Men

Selkies and mermaids were said to dwell in many places around the coast of Scotland, but the Blue Men are a phenomenon to be found in only one place. Between the Island of Lewis and the Shiant Isles lies a narrow strait, part of the Minch, which is known in Gaelic as *Sruth nam Fear Gorm*—The Stream of the Blue Men. Even when the seas all around are calm, the water in the Stream of the Blue Men can be rough and treacherous, and even today many skippers choose to steer clear of the strait and take a more circuitous route, for fear of the Blue Men. Anyone who has been at sea when the weather is wild, or has seen the force with which white-capped waves, several feet high, come crashing in to shore when a storm is blowing, can imagine how it is possible that sailors, caught in the teeth of a storm, might conjure up in their minds a picture of raging, white-haired blue figures attacking their boat. But if the Blue Men are no more than mental images which spring to into the heads of seamen in storm-tossed ships, then why are there no Blue Men anywhere else in the waters around Scotland, or even around the world?

The Blue Men were said to live in underwater caves in the Minch, and to occupy themselves by churning up the waters in the strait by the Shiant Isles. Sometimes they slept, and it was only then that the waters in the strait settled down to peace for a brief spell. As soon as the Blue Men awoke, the waves would rise. The Blue Men would stir the waters with their long arms, scattering spray and foam all around. They took particular pleasure in attacking boats.

They posted sentinels at the entrance to the strait and when a boat approached, the sentinels would signal to their companions lying in wait under the water, who would then come to the surface to stir up trouble. They would thrust their heads and chests out of the water and frighten the watching sailors. They would hurl abuse at the skipper, and jostle and shove the vessels to make them turn over, or pull on the rudder to force a ship off course and onto the rocks. Some folk referred to the strait as The Current of Destruction, and with good reason. Several boats were wrecked in the waters of the strait, and many times the blame for the disaster was placed upon the malicious activities of the Blue Men.

It was said that one way to outwit the Blue Men was to develop a skill in composing rhyming couplets, and the following tale illustrates this belief.

The Blue Men were lying dozing beneath the waves when the sentinels gave warning that a large ship was approaching. They swam to the surface in their hordes. They could see the great white sails of the vessel in the distance. It was a big ship, and they would have their work cut out for them if they were to capsize this one. The ship moved into the strait and several of the Blue Men dived below the surface and pulled on the keel, but the vessel moved on, sure and steady, and their efforts were to no avail. Others swarmed along the sides of the ship, thumping it with their fists, but the ship was built of the strongest, thickest timbers and they could not punch a hole in it. Nor could they move the rudder. The ship stayed right on course, steering a safe path through the strait. The chief of the Blue Men rose up out of the waves in fury. As he had done so often before with other ships, he challenged the skipper to a battle in verse.

> "Man of the black cap, what do you say
> As your proud ship cleaves the brine?"

The skipper did not hesitate to reply.

> "My speedy ship takes the shortest way
> And I'll follow you line by line."

The chief of the Blue Men continued the challenge.

> "My men are eager, my men are ready
> To drag you beneath the waves!"

But the skipper was undaunted. His response came back, quick as a flash.

> "My ship is speedy, my ship is steady;
> *If it sank it would wreck your caves.*"

The chief of the Blue Men knew he had been beaten. No skipper had ever been able to answer his challenges so quickly and so cleverly. He could have no power over such a skipper, or his ship. Reluctantly, he signalled to his men and they sank below the waves. The ship sailed on through the strait unharmed, its tall mast straight and true and its snow-white sails puffed out with pride.

Monsters

Nessie

The most famous monster in Scotland is the beast that is said to live in the deep dark waters of Loch Ness. Affectionately known as Nessie, the monster is generally referred to as "she," although there has never been an opportunity for anyone to determine the sex of this mythical creature. Nessie attracts visitors from all over the world, tourists, reporters and scientific investigators, and over the years has been subjected to more camera surveillance than any "reality TV" programme participant is ever likely to have to endure. In spite of this, she remains elusive, guarding her privacy carefully in the hidden murky depths of the loch, rewarding the thousands of hopeful spectators who come to see her with no more than the occasional tantalizing glimpse of what she might, or might not, look like.

The first written record of a beast in Loch Ness is in Saint Adamnan's biography of Saint Columba, which was written in the seventh century AD. According to Adamnan, Saint Columba was walking along the shore of the loch in 565AD when he caught sight of an enormous creature in the water, ready to attack a man who was swimming there. Saint Columba ordered the beast to depart in the name of God, and it obeyed him. On another occasion Saint Columba encountered the creature again, lying in wait for a victim. Saint Columba commanded the monster never to harm a human being again, and since then, there have been no reports of the Loch Ness monster having threatened anyone.

Over the years, the Loch Ness monster seems to have surfaced from time to time, giving rise to a number of stories about the beast in the loch, but it was only in the twentieth century that Nessie's name came to real prominence. In the

1930s, a road was built alongside the northern shore of the loch. This brought a growth in the number of people visiting the area and also afforded passers-by a clear view of the loch from their cars. In 1933, Nessie hit the headlines of the *Inverness Courier*. A couple who lived in the district claimed to have seen an enormous creature thrashing about in the surface waters of the loch. The article in the *Courier* marked the beginning of Nessie's meteoric rise to fame. It was not long before she had allegedly been sighted on land, casually crossing the road by the loch one day in early summer. Loch Ness Monster fever rapidly spread and Nessie became national headlines as groups of people swarmed to the shores of Loch Ness hoping to see, or catch, the creature who dwelt therein. In August of that year, when the fever was at its peak, there were no less than nine alleged sightings of the monster in the water. In July 1934, there were at least eight more. Less than a year later, however, the first wave of monster-hunting began to peter out after some plaster-casts of large animal footprints, which were said to belong to the monster, were exposed as hoaxes. How many of the claimed sightings had been fakes?

In spite of the skepticism of many, interest in the possibility of a mysterious creature dwelling in the loch did not go away entirely. Sightings continued to be reported from time to time in the years that followed, and in the 1960s, monster fever seemed to take a hold of the public imagination once again. With the resurgence in public interest came another increase in the number of alleged sightings. The summer of 1966 was particularly busy. The 1970s and '80s seem to have been a time of general cynicism, or short-sightedness, for scarcely a handful of sightings were recorded, but in the 1990s, armed with the wonders of sophisticated photography, video cameras, etc., members of the public took up the hunt once more.

So, if the Loch Ness monster does exist, or has ever existed, what sort of creature might she be? In the days of Saint Columba, she was seen (or imagined) to be one of the kelpies, or water horses, mythical creatures which were believed to prey on unsuspecting human victims, particularly children, luring them onto their backs before dragging them down into the water, never to be seen again. In more recent times, she has been described as having between one and three humps, which are somewhere between four and forty feet in length and are commonly said to resemble an upturned boat. She has been said to have a long tail and a long neck, around six feet long. Her mouth may be approximately one foot wide. When submerging and moving off, she makes a great splash and leaves a v-shaped wake behind her. Of course although the creature is commonly referred to as *the* Loch Ness monster (singular), it cannot be possible that there has only been one creature surviving nearly fifteen hundred years since the days of Saint Columba. There must have been, at least, a succession of breeding pairs over the centuries, and the fact that on a few occasions not one, but two "monster wakes" have allegedly been spotted simultaneously, seems to support this theory. The one identifiable creature which Nessie can be said to resemble most closely is the plesiosaur, which was a carnivorous marine reptile of the Jurassic and Cretaceous periods. Plesiosaurs could grow to around forty feet in length, had long necks and turtle-shaped bodies, and had paddle-like flippers to propel themselves through the water. There are many people who believe that Nessie is a plesiosaur, and although the survival of a family of such creatures in one isolated place in Scotland is hard to explain when all the others became extinct sixty-five million years ago, there have been attempts to demonstrate that such a thing is possible. One theory suggests that some plesiosaur eggs, long frozen in some deep, cold recess of the loch, could have thawed out and hatched to start the new dynasty. The cynics continue to contest the theory by stating that the loch does not have an adequate supply of food for such a creature, and so argument is met with counter-argument *ad nauseam*.

Loch Ness is huge, dark, and deep. Much of its waters are literally unfathomable, and this is perhaps the biggest hurdle, both for all those who wish to prove Nessie's existence, and those who wish to disprove it. The mystery is kept at the forefront of the public's imagination with boat trips and sightseeing tours around the loch on offer for visiting tourists, and a Loch Ness Monster Exhibition at the local visitor center. Alleged sightings are faithfully recorded in detail, and video footage of gloomy, unidentifiable shapes in the water is studied closely by enthusiasts and skeptics alike. For the real Nessie fan, the opportunity to look for the monster on webcam from the comfort of their own home has taken the hunt into the twenty-first century. The legend continues to grow.

Morag of Loch Morar

Loch Morar is not as large in surface area as Loch Ness, but the water there is deeper, and it is said that hundreds of feet below the surface of the loch lives another monster, who has come to be known as Morag. Morag has not reached the same dizzy heights of stardom as Nessie, and her history is not as long, but for those who are fascinated with mythical creatures of the deep, the possibility of her existence is no less exciting.

The earliest recorded sightings of the Loch Morar monster date from the second half of the nineteenth century. From time to time, fishermen out on the loch, or walkers making their way along its rocky shores, would claim to have seen one or more dark humps in the water, like upturned boats. Superstitions about death and dying were still very much a part of life in the Highlands in those days, and some said that these strange sights were omens of death, ghostly boats that warned of some tragedy to come. Others were not so sure, for they were convinced that the humps were a part of something living, some mysterious creature that rarely allowed itself to be seen. Years passed, and the rumors of the creature grew slowly. Eventually, as Nessie had done, this creature acquired a name, but still she remained reclusive, and she is still less sought-after than Nessie.

Many of the people who claimed to have seen Morag were fishing on the loch at the time. The sight of her hump (or humps), appearing and disappearing in the water, have caused great perplexity to a number of people over the years. In the 1960s, Morag was allegedly responsible for ruining an entire day's fishing for two young men. They were rowing out into the loch, and saw what the thought was a smooth, rounded rocky outcrop sticking out of the water, so they started to navigate their way round the obstacle with care. Their boat was hired, and they had no wish to pay for any damages they might incur with a careless bump. They were only half way round this miniature island when it suddenly moved, then sank, bumping into their little boat on the way down and making ripples of such a size that they almost capsized. Forgetting all about fishing, or the price they had paid for a day's boat hire, the two young men rowed back to shore as quickly as possible. There, with wide eyes and white faces, they returned the boat to its puzzled owner, muttering as they did so about the dangers "out there."

Descriptions of Morag, who has been seen mostly in the water, but also, on at least one occasion, on shore, make her sound very similar in appearance to her famous friend in Loch Ness. She is dark in color—brownish-black or black. Her skin is bumpy, like that of a reptile. She has been variously described as having one, two, three or four humps, and it is thought that she is around thirty feet long. Like Nessie, she has a long neck. One man who claimed to have seen her also said that he found her footprints in some soft ground on the shore, and they were diamond-shaped. A monster spotter with artistic leanings, Dr George Cooper, painted her portrait in 1958, but as Morag rarely reveals more of herself than a hump here and a neck there, it is hard to tell whether Dr Cooper managed to capture a true likeness. Those who have the time, energy and enthusiasm to continue the search will maybe be rewarded with the chance to see for themselves one day in the future.

Loch Morar is more remote and less easily accessible than Loch Ness, and most of the time, Morag is left in peace. Every now and then, another alleged sighting is logged in the records of keen cryptozoologists, but most visitors to the area barely give her more than a passing thought, and her presence is not advertized. For those who live close to Loch Morar, it is probably a good thing that Morag has not drawn the same attention to herself as Nessie. There is no monster exhibition, and local people are, for the most part, reluctant to exploit the monster rumors in any way. But monster enthusiasts are a die-hard bunch, and for them the legend lives on, even if it breathes more quietly than the legend of Nessie. And the theories about what she might be are much the same; like Nessie, she is now most commonly believed to be a plesiosaur—it may be possible, some say, that Nessie and Morag are related. It has even been suggested that far, far underground, there is a long water-filled tunnel that connects Loch Ness with Loch Morar and that the Loch Ness Monster and the Loch Morar Monster are one and the same creature, traveling between the two sites. Perhaps she likes to keep the visitors entertained. Or perhaps, in the way that all film stars do, the monster sometimes tires of all the cameras and attention. At times like these, we might imagine that she takes a break from life in Loch Ness and goes to Loch Morar to annoy a few fishermen for a change.

Nessie and Morag are the two most famous loch-dwelling monsters in Scotland, but, if we are to believe in their existence, we must also give some credence to the claims that in several other Scottish lochs—Loch Garten and Loch Oich, for example, similar creatures have been sighted. If all the claims are true, there could be as many as twenty loch monsters, perhaps even more!

The Linton Worm

There are a number of references to "worms" in traditional Scottish stories. The monster that is said to live in Loch Morar, for example, was once known as "The Great Worm." Several sites around the country are said to have been, once upon a time, the dwelling place of a worm. These worms were great serpents, which were said to terrorize the surrounding countryside, killing the farmers' animals and attacking humans. Some were believed to have magical powers. Others had rank, poisonous breath.

The story of the worm of Linton belongs to the Scottish Borders, where long ago, in Roxburghshire, it is said that a fearsome serpent used to live in a hollow on the slopes of Linton Hill near Jedburgh. For years the Linton worm blighted the lives of the people living in the district. Its breath was said to be so poisonous that if a man inhaled the slightest whiff of it, he faced instant death, so no-one dared approach it. Farmers stood by helplessly as their sheep and cattle dwindled in numbers, snapped up, one by one, by the ravenous jaws of the worm. No man had the courage to try to kill it, for it seemed like an impossible task, sure to end in death for anyone who attempted it.

Then a man called John Sommerville of Lauriston heard about the beast, and decided to come and see the worm for himself. Following the directions given to him be some people who lived nearby, Sommerville rode his horse cautiously towards the hollow where the terrible creature lay resting. He stopped his horse at a safe distance from the worm's lair and waited. The wind carried the scent of a human towards the sleeping beast, and slowly it woke up, and reared up its ugly head to find where the scent was coming from. Sommerville kept a tight hold of the horse's reins and remained perfectly still. At the sight of the man and the horse together, the worm seemed perplexed. It stretched out its neck and opened its jaws to their fullest extent, but it did not attack. It gave out a great puff of its fiery venomous breath, but Sommerville was too far away to feel its effects, and the poisonous gas dispersed in the air before it reached him. Still the serpent remained motionless, its jaws gaping helplessly. The sight gave Sommerville much food for thought. It was clear that although a single cow, or sheep, or even a man would make an easy mouthful for the beast, the prospect of man and horse together had it puzzled, for the two were more than its jaws could cope with.

As he turned and rode back home, a cunning plan was forming in Sommerville's mind. The next day, he went to the local blacksmith and asked him to make a special lance. The lance had to be much longer than such a weapon would normally be, for Sommerville had to keep a safe distance from the monster's breath. At the end of the lance was to be a spiked wheel made of the strongest iron.

When the lance had been finished to his satisfaction, Sommerville prepared to do battle. Taking his most loyal servant along with him, he rode into Jedburgh carrying his customized weapon and declared that soon the Linton worm would be dead. Not surprisingly, his claims were met with jeers and derision, for what he claimed, according to the people of Jedburgh, was impossible. Nonetheless, a number of townsfolk followed him out to Linton Hill, and selecting a viewpoint as close to the worm's hollow as they dared go, settled down to watch the action.

Sommerville rode closer to the worm's lair. His servant followed on foot. Sommerville reined in his horse and the servant took a ball of peat dipped in pitch from the bag he carried on his back, and stuck it firmly onto the spiked wheel at the end of Sommerville's lance. They moved a little closer. Just as before, the serpent caught the scent of human flesh and reared up its head. Just as it had done before, it stretched out its neck and opened its jaws to their fullest extent. At a signal from his master, the servant set fire to the peat ball on Sommerville's lance, and set it spinning.

Sommerville spurred his horse into a gallop, charged up to the open-mouthed worm, and thrust his lance as far as he could down its throat. The serpent writhed in fury and pain as the fiery peat ball seared his gullet and the spikes pierced his flesh, but it had been mortally wounded, and after one or two moments of desperate struggling, it stopped moving and died.

Sir John Sommerville had become a hero, and as reward for his courage, he was knighted, becoming the first Baron of Linton. At Linton Kirk nearby, a stone was carved to commemorate the great occasion when the people of Linton were saved from the worm. And on the landscape of Linton Hill, the strange undulating marks caused by the worm as it writhed and struggled before death still remain.

The Big Gray Man of Ben Macdhui

Ben Macdhui is the highest peak in the Cairngorms, and the second highest in Scotland. From its summit, the climber is afforded a magnificent panorama of the surrounding peaks; Cairngorm, Ben Avon and Cairn Toul. To the north west, the River Spey passes through Aviemore on its way to the Moray Firth. To the east, the Dee flows towards Ballater, Aboyne and Aberdeen. The mountain is popular with climbers who visit the region from many different countries, and its slopes offer a number of routes that are both challenging and rewarding, even to experienced mountaineers. But Ben Macdhui is well-known not only for its beauty and the sport that it offers its visitors. For over a century now, there has been much speculation that there may be something frightening lurking on Ben Macdhui. Over this period, several climbers claim to have witnessed a mysterious presence on the mountain; many believe it to be a physical one. This presence has been named *Am Fear Liath Mor*, more commonly known as The Big Gray Man.

On remote mountain slopes, far from the noise and bustle of centers of population, it is easy to give full reign to the imagination and let the mind wander to strange apparitions and monsters. There are plenty of things that the mountain climber encounters to provide fuel for the mind's journey; strange echoes in gullies, tricks of the light, shapes in the mist, ominous shadows cast as the sun moves across the unfamiliar landscape. Human beings are social animals, and solitude is alien to most of us. It can alter one's perceptions, especially in an unfamiliar environment, and fear of real, physical and recognizable danger can find itself accompanied by a fear of unidentifiable, intangible threats, which come from a realm far removed from man's knowledge of the physical world and its nature.

It is easier to dismiss the legends of monstrous apparitions in the mountains around the world than it is to give credence to them. The existence of the creatures in these legends has never been proved beyond doubt by material evidence or scientific fact. The Yeti in the Himlayas, Bigfoot in North America, and the Specter of the Brocken in Germany are all similar in this respect; they are beasts seen, but not captured, perceived but not touched. Some believe that there is a physical presence of some kind where these creatures have allegedly been seen. Most people, on the other hand, do not, and react to the legends with skepticism or derision. The Yeti and Bigfoot feature in cartoons from time to time, as cuddly figures of fun. The Specter of the Brocken in dismissed in more scientific fashion, as a shadowy illusion created by sunlight and mist.

The Big Gray Man of Ben Macdhui, like the other monstrous apparitions, has allegedly been seen and heard on a number of different occasions. But there is another more sinister aspect to the Gray Man, which the other apparitions do not share. The Big Gray Man's presence is not perceived by the physical senses alone. It can make itself felt in the spirits, in a manner that is generally claimed to be very disturbing. It is alleged that the Gray Man exerts a strong psychic influence upon those who encounter him. And several climbers, after having undergone the experience, have been reluctant to return to the mountain.

The first time the possible existence of the Big Gray Man of Ben Macdhui was mentioned in Scotland was in 1925. Norman Collie, a professor in Chemistry from London and an experienced and well-respected mountaineer, related his story to members of the Cairngorm Club at their Annual General Meeting. He recalled a solo climb on the mountain in 1891, and said that as he was making his way back down the mountainside from the summit through the mist, he became aware of the sound of footsteps behind him. For every three or four steps that the professor took, he heard one of these footsteps, as if whoever—or whatever—was following him taking much larger strides than himself. At first, he dismissed the sounds as nonsense, for he could see nothing, but as he continued downwards he could still hear them. At this point he was overwhelmed by a feeling of terror, and in blind panic, took flight, descending the rest of the mountain with more concern for speed than safety on the treacherous terrain. The experience had left him badly shaken, and determined that he would never climb Ben Macdhui alone again, for there was something "very queer" about the higher slopes of the mountain.

Collie had told this story once before, some years earlier in New Zealand, and it had been greeted with a moderate degree of interest and some understandable skepticism. But when Dr A M Kellas had heard about it, he was more than moderately interested in Collie's experience. Dr Kellas was another well-known figure in mountaineering circles, much respected for his achievements climbing in the Himalayas, who later died during the first expedition to Mount Everest in 1921–22. When Kellas heard Collie's story, he wrote to him to tell him of his own experience. Kellas had been on Ben Macdhui with his brother, and had been hammering out crystals from some rocks quite close to the summit when they had become aware of a large figure descending from above, out of the mist. The two men had then, like Collie, succumbed to a terrible feeling of fear and had been compelled to flee.

We do not know why Collie waited 34 years to tell his story to the Cairngorm Club, but it is reasonable to assume that he might have felt apprehensive about the reception it might get. Perhaps the letter from Kellas helped to give Collie the courage to relate his account of the experience. But at any rate, when he did finally speak out in 1925, he would know that there was at least one other knowledgeable, reasonable and experienced man who had testified to having had a similar encounter. Both men had spent extended amounts of time in remote mountain regions and consequently knew all too well the tricks that could be played on the mind when a person was alone, cold and tired. They were also familiar with the strange sights and sounds of such places; shadows in the mist, falling rocks, echoes and suchlike. But both strenuously denied that the phenomenon they had witnessed was anything like this.

There have been several reports of alleged encounters with the Big Gray Man since then. Some of them, undoubtedly, have been fantasy, or hoax. Others cannot be dismissed so easily. Some people claim to have heard strange voices, speaking in a foreign tongue, which has been said to resemble either Gaelic, or Urdu. Others have said that they could hear hauntingly beautiful music.

Alleged sightings vary from a vague description of a hazy, large, upright figure to a more precise picture of something akin to the Sasquatch or Yeti. In 1944, Captain Sir Hugh Rankin claimed to have met and spoken with the Big Gray Man on two separate occasions. According to Sir Hugh, who was a Buddhist himself, the Gray Man was a Bodhisattwa. [A Bodhisattwa is a being in an advanced degree of incarnation, next to that of a Buddha, who has achieved enlightenment and acts as a guide to others in their progress towards the same.] Sir Hugh was humbled, but unafraid. His experience of the Big Gray Man was apparently wholly benign. But most other climbers who have tales to tell of the Big Gray Man or of out-of-the-ordinary experiences on Ben Macdhui have shared feelings that are much different from those felt by Sir Hugh Rankin. Fear, sudden and overwhelming, has been commonly reported and openly admitted, even by hardened men of the outdoors. Sudden, terrible feelings of depression have also been described on a number of occasions. In some men's experience, these feelings have rapidly led to thoughts of suicide and frightening compulsions to self harm by falling or jumping off a ledge or into a gully.

This power that the phenomenon of the Gray Man seems to exert over people's minds is what makes it uniquely sinister and dangerous. Perhaps, knowing something about the phenomenon, the fear of an encounter with the Big Gray Man that has both triggered and inflamed the imaginations of many climbers on the slopes of Ben Macdhui, affecting their mood and convincing them that such an encounter has taken place. But that does not explain why Collie and Kellas felt as they did, on separate occasions and quite independently of each other. Nor will all climbers since then have known about the phenomenon before they set off up the mountain.

The phenomenon may be nothing more than a collection of misperceptions, or optical and aural illusions. It may be hallucination induced by fatigue, or hysteria. Norman Collie may have had a panic attack. Dr Kellas may have seen his own shadow in the mist. But their refusal to dismiss their experience as illusion or panic persisted until their deaths. Furthermore, there are several people still alive who claim to have experienced the Big Gray Man—whatever it is. And like Collie and Kellas, those among them whose claims were made in good faith are unlikely ever to be convinced that there is not "something up there."

The Fairy Realm

Belief in fairies was prevalent in Scotland in days gone by. Although they were spiritual beings, fairies were thought to resemble human beings in many ways; their physical appearance was similar, they lived together in social communities, they ate, drank, danced and sang, they could be kind, or malicious, charitable or unforgiving. Fairies were invisible to the human eye for most of the time, but when they did allow themselves to be seen, they were most commonly described as slender and pale, with gold-red hair, dressed in green. Most of them were, or appeared as women.

Opinions differed as to what, or who, the fairies were. Some people believed they were fallen angels, or demons. Others thought that they were the spirits of the dead. Other people simply saw them as another class of being, inhabitants of a world that existed separately from the human world, but from which they, at least, could come and go as they pleased. Few people thought of fairies as either intrinsically good or bad.

They were generally believed to be capable of behavior ranging from one extreme to the other. But it was always considered better to be cautious rather than casual about fairies. They could steal food, if it was left unprotected, and what was worse, they could steal an unbaptized child, and leave a fretful, wizened changeling in its place. It was generally considered prudent to take precautions against such things happening, with the use of charms against the fairy magic, or bribes of milk and food to appease them.

The fairy realm was most commonly thought to be a sub-terranean world, which the fairies reached through hidden entrances in hills, mountains, rocks and sometimes caves. It was generally thought to be a place filled with light, and with music, for the fairies were skilled musicians. It was a place where time seemed to stand still, or to pass very slowly. It was inaccessible to most human beings, and traditionally, those who did find their way into the fairy realm were unlikely to come out again. If they did, their lives were changed.

Thomas the Rhymer

Thomas the Rhymer is a very "weel-kent" figure in Scots story-telling and poetry, a man who is believed to have prophesied many major events in Scottish history while he was alive. He was said to speak the truth always, hence the other name by which he is commonly known, True Thomas. Although Thomas the Rhymer is a legendary figure, and is said to have lived in various parts of the country, it is most commonly believed that the legends originally grew up around a poet who lived in the Scottish borders during the thirteenth century. Thomas was born Thomas Learmont of Ercildoune. Ercildoune was a village now known as Earlston, situated in the Scottish border country, not far from the towns of Galashiels and Melrose. According to the most famous legend of his life, Thomas was not born with the gift of prophecy, but acquired it from the queen of the fairies.

Thomas was out walking in the Eildon Hills near his home one day, and he stopped to rest by Huntly Water, under the shade of the Eildon Tree. As he lay half-dozing in the shade, something caught his eye, and he turned to see a beautiful woman, clad in green silk and velvet, riding towards him on a white horse which had a bridle festooned with bright silver bells. There was something extraordinary about this woman, and Thomas was captivated by her beauty. As soon as he caught sight of her, he jumped to his feet, removed his hat and bowed before her. He thought she must be the Queen of Heaven, and addressed her as such. But the woman told him that she was not the Queen of Heaven, but the Queen of Elfland, where the fairies lived. Thomas was surprised to find that she knew his name, but he was even more perplexed when she declared that she had come expressly to seek him out. She dared him to kiss her on the lips, and Thomas did not hesitate. The Queen of Elfland now had him in her power.

"Now," said the queen, "you must come with me to Elfinland, where you will serve me for seven years, for good or for bad."

Thomas was entranced with his new acquaintance and climbed up behind her on the horse without another word. They rode on and on, until they were far from any place familiar to Thomas, and it seemed as if the journey might never end. When the horse finally drew to a halt, the lush, green summer countryside was nowhere to be seen and they were in a barren desert. The Queen dismounted with Thomas.

"Now," she said, "I have three wonders to show you." She pointed to three different roads that lay ahead of them, each going in a different direction. The first road was overgrown with thorns and briars. Travel along such a road would be painful and difficult, for the thorns made it almost impossible to make one's way along it.

"That road," the Queen told Thomas, "is the road to Righteousness. There are few men who choose to take it."

The second road was wide and easy to travel on. Lilies, their heads heavy with scented pollen, grew all along the verges.

"That road," the Queen said, "is the road to Hell, although many people do not believe it and mistake it for the road to Heaven."

The third road stretched ahead through a green landscape, covered in a dense blanket of ferns.

"That road," said the Queen, "is the road to Elfinland, where we are going. While you are in Elfinland, Thomas, you must remember one thing. You must never speak. If you utter a single word, you will never be able to return to your own land."

The Queen and Thomas traveled on into the night. It was a difficult journey, for they had to cross rivers and rocky countryside in the darkness, and there was no moon to light their way. Then they came to a river that was unlike all the others. As they waded through the murky waters, Thomas could just make out that the water was blood red.

"This is the river that carries away all the blood that is shed on the earth," the Queen told him.

They rode on until at last they game to a garden, which was full of trees laden with fruit of all kinds. The Queen went up to an apple tree and plucked a plump, red fruit from its branches and handed it to Thomas.

"Take this in payment," she said to him. "Eat it, and you will have a tongue that can never lie."

Thomas took the apple from the Queen and ate it, overawed at having been given such a priceless gift.

"Now Thomas," said the Queen, "remember, not another word." Thomas nodded. They mounted the horse and rode on, deep into the fairy realm.

Thomas was given a suit of green clothes and green velvet shoes, and so began his service to the Fairy Queen. The time he spent in Elfinland passed quickly, and it seemed to Thomas that only a few days had gone by when the Queen summoned him to her and told him that he was free to go. But time in Elfinland is not the same as time in the land of the humans, and the Queen told him that when he returned to his own land, he would find that he had been away for seven years. As he took his leave of the Fairy Queen, she bade him a fond farewell, but said that she would see him again.

"I will come again and call you back to Elfinland," she told him. "When the day comes, you will know."

And so Thomas the Rhymer returned to the land of humans, and not a word did he say to anyone of what he has seen and learned during his stay in Elfinland. His reputation as a prophet soon became known far and wide, and the accuracy with which he was able to foretell what would happen in the future was astonishing. He lived a contented life. He was a respected member of the community in which he lived, and his honesty and forthrightness were much appreciated by all those who knew him. He did not know when the day would come for him to return to the Fairy Queen, but he bided his time patiently, knowing that some day, a sign would be given to him.

And so it happened that one day, a young lad came running into the village, saying that he had seen a white hart and a white hind coming out of the forest nearby. Several of the villagers gathered together and went to see if what the boy was saying was true and sure enough, at the edge of the wood, they saw two white deer standing calmly beneath the trees, watching and waiting. The villagers called upon Thomas and told him what they had seen. They wanted to know if the unusual sight was an omen. When Thomas had listened to their news, he smiled, for he knew what it meant, but he did not explain. He simply bade his friends an affectionate farewell and walked off to the edge of the forest where the two creatures stood. Then all three moved off together and disappeared into the trees. Thomas the Rhymer was never seen again.

The Fiddlers of Tomnahurich

There was once a pair of musicians, who lived in Inverness-shire. They were down on their luck, and in spite of their considerable skills in playing the fiddle, had not found an audience to pay them well for a long time. And so it was that when they met an old man who said he could find them a night's work, they gladly took him up on his offer. The old man took the fiddlers up the hill at Tomnahurich, and in through an entrance in the hillside that they had never seen before. They followed him in and the entrance closed behind them. The fiddlers found themselves in a bright place, richly decorated and full of the sound of laughter, where beautiful slender women, handsome men and delicate-featured children were feasting. There was food and drink in abundance, and the two musicians were invited to take their fill before the dancing began. When they had eaten all that they wanted, they tuned up their fiddles and started to play. The dancing went on all night, and the fiddlers had as good a time as the revellers did. When it seemed at last that everyone had had enough, the old man paid them well for their trouble with a bag of gold coins, and ushered them out of the mysterious place into the gray light of dawn.

The fiddlers made their way back down the hillside in fine spirits, but when they got into town they were greatly taken aback by what they saw. New buildings had sprung up here and there, and the place looked completely different. They walked through the town without seeing a soul that they recognized, and that was most unusual. Everyone was dressed very strangely, and several people whom they passed commented on the fiddler's "old-fashioned" clothing. They heard the church bell ringing, calling people to worship, and decided to seek comfort in the familiar rituals of the church service. They walked into the church and settled themselves in their pew, still puzzled to notice that there was not a familiar face in the congregation. The minister came up to the pulpit and the fiddlers stood up with the other members of the congregation, ready to begin the morning's worship. But when the minister began to speak, and mentioned the name of God, the two fiddlers crumbled to dust.

They had not been away for just one night. They had been kept in the Fairy Realm for one hundred years. And the old man who had invited them inside was none other than Thomas the Rhymer.

Giant Lore

The countryside of Scotland is quieter now, for most of the giants are dead, or slumbering beneath the hills on which they used to sit. But in times gone by, the sound of their battles echoed across the glens and the noise made by the missiles that they threw at one another across lochs and estuaries here and there sent fishermen fleeing to the safety of the shores in their boats. These battles were a favorite form of entertainment for the giants. Two rivals, sitting on the tops of adjoining hills, or perched on promontories at either side of a bay, would take it in turns to fling their weapons—boulders, hammers, or great pickaxes—at one another. Sometimes one island-dwelling giant would pick a fight with another, living on another island near to him, and great stones would be hurled across the sea between the two.

The giants did little damage to each other, for we are told that the accuracy with which they aimed these missiles left much to be desired. All over Scotland lies a litter of stones that are said to have been left where they fell, after being hurled by one giant at another. Two great boulders, one white and one black, were left on opposite shores of Loch Ness after a feud between two giants who lived near there ended in stalemate. Another giant who lived in Kintail, once tried to hit a rival who lived across the water in Skye.

He missed, and the boulder that he flung crashed to the ground near Portree. There are giants' boulders on the east coast and the west, on the shores of the Cromarty Firth and in the Hebrides, in the Grampians, the Cairngorms, the hills of Fife and the Scottish Borders. On Law Hill, by Dundee, the "De'il's Stane" can be found. It is said that it was thrown across the Tay by a giant from Norman's Law at his rival on Law Hill, but fell short of its mark. At Ben Ledi, overlooking the town of Callander, a more amicable contest took place between a number of giants. A giant who was given the name of Samson lived there, and believing that he was the strongest of all, he challenged all comers to a shot-putting contest. The "shot" was a boulder of enormous size, which they took it in turns to throw from the summit of Ben Ledi. "Samson's putting-stone" lies where he last flung it, on the east side of the Ben.

The giants could be a terrible torment to humans, and they were notoriously hard to kill. Traditionally, they could be slain if their vulnerable spot—usually described as a mole—could be found. Otherwise, it took a combination of perseverance, brute strength, ingenuity and magic to kill them.

The Morvern Giant

Long ago, there lived a great giant in Morvern, which is on the west coast of Argyll, between Loch Linnhe and Loch Sunart. Across the sea from Morven, on the Isle of Mull, lived several more giants, whom the Morvern giant disliked intensely. He would often amuse himself by tossing boulders at them, across the Sound of Mull. He was bigger and stronger than any of the Mull giants, and he succeeded in causing one or two of them serious injury, much to his delight. The Morvern giant could pick up a cow or a bullock with one hand, and it made a fine meal for him. The sea provided another source of food for the giant, but of course, there was not a fish big enough to satisfy his appetite. When he went fishing, he was looking for a much bigger catch. His fishing rod was made from a tall, straight, silver birch tree, from which he had torn all the branches and roots. His line had been stolen from some fishermen, and it was the longest, strongest rope that they had. For a hook, the giant used an anchor. He had picked it up from the bottom of the harbor and snapped the rope that tied it to its ship. The ship had floated out into the sea in the middle of the night and had never been seen again. The giant would sit on a hillock by the water at the Point of Ardnamurchan, and cast his great hook and line far out to sea. Then one after another, he would haul great whales in to shore, roaring with laughter as they thudded onto the beach.

The giant was also a thief, and one day he stole some treasure from the king of Ardnamurchan. He did not need to sneak past the guards. He did not have to creep in under cover of darkness. He simply stuck his hand down a chimney and helped himself to all the gold and silver that was lying in the room below.

The king and his men gave chase, which was a very brave thing to do, considering the size and strength of the thief. The giant was heading eastward from the Point of Ardnamurchan, trudging along the northern shore of Loch Sunart, heading for the end. The king and his men knew that when the giant got to the end of the loch, he would turn south and west again, heading for his home in Morvern, and so they got in a boat and crossed Loch Sunart from north to south in order to intercept him. The cries of the king as he urged on his oarsmen alerted the giant to his pursuers. He picked up a great boulder and lifted it high above his head. Then he threw it into the loch, making great waves that tossed the king's boat from side to side like a twig in a torrent. But the king's men would not give up. With tremendous courage and tenacity, they battled through the raging waters to the other side of the loch, just as the giant was making his way up the hillside towards his home. Then the bravest warrior among the king's men called out to the giant, challenging him to stop and fight. The giant laughed, for he knew that he had the strength to crush every one of the king's men with his bare hands. He turned his face towards them, ready to answer the challenge with a scornful sneer. But when the warrior who had shouted out the challenge looked at the giant's face, he saw that there was a red mole right in the middle of his forehead, and knew that this was his weak spot. He drew his bow and, swiftly and surely, shot an arrow at the giant's forehead, hitting him right in the middle of the blemish. With a crash that echoed all across the peninsula, the giant fell dead to the ground. The king's men gathered up the stolen treasure and loaded it onto their boat. Then they cut off the giant's head and rolled it down the hillside to the shore. The weight of their load almost sank their boat as they sailed back over the loch to Ardnamurchan, with the triumphant giant slayer at the helm.

The Glaistig and the Kelpie

Highland folklore is animated by a wide variety of supernatural creatures, either harmful, or benevolent, and there are countless tales of man's encounters with them, some tragic, some humorous, some romantic. Two such creatures that feature in a large number of stories are the *glaistig* and the *kelpie* (*each-uisge*, or water-horse).

The glaistig was always female, a tutelary being who was believed to dwell in lochs and rivers, and to have a special attachment to animals and young children. When she did make herself visible to the human eye, it was said that she appeared as half-woman, half-goat, or as a woman with long fair hair, clothed in green. She watched over sheep and cattle, saving them from straying into danger. Often, as the adults went about their daily chores, the glaistig kept the children entertained with fun and games. It was commonly thought that glaistigs could attach themselves to particular families, as guardian spirits. In many parts of the Highlands offerings of milk or food were often left out for the glaistig to ensure that her loyalty to those under her protection remained steadfast. There was another side to the glaistig, however. She could tease and torment, and sometimes, she could do harm. The story of the glaistig's curse illustrates this belief.

The kelpie, water-horse or *each uisge*, was another water-dwelling creature. It was widely thought to be malevolent, capable of luring many innocent souls to their deaths in its sub-aquatic lair. Although it was sometimes said to have the power to transform itself into the shape of a man, it generally appeared on land as a magnificent horse and tempted weary travelers to try to ride upon its back. Once they had mounted, they found that they could not dismount and were dragged, helpless, underwater by the kelpie. There they would be devoured. Sometimes evidence could be found of the victim's fate. It was generally thought that the kelpie did not eat all of its victims, but left a small part of them—the liver, some said, or the heart—and these would be washed up at the water's edge where searchers could find them. One story tells of a number of children who encounter a kelpie while playing at the water's edge. All but one of them climb on the creature's back. The last child reaches out to stroke the creature's head, and as his first finger touches it, it becomes stuck fast. The child draws his knife and cuts off his finger in order to save himself but can only stand and watch as his companions disappear beneath the waves on the kelpie's back. In another version of the same story, six little girls are lured on to the kelpie's back, but the seventh child, a boy, is too cautious to risk it. The kelpie tries to catch him, but he manages to escape. Most kelpies appeared as black horses, but the River Spey was thought to be the home of a kelpie that took the form of a great white horse. The deaths of many people who drowned in the river's white-flecked, tumbling waters were blamed upon the kelpie. The majority of stories about kelpies depict this mysterious

creature at its worst; a mortal enemy of man, who may sometimes be outwitted, but should always be feared. The story of
the Kelpie of Loch Garvie is different.

The glaistig of Ardnadrochit

There was once a glaistig who lived in Ardnadrochit on the Isle
of Mull. She was a guardian of the Lamont family and looked
after all the cattle that belonged to them. She was devoted to
her duties. One day, as the glaistig was out herding the cattle,
she saw some men approaching. They were cattle raiders from
Lorne, and they had come to steal the beasts away from her.
The glaistig could not move the cattle fast enough to get them
to safety, but she would not allow the raiders to take them
away. She struck the animals on their backs with her magic
wand, and turned them all, one after another, into great gray
stones, which are still lying where she left them.

The glaistig had foiled the thieves but the loss of her animals
broke her heart and there was nothing that the Lamont family
could do to console her. She pined away and died, and they
buried her close to the stones.

The kelpie of Loch Garve

The kelpie of Loch Garve lived in a cold, dark, underwater
lair, hidden from sight in the very deepest part of the loch. He
liked his home just fine, and although he ventured onto land
from time to time, he was always glad to get back to familiar
surroundings, where his wife waited for him. But the kelpie's
wife was not happy. She felt the cold terribly, and life in the
lair was miserable for her as she shivered and shook, trying,
and failing to get warm. She complained to her husband, but
he did not feel the cold like she did, and at first he thought
that she was just making a fuss over nothing. Time went on,
and the kelpie's wife became more and more unhappy. At last,

he realized that if he wanted to keep her, he would have to do something to make the place a little more comfortable for her. He left home the very next day, and swam to the surface of the loch, where he turned himself into a beautiful horse. Then he went to the house of a man he had heard of, a builder who knew how to construct all sorts of useful things. When he got to the builder's house, he stamped on the ground until the man came out.

The builder was surprised to see such a beautiful horse on his doorstep. It seemed to be waiting patiently for him to mount it, and so he climbed on. As soon as the builder was sitting upon his back, the kelpie took off like the wind. The builder was terrified, for he realized that he was stuck fast to the kelpie's back, and they were heading towards the loch. He muttered a silent prayer as the kelpie plunged into the water, and he felt himself going down, down into the cold and dark. But the kelpie did not want to harm him. When they got to the bottom of the loch, he let the builder dismount. Then he explained his problem to him. He told him how his wife could not get warm in their home deep down in the loch, and how unhappy she was. And he asked the builder to help. If the builder could make something to help the kelpie's wife get warm, then he would be able to return safely to dry land, with a promise of a plentiful supply of fish from the loch to eat, whenever he wanted it.

The builder set to work at once, and made a great big fireplace in the kelpie's lair, with a great big chimney to carry the smoke to the surface of the water. When the work was complete, and the fire was lit, the kelpie looked at the smile on his wife's face with pleasure. He returned the builder safely to his own home on dry land, and true to his word, kept the kindly tradesman supplied for the rest of his days with plenty of fine, fresh fish from the loch. They say that even in the coldest of winter weathers, when all around is frozen, there is one small area of water on Loch Garve that stays free from ice. That is because far below the surface, a fire is burning merrily in the kelpie's home, and the heat which rises up from it stops the water on the surface from freezing.

The killing of the kelpie of Raasay

There was once a blacksmith who lived on Raasay. He owned a number of cattle and some sheep, and from time to time, one of the beasts disappeared. The smith knew that the likely culprit was the kelpie who dwelt in the loch nearby. He was angry, but felt that he could do little to stop it happening. Then one day the kelpie went too far. The smith's daughter had been out working with the animals that day, and she did not return home at the usual time. Evening turned into night and still there was no sign of her.

The smith waited anxiously for many hours, then as soon as the dawn came up, he went with his son to look for her. When they reached the edge of the loch, they found the girl's liver lying amongst the pebbles and realized at once that the kelpie must have taken her.

The smith's fury knew no bounds. He made up his mind to destroy the creature. With the help of his son, he lit a great fire at the water's edge, and used it as a makeshift forge to make a number of large iron hooks. Then the two men set up a spit on which they put a sheep to roast. As the sheep's carcass began to cook, sending an appetizing aroma over the waters of the loch, the smith set the hooks in the fire to heat until they were red-hot. The greedy water-horse caught the scent of the cooking meat and surfaced. It swam over to the fire and made a grab for the sheep's carcass with its jaws and as it did so, the smith and his son set about it with the red-hot hooks. At last it was dead, and they turned away, leaving its inert body lying on the shore. The next day, the smith and his son returned to the lochside but could find no trace of the kelpie's body. All that was left by the ashes of the fire was a heap of starshine.

Scottish Witches

A Charmed Life: Superstition And Witchcraft

WHETHER or not we admit to being superstitious, there are few of us who do not pay some sort of homage to superstitious practises and beliefs—we might cross our fingers or touch wood, for example, throw spilled salt over our left shoulder, or have in our possession "lucky" items of clothing, coins, stones or talismans.

Superstitious behavior is almost as old as man and is practised in societies in every corner of the globe. As man has struggled to forge a living in a world he does not fully understand, and against elements and occurrences over which he has little or no control, he has sought to explain the inexplicable through beliefs in external, unworldly forces; to predict the unpredictable and to control the uncontrollable through practises aimed at manipulating good and evil towards his own ends; appeasing the forces that might work against him, nurturing the forces that could benefit him.

In Scottish culture there is a great wealth of customs, sayings and actions that have accumulated through centuries of superstitious belief, and many of which are still practised by people today. Some people will still plant rowan trees, believed to provide protection against evil spirits, outside their homes. When a mother takes her new baby out for the first time, neighbors and friends might still place silver coins in the prams of new infants, for giving a gift to a newborn child, especially one of silver, is thought to bring both the giver and the child good fortune. But when can a superstitious practise be considered a spell, or a charm of witchcraft?

Witchcraft is believed to invest the practising individual with certain powers, whilst superstitious practises offer protection. Sometimes, moreover, the protection sought through superstitious practises is against the perceived evils that witches might be believed to cause. However, the two are still strongly tied to each other—they have much in common. Talismans, symbols, incantations or sayings, rituals—these are elements shared by witchcraft and superstition. It is not always clear which is which. When we see a solitary magpie and politely wish it "good morning" to avert ill-fortune, are we merely being superstitious, or are we casting a spell?

When Christianity was introduced to Scotland, superstition was already deeply rooted, and the practise of magic already hundreds of years old. And whilst Christianity dismissed the pagan gods from the converted people's minds, it did not altogether supersede superstition. Nor did it entirely dispel beliefs in magic. Indeed, it can be argued that superstition continued to exist quite comfortably alongside Christianity in Scotland. Some of our superstitions, such as avoiding having thirteen guests seated at the same table, have their origins in the Christian religion. Many old Scottish traditional practises carried out in the celebration of milestones in life, or special festivals, combined religious belief with an abiding indulgence in superstition. For example, in some parts of Scotland, where a boy and a girl were both presented for baptism on the same day, the girl had to be baptized first. If the boy's baptism were to precede the girl's, it was believed that the girl might grow a beard in later life. There were careful precautions taken for the protection of new-born infants, and certain procedures to be followed around the time of their birth, to prevent them from being taken away by fairies. When a death had taken place an equal number of precautions were taken to ensure that the spirits of the newly dead were protected from the forces of evil until a proper funeral sent them safely into the afterlife. In times gone by it was not necessarily considered enough to put your trust in God for protection against malign forces.

With the advent of Christianity, the role of the practitioners of magic gradually changed over the centuries, both in their own eyes and in the eyes of others. As far as the authorities of the Christian Church were concerned, witchcraft was heresy.

Like superstition and witchcraft, religion has its rituals, symbols, incantations and over time, we find that witches in Scotland began to integrate some elements of Christian services or prayers, albeit in adapted form, into their own practise. After the Reformation in Scotland, when the practise of Roman Catholicism was abhorred by so many leading Protestants, practitioners of magic frequently found they were considered guilty of a twofold heresy—i.e. practising witchcraft and acknowledging the rites of Roman Catholicism. Witches still commonly used, or misused, elements of the Roman Catholic mass in their rituals and charms. The idea of the Demonic pact—that witches had actively renounced their baptism and transferred their allegiances to Satan—was one which is thought to have originated in Europe and influenced Scottish witch-beliefs in the late sixteenth and early seventeenth centuries. Charges laid against accused witches and the confessions of the accused themselves, reflected how this belief had become practise. Along with the idea of the Demonic pact came that of the sabbat. Although the sabbat of the "black" witches was not a true subversion of the Christian mass, it would frequently be conducted on sacred ground, and the prayers and incantations recited by many witches, whether these be "white," healer witches or "black" witches whose practise was largely malevolent and who admitted to being active devotees of Satan, frequently contained elements from, or were little more than adulterated versions of prayers that were commonly recited in the pre-Reformation Christian church.

Gradually, skepticism regarding the effectiveness and hence, the real threat of witchcraft began to overtake the fear. Whilst the church authorities might still rail against the witches as heretics and enemies God, the law makers and enforcers gradually came to the conclusion that connections like those which had been made in past years between misfortune and witchcraft were spurious, and that the practise of witchcraft itself, unless accompanied by physical violence, could not cause physical harm or death. In short, whatever the intent of the witch, whether good or evil, witchcraft did not work, and people could not commit crimes using witchcraft alone. Accordingly, the crime of witchcraft was removed from the statute books.

The period of the witch-hunts did not stamp out witchcraft in Scotland. Superstition and witchcraft alike had already shown themselves to be adaptable to change. They had modified over the centuries to absorb the influences of changing religious beliefs and practises, and of foreign witch beliefs and superstitions. In the centuries since the witch hunts, witchcraft has continued, and whilst elements of traditional magic are retained, it still continues to evolve, incorporating a fluid and changing variety of beliefs and practises into its whole.

Wicca and Modern Witchcraft

Wicca is a modern attempt to reconstruct what its followers believe is the world's oldest religion—witchcraft. This religion finds its origins in northern Europe and is centerd on a belief in a fertility goddess, sometimes known as the Earth Mother or even May Queen, and her consort, the God of the Hunt, also known as the Green Man.

Despite this connection with the distant past, Wiccans are generally under no illusions that their "craft" is anything other than a modern take on an old faith, much of which was systematically wiped out by the early Christian movement.

That Wicca should emerge in the late 1940s after, perhaps thousands of years of lying pretty much dormant can be partially attributed to the increasingly secular nature of our society from the Industrial Revolution onwards.

That, and the advent of a series of writings that once again sparked people's interest in a long-lost religion promising a closer understanding of the natural world and a way of living in peace at a time when, all around, the world was at war.

Margaret Murray's books, including *The Witch Cult of Western Europe* and *The God of the Witches*, published in the early decades of the twentieth century, put forward the idea that the witches who were persecuted in the 16th and 17th centuries were not the unfortunate victims of mass hysteria so much as occasional practitioners of a much earlier, comprehensive pan-European religion.

Most historians laughed in her face but her works endured.

Whatever enthusiasm Murray may have ignited was fanned into flame by Gerald Gardner, a civil servant and Wiccan coven member who published several books detailing Wicca's origins, beliefs, rituals and concepts.

It was he who first related modern witchcraft to the ancient worship of the fertility goddess and her consort. He went on to describe Wicca as a religion whose rituals related to the moon. Wiccans celebrate the full moons and sometimes also the new moons, as well as the spring and autumn equinoxes.

Curiously, Druidic worship, which must have existed at the same time, centerd itself on the activities of the sun, which Druids believed was hugely powerful and no less than the bestower of life.

Gardner claimed, controversially, that the link between ancient and modern witchcraft had never been broken. Many others then and since dispute this, insisting that modern witchcraft is a restoration based on the fragments of information and ritual that were not extinguished by churches, and incorporating elements of other belief systems, including rituals taken from the Masonic Order and ceremonial magic.

Wiccan beliefs and rites

Wiccans believe ...

1 ... that the divine can be seen in everything, from a blade of grass to a shower of rain to a child's smile. They are not concerned with demonic rituals and calling up the devil, and are hence also known as white witches. Instead, they concentrate their energies on healing, teaching, learning and offering protection against malevolent forces.

2 ... in the three-fold system, also known as the "law of three," whereby anything that they put out into the world will return to them threefold. This, as you can imagine, works as a very powerful disincentive to using Wicca to perpetrate evil or cause harm to others. In fact, Wicca is a very reflective religion in which practitioners are encouraged to consider the import of everything they do, and how it impacts on others.

3 ...in a god, or single deity, whom they consider to be "unknowable." The fertility goddess and her consort are seen less as deities and more as intermediaries between earth

and a higher realm. However, most prayers are issued to these two figures, rather than directly to the deity.

Thus, some Wiccans can reconcile their practise of modern witchcraft with a Christian faith.

Wicca rituals include baptisms, though in this case the child is not committed to the religion. Indeed, Wiccans only accept members aged 18 or over, when they are sufficiently mature to exercise an independent and informed decision, and an adult baptism is enacted.

Wiccans also have their own marriage ceremonies.

4 ... that, as long as you harm no-one else, you can do as you wish. This is known as the Wiccan Rede, and relates to the Wiccan idea of personal responsibility.

Spells, for instance, should not be constructed so as to force anyone to do anything, as this violates the Wiccan Rede's invocation against manipulation and control. So if you are in the market for a love potion or to have a rival turned into a toad, you will need to look somewhere else.

In fact, Wicca does not have a set repertoire of spells though Wiccans may contruct ones which, for instance, would help a lonely person become more open to love, or a jealous person find solace through something more positive than revenge.

5 ... in sexual equality and tolerance of sexualities, including homosexuality and bisexuality.

6 ... in the reincarnation of the human soul. Rather than the heaven and hell system of Christian faiths. Wiccans, like Celts, believe that life and death are part of the same, endless cycle and that the dead should be revered, not feared.

Though Wicca is a recognized religion, it is not easy to access as covens are not listed in phone directories the way regular religious organizations are. The best way to contact them is through word-of-mouth, or by attending pagan festivals where you should be able to get talking to like-minded individuals. But non-Wiccans are warned, as with mediums, to check a person/group's credentials before committing themselves.

Though Wicca remains a little elusive, it has hit the headlines recently, when Scotland became the location of the first authorized Wiccan wedding.

Paul Rickards and Louise Schender, from Canada, were married in 2004 in a Wiccan ceremony held in Edinburgh's underground vaults and conducted by the Niddry Street Temple of the Source Coven of the Blue Dragon, by George Cameron and Lady Felina, the coven's High Priest and High Priestess.

Commenting, a spokesperson for the General Registry Office of Scotland said: "It is the first Wiccan wedding to be authorized in Scotland. It is a recommended form of religion. The Registrar General for Scotland attaches great importance to the principle of marriage."

As did the happy couple who, though not practising Wiccans, found the belief system on which it is based very much to their taste.

White Witches

There are other "categories" of white witches still practising today, some of which are as follows:

Kitchen witches

Kitchen witches have more in common with herbalists than Wiccans in that their witchery is very much focussed on the utilization of herbs and plants for healing and restorative purposes. They also tap into earth energies and the elements of fire, wind and water, and base their activities round the kitchen hearth, hence their generic name. They are sometimes referred to as green witches.

Hereditary witches

Some practising witches claim to have inherited their knowledge and skills from family members, who passed this lore down through the generations. Many such were wiped out during the time of the witch-trials, when such knowledge was viewed more as a curse than a blessing. Many others dropped the familial tradition, believing it flew in the face of Christianity.

Eclectic or solo witches

Eclectic or solo witches do not belong to a coven or work according to an established set of beliefs. Instead, they prefer to work alone, picking and choosing whatever elements of witchcraft work best for them.

Correllian nativist tradition

Unlike other forms of modern witchcraft, the Correllian Nativist Tradition, which is based on Wicca incorporating beliefs and rituals from Native American religions, favor the idea of Wicca operating on a worldwide, organized basis rather than through isolated groups. To this end, they have established a unified tradition with a single leadership. They pride themselves on their accessibility and are great promoters of Wiccan education, even offering correspondence courses via the internet.

Dianic tradition

Dianic witches belong to female-only covens and devote themselves only to the goddess of fertility. They have similarities with the Dryadic witches, another female-only sect, who draw much of their ideas and beliefs from fairy lore.

Pagan Festivals

As church attendance continues to decline in Scotland, one area where religious observation appears to be on the up is in Paganism, which has many similarities with Wicca in that it is centerd around the natural world and is essentially benign, concerned with doing good not evil.

Pagans celebrate eight major festivals a year, at six to seven week intervals, giving the year a rhythmic structure. This structure is known as the Wheel of the Year, which accords with the Wiccan idea of life being, in essence, circular.

Imbolc (February 1 or 2)

Imbolc is also known as the day of bride, the goddess of fire, and Pagans mark it by lighting fires to hasten the return of the sun after the long winter so as to ensure that the spring planting goes well.

It is a time when many attend to domestic tasks, such as sweeping out the house—the basis of our modern-day concept of spring cleaning—and making candles.

Imbolc was assimilated into the Christian calendar, becoming Candlemass, where candles are lit to honor the purity and holiness of the Virgin Mary.

Spring Equinox (March 20 or 21)

This is the day when spring officially begins, as the length of the day now equals that of the night. Christianity appropriated this one too, turning it into Easter, the celebration of the Resurrection and incorporating many Pagan rituals associated with the idea of birth and regeneration, such as egg painting and seed planting.

Beltane (April 30 or May 1)

This is the great fire festival to welcome in the summer. Fire, to the Pagans, is linked to fertility and purity and many love matches were sealed at this time of year. Mayday, celebrated particularly in England, typifies Beltane's delight in sexuality and fecundity.

In Edinburgh, Beltane attracts thousands of people to Calton Hill every April 30, where fires are lit and crowds gather to watch the May Queen arrive with the Green Man. The Queen crowns him, after which he sheds his winter clothes and they both get married.

Lughnasadh (August 1 or 2)

Like Lammas, or the loaf mass, this is a harvest thanksgiving essentially, celebrated with singing, dancing and feasting. It is also a time for prudence, and for making plans for the winter.

Autumn Equinox (September 20 or 21)

The equinox marks the end of summer and is a time for reflection.

Samhain (October 31 or November 1)

This is the beginning of the Pagan year, when gods or spirits were thought to roam the earth, mingling with human beings. This undoubtedly gave rise to Hallowe'en, which is characterized as a wild night when the spirits rise again, before scurrying away in the face of All Saints' Day on 1st November.

Pagans celebrated with feasting and dancing. However, many modern Pagans are vegetarians, factory-farming having little correlation with a holistic view of man and animals, and the kind of drunkenness associated with ancient rituals is often foregone too.

Winter Solstice (December 22)

This is the shortest day of the year, when the sun "dies" at sunset, only to be reborn the following morning, marking the "return of the sun." Rituals included gathering at sacred sites to watch the sun go down, and lighting a Yule Log—a log that burned for days—to banish the darkness.

Many other traditions grew from this, including that of Father Winter, a rather malevolent old man who wandered from house to house, demanding to be entertained. If he was turned away, he would stick around, ensuring the winter was perpetual. He was later sanitized, with a little help from St Nicholas, into our modern day Santa Claus.

The Hunted

In sixteenth- and seventeenth-century Scotland any distinction between "white" and "black" magic became irrelevant, and any notion of magic working independently of either God or the Devil was dismissed. The practise of magic was the work of the Devil, God's greatest foe. Curing, harming, charming, cursing, foretelling the future and talking to spirits of the dead were equally suspect activities. Those who claimed to do any such things, those who were seen to do any such things, and those who were said to have done any such things were equally liable to find themselves in danger from the wrath of the church authorities and the courts.

What was a witch, in the eyes of those who led the witch hunts of the sixteenth and seventeenth centuries? Who were these people who were persecuted in their hundreds?

The statistics that can be calculated from surviving records of witch trials reveal, to a certain extent, certain factors that were held in common by a significant number of the accused.

Firstly, although men were prosecuted for witchcraft, it is true to say that the majority of those who were tried for such crimes were women. Throughout the period of witch persecutions, around 80 per cent of those suspected of witchcraft were female. This is sometimes interpreted as sign of women's inferior status in society, or of "institutional misogyny" on the part of the church and the courts. But the figures may simply illustrate social perceptions of witchcraft at the time; it was seen primarily as a woman's crime. That is to say, because of the things that people believed to be true about witches, women were more likely suspects, and therefore more women were apprehended.

The age of a "typical" Scottish witch is not so easy to tell. Some were old, some were little more than girls, but there are indications that the majority of those who were accused were in the "middle-age" bracket. Most were married, or widowed, and were therefore clearly adults. Several had children, many of whom were adults themselves. There were certainly several old women who found themselves on trial for witchcraft during the period, but any notion of the typical Scottish witch of the sixteenth and seventeenth centuries being a wizened old hag would be wrong.

If there is one thing that can be said to be true of all the alleged witches who were prosecuted in Scotland in the sixteenth and seventeenth centuries, whether they saw themselves as witches or not, it is perhaps that they were all people who (through their own fault or otherwise) found themselves with enemies, and who then fell foul of a belief that pervaded all ranks of society at the time: the belief that witchcraft entailed real and *effective* practises, that could be used for good or for evil. Had that belief not been as prevalent as it was, whether they were innocent of practising witchcraft or guilty, these people could never have been successfully prosecuted in such large numbers. Had that belief not been as prevalent as it was, we might argue that it is unlikely that the Witchcraft Act of 1563 would ever have been passed.

Two Famous Witch Trials

The North Berwick Witches

The story of the North Berwick witch trials deserves to be singled out for special attention for a number of reasons. It was the first mass witch-trial to take place in Scotland and is notable for the numbers of people who were alleged, in the confessions of those who had been apprehended, to have been taking part in witchcraft in the area around East Lothian. The case also quickly achieved notoriety, even in those cruel times, for the manner in which some of those who were charged suffered for the accusations that had been made against them. The charges that were laid against the people accused of sorcery at North Berwick, and the confessions that were given by some of these people, not only demonstrate quite clearly how hard it is to distinguish the difference between fantasy and fact in cases of this nature, but also bring in an element that had not featured in previous witch trials in Scotland. This was the notion that the persons involved had been taking part in ceremonies and rites in which the Devil was said to have appeared; they had been consorting with and acting directly upon the wishes and demands of Satan himself.

Mention was made, for the first time in a Scottish witch trial, of the Satanic Pact, which swiftly became a major factor in establishing guilt in later prosecutions.

The North Berwick trials were also unique because of the personal part that King James VI played in the investigations and because the events that lead up to the trials involved two countries, Denmark and Scotland. Finally, but not least importantly, the trials of the North Berwick witches are particularly notable because the accused were charged not only with sorcery, but with treason, and the involvement of one of the accused, Francis Stewart, Earl of Bothwell, has been the subject of much debate amongst historians in the years that have passed since.

King James VI had chosen a wife for himself; the fourteen year-old Anne of Denmark. She was to be brought over to Scotland to marry him in 1589, but a succession of storms prevented the boat that was to bring her from setting sail. The Danish authorities blamed witchcraft for the unfortunate weather and consequently a number of people were arrested and brought to trial in Copenhagen. Eventually, King James agreed in the autumn of 1589 to travel overseas to Denmark to meet his betrothed and bring her back to Scotland himself. After a stay of some six months he returned with Anne, now his wife, to Scotland. His journey had been successfully accomplished, but it had been hampered by bad weather, both on the outward and return voyages. On the return voyage one of his ships, carrying wedding gifts for the new queen, was sunk.

In the closing weeks of 1690, the king received some disturbing news. It seemed that the evil that had hindered his marriage plans was not only to be found in Denmark. In his own land, witchcraft and treason were afoot. In North Berwick, a fishing port on the east coast of Scotland, a coven of witches had been working against the king, trying to cause his death through sorcery. The discovery had come to light in the following manner.

Suspicion had fallen first on a woman from Tranent, a servant of David Seton called Geillis Duncan, whose behavior had caused her master some concern. The rather gruesome pamphlet *"Newes from Scotland"* published in 1591, described how the first suspicions were raised as follows:

> *"Within the towne of Trenent, in the kingdome of Scotland, there dwelleth one David Seaton who, being deputie bailiffe in the said towne, had a maid called Geillis Duncane, who used secretlie to absent and lie forth of hir maisters house every other night: This Geillis Duncan tooke in hand to helpe all such as were troubled or grieved with anie kinde of sicknes or infirmitie, and in short space did perfourme many matters most miraculous; which things, for asmuch as shee began to do them upon a sodaine, having never done the like before, made her maister and others to be in great admiration, and wondered thereat: by meanes whereof, the said David Seaton had his maid in great suspition that shee did not those things by naturall and lawfull waies, but rather supposed it to bee done by some extraordinarie and unlawfull meanes."*

So far, then, Geillis was not obviously guilty of malefice. She kept disappearing at night, and she seemed to have a new and inexplicable ability to heal the sick. But if she could heal people, then she must also be capable of harm. On Seton's orders, Geillis was tortured—in all likelihood illegally—and examined for the Devil's mark, which was found on her neck. Following interrogation she confessed to having acted with others.

More people were apprehended for investigation and over a relatively short space of time, a large number of names were produced, including the following: Agnes Sampson from Haddington, Agnes Thompson from Edinburgh, Doctor Fian from Prestonpans; the wife of George Motts from Lothian; Robert Grierson; Janet Sandilands, a potter's wife, a smith,

Euphame Macalyean, Barbara Napier and several others from Edinburgh and East Lothian.

Agnes Sampson was the oldest and she was brought before King James himself for examination. She refused to give in to questioning and accordingly His Majesty ordered that she be taken to prison to be examined for the telltale mark of a witch and tortured until she confessed. The Devil's mark was found, and after suffering terrible tortures at the hands of her interrogators, Agnes admitted that she was a witch. She was brought in front of the king once more, and this time willingly told him about the treacherous and devilish deeds of which she and her accomplices were guilty.

On Hallowe'en, 1589, she and several others had sailed in sieves, drinking and carousing all the way, to North Berwick. Dr Fian had taken the lead in the procession, with Geillis Duncan playing her jew's harp as musical accompaniment. The assembly of witches had danced their way towards the kirk, singing. This story was to be confirmed by Geillis Duncan, who was brought before King James to play her instrument for him to hear.

At the gathering in North Berwick, none other than Satan himself had been present. He had ordered that the king should be killed, and in a strange ceremony which had entailed the removal of joints from bodies buried within and without the kirkyard, the assembled persons had agreed to his wishes, sealing their promise by kissing the Devil's buttocks.

The king initially had strong misgivings about the reliability of Agnes Sampson's confession. He called her a liar. But Agnes, apparently, having previously refused so vehemently to give up a confession, was now quite eager to prove her guilt. She whispered in King James's ear the words that he had exchanged with his wife on their wedding night. Now would he believe that she was a witch? Of course he would.

The meeting at North Berwick might have been the largest meeting—accounts vary, but somewhere between forty and two hundred people were said to have attended—but it had not been the only one, according to the growing testimonies of various of the accused. At one other meeting, Dr Fian, Robert Grierson, Agnes Sampson and others had gone out to sea and had thrown a cat, delivered by the hand of Satan, into the water to try to prevent the king's ship from arriving safely back in Scotland. At another, with the Devil present, a stolen picture of the king was passed from hand to hand and trouble wished upon him.

At another meeting, a wax likeness of King James VI was produced. And on yet another occasion, venom from a toad which had been hung upside-down was mixed with urine and "the thing in the forehead of a new-foaled foal" in an oyster-shell, ready to be left where it might fall upon the king and bring about his destruction.

Agnes Sampson, who had a reputation as a practising witch before the trial, was acknowledged in both age and status as the most senior of the women who were accused. She calmly gave long and detailed accounts of the witches' treasonable and maleficent activities, but her compliance did not bring her any benefits. She was strangled and burnt.

Dr Fian, the Prestonpans schoolmaster, proved to be equally forthcoming under torture and interrogation. He was generally acknowledged as the Devil's clerk in the proceedings at North Berwick—no doubt because he was one of the most educated among the gathering. He gave further information about the meeting at North Berwick kirk.

It transpired he had a reputation as a womanizer and as a sorcerer and evidence was offered up by others against him to this effect. Shortly after his confession had been secured, Fian escaped. He was caught again and in spite of his protests that his confession had been false, after further torture he faced the same fate as several of his co-accused.

Barbara Napier was a well-connected woman. Her husband, Archibald Douglas, was a respected citizen of Edinburgh. Her brother-in-law was an advocate. She admitted a connection with Richard Graham, one of the other accused, confessing that she had used his services as a magician on one occasion. She also admitted that she had had similar contact with Agnes Sampson. But throughout the entire proceeding, she denied taking part in any of the treasonable activities of which she had been accused. She had consulted witches, she said; but she was not guilty of practising witchcraft herself. She was initially cleared of the charge of treason, but following the intervention of the king, she was finally found guilty and executed.

Like Barbara Napier, Euphame Macalyean was a member of the Edinburgh gentry; the illegitimate daughter of one advocate, the wife of another. The accusations against her not only involved her alleged participation in the activities of the North Berwick witches, but also her alleged conspiracy to kill her first husband with witchcraft and her use of witchcraft in matters of love and personal dispute. In spite of a powerful legal defence, Euphame Macalyean was found guilty and burned alive.

Richard Graham, another of the accused, also had a reputation as a sorcerer. He was already an excommunicate. He was acknowledged as one of the most powerful figures in the group and may even have been the leader. It was he who commanded Geillis Duncan to assemble with the other witches at North Berwick. He was acquainted with several members of the Scottish nobility who were said to have recognized and at times made use of his magical powers. He confessed to having "raised the Devil" on more than one occasion. Graham survived longer than most of the other accused, but he, too was eventually executed in 1592.

The confessions of Agnes Sampson, Geillis Duncan, Richard Graham and others all named Francis Stewart, the Earl of Bothwell as the man behind their attempts to kill the king. Bothwell was a powerful figure in Scotland, and had been one of the members of the Regency Council in charge of Scottish affairs while James was away in Denmark, but his relationship with the king was not a comfortable one and it was believed by many that he did indeed pose a threat to the king's security. Whether he had been the figure behind all the intrigue, or whether the allegations of his involvement in the affair were prompted, or manufactured by his political enemies will never be known. He did acknowledge that Richard Graham was known to him, but strenuously denied any part in a magical conspiracy against the king. And whilst proceedings against the other accused moved quite swiftly to a conclusion (although Richard Graham was not executed until 1592, most of those who had been found guilty had been executed by spring 1591), Bothwell's case was to occupy the king's mind for considerably longer. Richard Graham had told in his confession of several meetings which had taken place at which he and Bothwell had discussed how best the king's death might be caused by enchantment. During his period of imprisonment, he also claimed that Bothwell had sent him money in an attempt to bribe him into keeping silent about any such activities.

Bothwell was eventually arrested in May 1591 and imprisoned in Edinburgh Castle. He had several points to bring up in his own defence: Graham was an unreliable witness, as were the other witches who had named him; Graham had been persuaded to make the allegations against him with promises of avoiding execution. But by June, James had been convinced that Bothwell was guilty of treasonable conspiracy, and plans were made to send him into exile abroad. Bothwell foiled the king's plans to send him out of harm's way, however, for he managed to escape and went north into hiding. The king had him declared a traitor and his goods were forfeited to the crown, but Bothwell remained at liberty for two more years, tormenting King James in mind and, on one occasion, threatening him in person at Holyrood Palace. Finally, in 1593, he was brought to trial. King James was not to see Bothwell brought to justice on this occasion either, however, for Bothwell maintained his innocence. His case rested principally on Graham's proven reputation as a sorcerer and hence his unreliability as a witness, and on the claim that Graham had been coerced into manufacturing evidence against him. Bothwell was not short of powerful supporters and few people were surprised when he was acquitted of the charges against him.

It is quite likely that there was a conspiracy to kill King James in 1589–90, and that those who took part in it sought to achieve their ends through the use of black magic. Just how much of the confessions of Agnes Sampson, John Fian, Geillis Duncan and others can be taken as fact will never be known. If everything that was laid against those that were accused is to believed, then the conspiracy was certainly far-reaching. From Edinburgh, to Prestonpans, to North Berwick, there were groups of people from all walks of life who had some part in the affair. Just how many people really were involved will also remain a mystery, for although we know the fates of the more notable figures in the case, we do not know how many others were apprehended and tried for their alleged role in the sorry business.

The role of the Devil in the witches' activities continues to invite speculation. Was this one individual coordinating all efforts, appearing to the witches in demonic guise? Might it have been different men (for the Devil appeared in the form of a man) on different occasions—Richard Graham on one occasion, someone else on others. Or might it even have been Bothwell himself? Did Bothwell instigate the whole affair, or were the allegations of his involvement the result of his enemies, or more specifically, supporters of the king, conspiring to put him out of harm's way? Did Agnes Sampson, Richard Graham and the others who named Bothwell, willingly volunteer Bothwell's name or was it suggested to them? Bothwell was known as a loose cannon, to say the least, and had already been involved in rebellion against the king before 1589. He did know Richard Graham, and had even made use of Graham's skills as a sorcerer in the past. Might he have called upon Graham to help him to get rid of the king and throw the country into chaos? If so, why? Historians are likely to be intrigued by the case for years to come.

The Witches of Pittenweem

By the turn of the eighteenth century, prosecutions for witchcraft were becoming increasingly rare. But in the East Neuk of Fife, in the fishing village of Pittenweem, it appears that witch-fever had not yet burned out.

In 1704, a young boy called Patrick Morton, an apprentice blacksmith who lived in Pittenweem, fell foul of the ill-temper of a woman called Beatrix Laing. She had asked him to make some nails for her, but he had been unable to oblige immediately, his time being taken up with another job on which he was already working. Beatrix took umbrage at his refusal and went away, muttering under her breath. At this point, it seems that the lad's imagination began to take over. He feared that Beatrix was cursing him. Shortly afterwards, when he saw Beatrix tipping hot embers into a bucket of water, he became convinced that she was uttering charms to herself, and assumed that the charms were against him. Some days later, the lad fell ill. He was struck by some mysterious weakness, followed by paralysis and fitting. His body became alarmingly swollen, his head turned to an awkward angle, and he had difficulty breathing. Whatever illness it might have been that Patrick Morton was suffering from, he believed it had been caused by Beatrix Laing. She had bewitched him. He confided his fears to the local minister, Patrick Cowper, and along with Beatrix Laing, he accused another woman called Janet Cornfoot.

Beatrix Laing was the wife of a respectable burgess of the town. Her husband had served as treasurer of the council. But her position in society was not enough to offer her any protection against Patrick Morton's accusations. It is quite possible that she had already been suspected of witchcraft. She was taken into custody for the process of interrogation to begin. The minister Patrick Cowper, eager to have his conviction, proved to be a cruel tormentor and Beatrix was denied sleep for five days, and subjected to torture. At length, the poor woman gave her interrogators the confession they wanted, naming, as she did so, certain other people, including Janet Cornfoot, Isobel Brown and Nicol Adam. Once her torment had come to an end, however, Beatrix withdrew her confession, on the grounds that it had been obtained under unreasonable duress. This did her no good, for she was subjected to further abuse and then thrown into a dungeon, where she stayed for a period of five months while Cowper made application to have her, and others among her co-accused, tried in Edinburgh. Her case never came to trial in the High Court. It seems that, in Edinburgh, reason prevailed and the Privy Council decided against taking the matter any further. Beatrix was ordered to pay a fine and was released. But justice (or justice as he saw it) was still uppermost in the mind of the minister and good citizens of Pittenweem, and upon Beatrix Laing's release, with the blessings of Mr Cowper, an angry mob hounded her out of her home town.

Isobel Adam was also forced to confess, but she too, in spite of her confession, was able to secure her freedom after payment of a fine. Her fate thereafter is not known, but it is reasonable to assume, in the light of Beatrix Laing's treatment, that she, too, found herself banished from the community.

Another of those who had been apprehended, one of the people whom Isobel Adam named in her confession, was a man called Thomas Brown. He died while in prison in Pittenweem—in all probability his death occurred as a direct result of his treatment while in custody.

Of all those who were accused, Janet Cornfoot suffered the most terribly. She was apprehended following Patrick Morton's accusations, tortured and detained for trial. When, along with that of Beatrix Laing, her case was referred to Edinburgh, she was also released, but she was immediately taken into custody in Pittenweem again. Patrick Cowper was determined that she be re-tried and found guilty. The minister must have had a sadistic streak, for he took it upon himself personally to administer the harshest of floggings, in order to force a confession from her. For a short time, it seemed as if Janet might yet be able to save her own life, for somehow, she managed to escape from prison. But as soon as the news of her escape spread through the town, a frantic search was begun, and before long, the terrified creature was found, dragged out from hiding and hauled down to the beach by a raging mob of townsfolk, baying for her blood. All thoughts of true justice had deserted the people of Pittenweem and Janet's neighbors had become her lynch-mob.

Janet's hands and feet were tied, then she was strung onto a rope stretching between a ship in the harbor and the crowd on the shore. Swinging her outstretched body from side to side, the mob hurled stones at her. When the novelty of this had worn off, they untied her and dumped her, battered and bruised, on the shore. Then they placed a heavy door on top of her, piling boulder upon boulder onto the door until all signs of life in Janet's crushed body were finally extinguished. The good minister and the lawmen did nothing to prevent the horror.

The case of the Pittenweem witches is a particularly horrific episode in the history of the Scottish witch-hunts. The records are full of accounts of ill-treatment, cruelty and injustice, but this stands alone as an example of the terrible consequences of mob hysteria. It is all the worse for the fact that the events took place at a time when in most other parts of Scotland, reason was beginning to prevail. In only thirty years' time, the crimes of which Janet Cornfoot and Beatrix Laing had been accused would no longer be recognized in law.

Second Sight, Prophecies and Curses

I F THOSE of Celtic blood are more likely to be gifted
with psychic "sensitivity" then surely it follows that they
are also more likely to be blessed with "second sight"?

One of the most celebrated of all seers, Kenneth Mackenzie,
more familiarly known as the Brahan Seer, hailed from these
shores, setting an almost unsurpassable precedent for generations of seers to come.

Maybe it is in the genes. Tradition has it that second sight,
called *Da Shealladh* in Gaelic (lit. "two sights"), is passed down
through the tentacles of families like a curious heirloom, or
gifted by a supernatural source for one lifetime only.

Then again, perhaps it is down to the land itself, to the
fact that even now many people live in isolated communities,
at the mercy of the land, and are still bound together by the
old ways of life and the old legends and stories that attach
themselves to them.

Maybe the ability to divine the future is part of this stock
of ancient lore, an ability we all once had but have lost as our
civilization has progressed towards modernity? Certainly it
seems that divination thrives amongst those who live close to
the land and away from the cut and thrust of contemporary,
urban life.

Most prophecies relate to death, with shrouds and bodies
being the most commonly cited visions.

One typical case was recorded by a Rev Dr Stewart, of Nether
Lochaber, who was visited by one of his women parishioners
who bade him look at a rock by the sea. This rock appeared to be
glowing, as if illuminated by phosphorescence. He assumed this
odd visual effect was produced through some natural agency

but his visitor was adamant that it foretold a death, and said a body would be laid on that spot by nightfall tomorrow.

The next day, a boat arrived bearing a dead body for burial. The corpse, as the woman parishioner had predicted, was laid at the foot of the rock.

Many books have been written on the subject of second sight, notably the Rev Mr Kirk's *The Secret Commonwealth*, of 1691, which was later edited by no less than Sir Walter Scott. Even such a notable diarist as Samuel Pepys was fascinated by the subject, attempting at one stage to produce a quasi-scientific analysis of it.

However, though a subject of great interest, second sight was not something that people readily owned up to. One reason being that, so legend has it, if you speak out a prophecy before it happens, you lose the ability to see the future! Which just goes to show that the best predictions really are those we hear about afterwards.

Another reason for reticence was the punishment meted out to those who foretold things people did not want to hear.

Though the ability to see into the future is one that has always been envied and highly prized, seers, particularly in the past, have often had less than an easy time of it. Many were blamed for the messages of doom they sometimes had to impart, others were accused of witchcraft or sorcery, still others were written off as deranged.

Thankfully, these days we have a more tolerant attitude towards those who can look into the future and read us our fortune.

Though there are thousands of unattributed tales of people foreseeing deaths and crop failures and famines, only two visionaries have stood the test of time, one ancient the other modern, and their stories are as follows.

The Brahan Seer

The gift of prophecy

Kenneth Mackenzie or Coinneach Odhar, generally referred to as the Brahan Seer, is Scotland's most legendary fortune-teller. Some of his predictions read strangely today, written as they are in often rather impenetrable verse. But others are startling in their accuracy.

Mackenzie foretold, amongst other things, the bloody outcome of the Battle of Culloden, the construction of the Caledonian Canal and the Highland Clearances.

Thus he is often hailed as the Gaelic Nostradamus, in reference to the great 17th-century prophet who is claimed to have foretold the rise of Hitler and the Russian Revolution, albeit in cryptic stanzas known as quatrains.

Mackenzie was born on the Isle of Lewis sometime in the early 1600s. Or at least, so the story goes. In fact, there is no actual record of his having existed at all.

There is a Scottish Parliament record, dated 1577, of a Coinneach Odhar, described as an "enchanter," with two writs issued for his arrest. This relates to the case of a Catherine Ross of Balnagowan, married to Robert Mor Munro of Foulis, who had six children by his first marriage and six by his second, to Catherine.

Catherine, it seems, was ambitious for her own children, and hatched a ruthless plan to rid herself of her stepchildren, who stood in the way of their inheritance. She engaged 26 local witches who, the record suggests, were unsuccessful in their endeavor. Coinneach Odhar, whom she engaged subsequently, did a rather better job, providing her with poison.

Alas, the record does not tell us if he was ever caught, though he would most certainly have been burnt alive if he had been, and at a town called Fortrose, because Foulis fell within the jurisdiction of Fortrose Cathedral.

Which is where this real record dovetails to some extent with the Brahan Seer legend, as Kenneth Mackenzie is said to have been burnt alive in a spiked tar barrel in Fortrose, and there is a stone slab by Chanonry Point, near the town, which marks where he allegedly died.

However, the dates are a little awry. This Coinneach Odhar was a little early for our seer, leading some to speculate that the sorcerer was possibly the grandfather of the prophet, his supernatural gifts being put to rather less murderous use a couple of generations on.

However, the two most famous explanations of how Mackenzie gained his gift do not take a family gene pool into account.

The first story has it that Mackenzie's mother was out one night, tending to her cattle. It was nearing midnight when she approached a local hill called Cnoceothall, which overlooked a burial ground. As the witching hour struck, she saw the graves open up and the dead rise, their ghostly forms drifting away in all directions. An hour later, they all returned, their graves shutting up behind them.

All but one, that is. Mackenzie's mother walked up to this one and placed her staff across it, thereby preventing the spirit from re-entering its resting-place. Shortly afterwards, the ghost of a beautiful woman drifted into the graveyard and, seeing the barrier in her way, begged for it to be removed. Mackenzie's mother, clearly possessed of a typically Highland curiosity, said she would, but only if the ghost first told her why she had returned so much later than the others.

The ghost-woman explained that she had been to Norway, and was in fact the King of Norway's drowned daughter. Following the tragic accident, her body had been borne across the sea, finally washing up on a nearby shore. Hence her burial here in Lewis.

She then promised that, if she was allowed to pass, she would reward her interlocutor with a "valuable secret," instructing Mackenzie's mother to go to a nearby loch and seek out a small, round blue stone which she should then pass on to her son, Kenneth. This, said the ghost, would give him the power to predict the future.

This she did, presumably having let the poor ghost pass, and her son was duly blessed with the gift of second sight. As an adult, Kenneth Mackenzie moved to Brahan, an estate on the mainland near Inverness, where he worked as a laborer, yet told the fortunes of some of the richest families in the land. Which gives us an indication of the strict social order of those days; "upwardly mobile" was not a familiar concept to our 17th century forebears.

The second story, cited by—amongst others—Hugh Miller, resident of nearby Cromarty and known as one of the fathers of geology as well as an enthusiastic and important chronicler of Highland lore, has it that Mackenzie received his gift whilst working on the Brahan estate.

He was cutting peats one day, peats being the primary source of fuel in the Highlands in those days, in a location some distance from his master and mistress's house. It being so far away that he would lose valuable daylight hours returning to the house for dinner, his midday meal was taken out to him by his mistress, who had taken the opportunity to lace the repast with poison.

The background to this story being that Mackenzie had made a nuisance of himself, teasing the mistress to the point where she found him unendurable. However, her plan to poison him was foiled because he fell asleep beforehand and, upon waking, felt something hard pressing on his heart. The source of the pressure was a hard white stone, with a hole in the middle, which had mysteriously appeared in his waistcoat pocket.

Looking through the hole, he had a vision of his mistress lacing his food with poison and was thus forewarned. Just to make sure, when the meal did arrive, he fed it to his faithful hound and watched, in dismay, as the unfortunate creature died in agony in front of him.

The stone is alleged to have left him blind in one eye, but with the other he was to see many incredible things indeed.

Most storytellers agree that the gift of prophecy was bequeathed by the stone but Miller, who was nothing if not a rational man, believed it was more of a gimmick designed to lend Mackenzie gravitas and that the gift, if it existed, was inherent.

"If Kenneth was really possessed of the power of prophecy, he more than likely used the stone simply to impose upon the people, who would never believe him possessed of such a gift unless they saw with their own eyes the means by which he exercised it."

Kenneth Mackenzie made many uncanny predictions, some relating to the future of wealthy families of the area, some to changes that would occur in the local area in years to come, and others reaching far into the future, touching on the Industrial Revolution, the reign of Victoria, even the modern age of oil platforms and aviation.

The Caledonian Canal

Tomnahurich is a large hill sited near the Highland capital of Inverness. For many centuries it was regarded as a "fairies' hill" into which human beings could be enchanted by fairies, often never to return.

Though it was situated reasonably near a series of inland

lochs, it was very much a landlocked hill. So it came as a great surprise when Mackenzie declared:

"Strange as it may seem to you this day, and it is not far off, when full-rigged ships will be seen sailing eastward and westward by the back of Tomnahurich, near Inverness."

Yet it came to pass.

In the early nineteenth century—1802–1833—Thomas Telford designed and built the Caledonian Canal, connecting those inland lochs to the sea. It was created to provide safe passage for Royal Navy ships during the Napoleonic War, so there would indeed have been fully-rigged, sea-going vessels seen navigating around Tomnahurich, both eastward and westward.

Strathpeffer Spa

"Uninviting and disagreeable as it is, with its thick-crusted surface and unpleasant smell, the day will come when it shall be under lock and key and crowds ... will throng to its portals."

Here Mackenzie was describing the sulphur springs at Strathpeffer, a small Highland town near the Brahan estate. These springs were a source of disgust in the 17th century with their loathsome rotten egg smell.

But reel two centuries forward, and Strathpeffer had become one of the Victorians favorite spas, a place where the afflicted came flocking to "take the waters," believed by then to have great restorative powers.

These days, you can still taste the waters, and the smart Victorian hotels, railway station and town-houses are testament to how truly Mackenzie's bizarre prediction came true.

The Highland Clearances

In Mackenzie's day, the Highlands and Islands of Scotland

were populous places, a patchwork of small subsistence crofts and townships, where generations succeeded generations.

These days, the Highlands are considered Europe's only wilderness. You can travel for miles in any direction and not encounter a single person. Instead are acres upon acres of empty, untended land, marked with the occasional ruined homestead.

What happened in between times was one of the most terrible crimes against humanity witnessed in Scotland, when thousands were swept off the land they had tended for centuries by landlords grown greedy for profit. Many died, of starvation or being burnt alive in their own homes. Others migrated to the cities, or to the New Worlds in Canada and Australia.

Mackenzie saw it all.

"The day will come, and it is not far off, when farm-steadings will be so few and far between that the cock of a crow shall not be heard from one steading to the other."

He even predicted what would take the place of man—sheep. Though his phraseology is perhaps a little brutal on the poor Highlanders who saw their crops burnt and their wives mistreated before their very eyes.

"The clans will become so effeminate as to flee from their native country before an army of sheep."

Culloden

One of Mackenzie's most famous predictions is that of Culloden. A vision seized him one day, as he was passing Culloden Moor, near Drumossie, on the far side of Inverness.

"Oh! Drummossie, thy bleak moor shall, ere many generations have passed away, be stained with the best blood of the Highlands. Glad am I that I will not see the day, for it will be a frightful period; heads will be lopped off by the score, and no mercy shall be shown or quarter given on either side."

He was not far wrong. Only a century after his passing, in 1746, was the Battle of Culloden, the last to be fought on British soil. The Hanoverians, in the pay of the English king, routed the forces of Bonnie Prince Charlie, comprised mostly of Highlanders.

Because the Jacobites had been such a thorn in the Hanoverian side, the Duke of Cumberland was given strict instructions to show no mercy in victory and he carried those orders out to the letter. Not only were the Highlanders soundly defeated, those left wounded on the battlefield afterwards were butchered where they lay.

So many died that day that bodies were simply identified by clan and tossed into mass graves, the markers of which can be seen to this day.

Piper Alpha and the Lockerbie disaster

Kenneth Mackenzie once predicted that "when the ninth bridge crosses the River Ness, there will be fire, flood and calamity."

And for years, the civic planners of Inverness resisted building a ninth bridge, lest they tempt fate. However, by 1987, it seems that Mackenzie's words were forgotten and construction began on a new bridge across the River Ness.

That year, the oil platform Piper Alpha exploded in the North Sea, killing 187 men. Survivors describe how the platform went up like a ball of flame, and how they could only escape by diving into what looked like a sea of molten fire.

A year later came the calamity, when Pan-Am flight 103 blew up above the small town of Lockerbie, its falling wreckage devastating the town below and adding local residents to the death toll of passengers. In total, 279 people died.

Then came the flood. In 1989, a huge spring rainfall caused dreadful flooding, finally washing away the rail bridge and thus, temporarily at least, returning the River Ness bridge tally to eight.

The tale of the Jaw=bone

"The day will come when the Lewsmen shall go forth with their hosts to battle, but they will be turned back by the jaw-bone of an animal smaller than an ass."

This was one of Mackenzie's most incomprehensible predictions yet it came true, and in a quite remarkable way.

In 1745, information was received by those loyal to Bonnie Prince Charlie that he was about to land in Scotland in a bid to raise an army and once again lead a rebellion.

The Earl of Seaforth had previously been a great supporter of the Young Pretender, an allegience that had temporarily cost him his lands. Having had them recently restored to him, he was advised against being seen to join up with the Jacobite forces again.

However, he had already issued private orders to Stornoway to have his men, the famous Lewsmen, sent in readiness to assist Charlie. Keen to put the brakes on the venture, he hurried towards the West Coast and saw two ships on the horizon, armed to the teeth with battle-ready Lewsmen.

As it happened, Seaforth had just been dining on a sheep's head, and so he used the jaw-bone to signal to the ships to turn tail at once.

Thus the brave Lewsman were turned back from battle by a jaw-bone of an animal smaller than an ass.

The Curse of the Seaforths

The last, and perhaps most epic, of all the Brahan Seer stories is that relating to the Seaforths, an ancient and landed family whose estates sprawled across the Highlands.

The events occurred shortly after the restoration of King

Charles II, when Kenneth, the Third Earl of Seaforth, was summoned to Paris on business, leaving his wife the Countess at home alone at Brahan Castle.

But he tarried and he tarried in the French metropolis and she became anxious, finally calling in the Seer to ascertain whether her husband was safe and well.

Looking through his stone, Mackenzie saw that the Earl was thriving in Paris, thanks to fine wine and even finer women. Chuckling to himself, he assured the Countess that, yes, the Earl was safe and well.

The Countess was not satisfied with this and besides, Mackenzie's smirking manner had raised her heckles. Mackenzie, knowing that what he had seen would only raise her ire still further, bade her be satisfied that her Lord was safe and well and ask no more.

But she insisted, growing increasingly angry with the Seer, who responded reluctantly:

"As you will know that which will make you unhappy, I must tell you the truth.

"My lord seems to have little thought of you, or of his children, or of his Highland home. I saw him in a gay gilded room, grandly decked out in velvets, with silks and cloth of gold, and on his knees before a fair lady, his arm round her waist, and her hand pressed to his lips."

This did not please the Countess, especially as she realized she had made him reveal all in front of the servants. The gentry were notoriously class and status-conscious in those days and there were few things worse than being humiliated in front of your domestic staff.

She determined, therefore, to discredit Mackenzie as this, she hoped, would put paid to any sniggering rumors about her husband's infidelity. How she was going to discredit him we will never know because her ill temper got the better of her and she lashed out with the strongest punishment in her gift...and sentenced the Seer to death.

"You have spoken evil dignities, you have vilified the mighty land; you have defamed a mighty chief in the midst of his vassals, you have abused my hospitality and outraged my feelings, you have sullied the good name of my lord n the halls of his ancestors, and you shall suffer the most signal vengeance I can inflict—you shall suffer death," raged the Countess.

At first, Mackenzie was not unduly alarmed. He assumed she would recover her good spirits and quietly release him. But she never flinched from her vengeful purpose.

He was not allowed to make the case for his defence, nor was there time for anyone of noble standing to intervene on his behalf. The orders were given, and Mackenzie was led out for immediate execution, which took the form of his being burnt alive in a barrel of tar.

Before he went to his doom however, he pulled out his white stone and, looking into the future, declared:

"I see into the far future, and I read the doom of the race of my oppressor.

"The long-descended line of Seaforth will, ere many generations have passed, end in extinction and in sorrow. I see a chief, the last of his house, both deaf and dumb. He will be the father of four fair sons, all of whom he will follow to the tomb. He will live careworn and die mourning, knowing that the honors of his line are to be extinguished for ever, and that no future chief of the Mackenzies shall bear rule at Brahan or in Kintail.

"After lamenting over the last and most promising of his sons, he himself shall sink into the grave, and the remnant of his possessions shall be inherited by a white-coifed (or white-hooded) lassie from the East, and she is to kill her sister.

"And as a sign by which it may be known that these

things are coming to pass, there shall be four great lairds in the days of the last deaf and dumb Seaforth—Gairloch, Chisholm, Grant and Raasay—of whom one shall be buck-toothed, another hare-lipped, another half-witted, and the fourth a stammerer. Chiefs distinguished by these personal marks shall be allies and neighbors of the last Seaforth; and when he looks around him and sees them, he may know that his sons are doomed to death, that his broad lands shall pass away to the stranger, and that his race shall come to an end."

It was, by any measure, a fine and dramatic exit and, it seems, came to pass just as he said, but not for over a century.

Indeed, it seemed that the Seer was to be defied as the Seaforths thrived, even surviving—as previously mentioned—the confiscation of their lands following the 1715 Jacobite uprising.

But then, in 1794, was born Francis Humberston Mackenzie, who was to become known as the "last of the Seaforths." He was born with all his faculties intact but following a childhood bout of Scarlet Fever, was left deaf. Though he was still able to speak, he lost that power towards the end of his life.

Nonetheless, he had a successful career in the military, made a good marriage, to Mary Proby, and fathered four sons and six daughters. It was such a good life that he was not alarmed by the fact that four Lairds of his acquaintance, namely Gairloch, Chisholm, Grant and Raasay, had the exact physical peculiarities of which the Kenneth Mackenzie had made mention.

But the prophecy would out. One of Seaforth's sons had died young, and the other three followed him to the grave in time, the last enduring a long illness before finally dying.

Broken-hearted and haunted by the Seer's words, Lord

Seaforth followed him to the grave in 1815. Thus the name of Seaforth died out and the lands were indeed inherited by Seaforth's daughter, by then a young widow, often referred to as a "white-hooded lassie," whose married name was Hood.

Upon her second marriage, the Seaforth lands passed into the Earl of Galloway's line, with the Island of Lewis being sold off to a Sir James Matheson.

All of which left only one portion of Kenneth Mackenzie's curse outstanding, that this white-hooded lassie would kill her sister.

This happened some time later. Mrs Stewart Mackenzie as she now was, was driving her young sister Caroline in a horse-drawn carriage through the Brahan estate woods when the horses took fright and bolted, and she lost control.

Both sisters were thrown from the carriage, Mrs Mackenzie recovering at length, but Caroline dying of her injuries.

It was not her fault but because she was the driver of the carriage, the white-hooded lassie could be said to have indeed killed her sister.

So famous is the tale of the Curse of the Seaforths that Sir Walter Scott, the author of the Waverley novels, wrote a poem about it, the Lament for "The Last of the Seaforths."

Modern Prophets

There have been none since who match Kenneth Mackenzie's fame or uncanny ability to lay his finger on the future. Then again, it has to be remembered that many of the Brahan Seer's predictions took a century of two to play out. So perhaps we will have to wait and see.

However, one seer worthy of mention is Swein MacDonald, who lives in the Highlands, in fact not far from the 17th century home of Mackenzie himself.

MacDonald did not receive his gift in the magical way attributed to the Brahan Seer. Instead, he says, he has always been able to see into the future, a gift passed down through his family, which he can trace back to the 1720s in Sutherland.

His mother had second sight but such was the strength of her Presbyterian faith, she was reluctant to practise it. Her father however, Swein's grandfather, was famous for his ability to predict who would die next. A handy skill given that he worked as a grave-digger.

As a child, MacDonald could see the dead, and even predict occasional, random events, but it was not until much later that he took up this calling seriously.

Though he was born in Elgin, in the North East, MacDonald worked for much of his adult life in Glasgow, as a civil engineer for the Clyde Navigation Trust, before an industrial accident put paid to that. A skip containing a ton of bricks was swinging from a crane when it hit MacDonald, very nearly to his fatal injury.

These days, he walks with a stick and has an impaired sense of both taste and smell. But somehow, this brush with mortality heightened his other senses, notably that relating to prophecy.

He developed tunnel vision, a not uncommon result of severe head injuries, and this in turn seemed to develop what he calls his "third eye," the orifice through which he sees the world to come.

When clients visit him at his home, a small croft overlooking the Dornoch Firth, he ushers them into a consultation room, containing two chairs, which sit facing each other.

Once he and his client are seated, MacDonald offers them pen and paper to take notes if they so wish. Then, without preamble, he begins to talk and many have been astounded by the accuracy with which he describes their lives, family and circumstances.

He then ventures on to the future, offering advice and an insight into critical events to come, finally inviting his sitter to ask him any questions.

The future, he says, reels before him like images in a film but, though he is happy to see anyone and try to help them, he has one hard and fast rule: he will not deliver a bad fortune. If he looks into someone's future and sees only darkness, he will tell them nothing. As many mediums and psychics also say, the future cannot be changed and knowing an ill fate will do nobody any good.

One example of his withholding of evidence, as it were, is cited in Roddy Martine's *Supernatural Scotland*.

Two women had traveled all the way up from Glasgow to see the Dornoch Seer so the second was very disappointed when he told her that he was now exhausted and could not therefore also give her a reading. Despite her earnest pleading, he continued to beg off, citing tiredness. However, when she began to cry with frustration, he relented, saying he would not give her a reading exactly, instead writing down a prophecy on a piece of paper, then sealing it in an envelope. Her part of the bargain was that she must promise not to read it till she got home to Glasgow. This she agreed to, and the two women left, somewhat mollified.

The second woman, who was the driver, slid the sealed prophecy into her handbag before they drove off. On the way home, the car was involved in a horrendous, head-on collision that killed the driver outright, though the passenger survived.

A long time later, this first woman was going through her friend's handbag, just part of the traditional clearing out of a dead person's effects, and chanced upon the sealed prophecy. Under the tragic circumstances, it is no wonder she had forgotten it until now.

Opening it, she found herself staring, not at a prophecy, but at a blank sheet of paper. MacDonald had seen the woman's death and could not bring himself to tell her.

Another time, he forebore to tell a young woman that her parents were soon to die in a car accident. She returned to see him some time later and asked why he had failed to warn her. He responded that he could not tell her something that she could not bear to know, given that she could do nothing to prevent it.

Though MacDonald offers advice on the future, he is firm in his belief that destiny cannot be altered once it is set in motion.

MacDonald has been involved in police work, specifically in tracking down missing persons. In one case, he was asked by an anxious couple in Lanarkshire if he could pinpoint the whereabouts of their runaway son.

Through his third eye, MacDonald saw the young man surrounded by "tall buildings" and knew that he was perfectly safe and would return soon. The only problem he had was a sore shoulder.

As predicted, the son did turn up, complete with sore shoulder. He had been in Castlemilk, a housing scheme in Glasgow, famous for its high-rises.

MacDonald was also consulted by the police when they ran out of leads in the Renee MacRae disappearance of 1976. Renee and her young son had apparently left Inverness one evening but the only trace that has ever been found of them is a burnt-out car in a layby on the A9, the main motorway from Inverness to the South. So far, the case remains a mystery.

Another story involves the discovery of a body in the Cairngorm mountains, near Aviemore. A young man had been reported missing in Inverness and his description matched that of the dead man. His distraught father came to identify the body and, through confirming that it was his son, enabled the police to close the case.

However, a woman in London had recently sought out MacDonald's assistance in tracking down her missing son. She sent him a photograph and, the minute it was in his hands, the seer had a vision of a young man lying dead in a mountain landscape.

He had died of hypothermia, a likely enough death in such harsh conditions, but the telling details were that one of his boots was missing and one of his trouser pockets contained a Swiss Army knife.

MacDonald says that when he divines where a missing person is "you get this strange, strange feeling about it. Just once. If anybody is living, it's a good feeling. If somebody is dead, it's a bad feeling. You get this feeling of tension."

Swein phoned the police and convinced them, just through the sheer detail of his description, that the Cairngorms case needed further investigation.

The body was exhumed and a photograph taken was identified by the London woman as indeed that of her son.

Meanwhile, the now quite overwhelmed father learnt that his son had not perished on the hillsides but been on a week-long drinking bender in Inverness.

Curses

The Brahan Seer was not alone in his ability to deliver curses that appeared to come true. Many insist that curses, because they become embedded in the minds of the cursed, operate simply as self-fulfilling prophecies. The following stories perhaps shed a little doubt on that comforting theory.

Bonnie Dundee—ominous sights

Two stories have been told about the death of John Graham of Claverhouse, Viscount Dundee, "Bonnie Dundee," the persecutor of the Covenanters who was killed at the Battle of Killiecrankie, a landmark in Scottish history.

The night before the battle, it is said, as Graham slept, he was disturbed by two things. First, he saw a strange red glow in the darkness, which could not be explained by human activity. This same glow has been reportedly seen by visitors to the site on the anniversary of the battle in years since. Ghostly lights are quite a common phenomenon, as has already been mentioned, both as signs of approaching death (death candles) and as spectral "markers" of places where bloodshed and death have occurred.

The second thing to trouble Graham happened towards the hours of dawn, we are told. He saw a vision of a man by his bed, blood dripping from a head wound. The terrible figure pointed at Graham and cried:

"Remember Brown of Priesthill!"

Brown of Priesthill was a man called John Brown, a Covenanter who was killed for his beliefs. It is said that when the men in the firing squad saw Brown's steadfast courage and unfailing religious conviction in the face of imminent execution, they faltered, and Viscount Dundee himself fired the fatal shot.

Graham was greatly disturbed by the specter of Brown of Priesthill. Thinking (hoping) that what he had seen had not been a ghost but instead some devious trick by his enemies, he got up and inquired of the sentry whether there had been intruders in the camp. The guard outside, however, said that all had been quiet and that nobody had approached Graham's tent.

The figure that Bonnie Dundee had seen had been a

sign—its appearance, along with the eerie red glow, foretold his death in battle the next day.

Another person, many miles away, had a vision to tell him of John Graham's death. He was Lord Balcarres of Colinsburgh, unable to join his acquaintance in battle because he was under arrest on the orders of parliament. On the night after the battle, he was roused from sleep by a sound by his bed. He looked up and saw his comrade, Viscount Dundee, standing by the bed. He rose to greet him but the figure turned away and then disappeared. It was only later that Lord Balcarres found out that Viscount Dundee had been killed in battle that very day.

Sir Walter Scott

Sir Walter Scott had a keen interest in the supernatural, and during his lifetime he witnessed a ghost in his own home. A man from London, called George Bullock, was appointed by Scott to take charge of many of the building works at the writer's home, Abbotsford. George Bullock died in London in 1818, while work was still in progress at Abbotsford, fourteen years before the author's own death.

On the night of Bullock's death, Scott told of being woken by violent noises in the house. Although it was the middle of the night, it sounded as if builders were at work. Scott got up to investigate, but as he made his way through the house apprehensively, sword in hand, he could find nothing to explain the disturbance. The house was quiet again, and there were no signs of any disturbance.

Later, Scott was to discover that the bizarre events coincided with Bullock's death in London. The ghost of Bullock is said to have put in an appearance at Abbotsford on a number of occasions since then.

Visions of the dead in Galloway

Two stories that originate from Galloway in southwest Scotland echo the story of Mr Swan (*see* A Haunted Capital—Ann Street).

The first story concerns an old man, a smallholder, who was working out in the fields on the hillside one afternoon when he caught sight of his son below him in the distance, heading towards their home. The old man called down to his son, but obviously the lad was too far away to hear him.

The old man was consumed with curiosity. His son was a sailor, and the old man was sure that he was supposed to be on a long voyage, still at sea for some weeks to come. All the same, the old man had work to attend to. The potato crop had to be brought in. He hurried on with his task—the sooner he finished, the sooner he would be able to go home and see his son.

The old man had finished his work by lunch time. He hurried back to the cottage to greet his son and hear all his news. But when he got home, there was no sign of the lad. The old man's wife was preparing a meal for two people, just as usual. The old man asked whether their son had been home, but his wife said no.

The old man decided that his eyes had been deceiving him—he had, after all, been high up on the hillside. What he thought had been the figure of his son was probably just a passer-by with a similar appearance.

Some time later, however, the old man and his wife received the tragic news that their son had been killed overseas in an accident—at the time at which his father had thought he had seen him.

The second story concerns a boy who was staying with his grandparents for the summer. The boy was sitting outside in the yard one afternoon, whittling some wood, when he saw his grandfather come out of the house. The old man paused to watch the boy for a few moments, then, without saying a word, walked off out of the yard towards the fields. The boy remarked to himself that the old man seemed uncharacteristically quiet, but he was too absorbed in what he was doing to give the matter much thought.

A few minutes later the boy went back into the house. He was quite taken aback when he saw that his grandfather was there, sitting in his favorite chair by the fire. Hadn't he just seen the old man walk away from the house, dressed in exactly the same clothes? It was the strangest thing—after all, the old man could not be in two places at the same time. Had the boy been dreaming or had his eyes been deceiving him?

Quite unexpectedly, the old man fell ill that night and very shortly afterwards he died. The boy now understood that when he had seen the figure of his grandfather walking away he had been forewarned of the old man's departure to another life.

The Cursed Mill

Many years ago, near Newtonmore, there was once a mill that was said to be cursed. The curse had been placed on the mill, it was said, by an old witch who had a grievance with the man who owned the mill at that time.

The curse wreaked havoc for some years after that. The first miller was killed in a fire. His successor died of a sudden and mysterious illness, after which the mill was burned to the ground. When the mill was rebuilt, the witch's heart softened a little and she weakened the curse. Now the mill would be safe from further problems as long as it was left idle for one day every year. Woe betide the miller who dared to use the mill on the forbidden day.

Many years later, the mill was bought by an ambitious miller who wanted to expand his business. He already owned one mill and wanted to improve his prospects with the purchase of a second one. He did not hold with superstition, nor did he like the mill at Newtonmore standing idle when he could be making money from it. The so-called witch was long dead, and the miller could not see what harm she could do from the grave.

In spite of warnings not to do so, the miller prepared to keep the mill working on the forbidden day. Hardly had he set the machinery in motion than there was a terrible grating sound and everything came to a halt. The small amount of meal that had been ground was full of grit, and one of the grinding stones had, incredibly, broken into several fragments.

Unwilling to admit that he might have been wrong, the miller denied to all and sundry that he had had any problems. He quietly arranged delivery of a new grinding stone and carried on working for another year.

The next year the miller was still determined to keep the mill working on the forbidden day. But this time not one piece of machinery would function in spite of the most careful maintenance. Nothing seemed to be wrong, but, all the same, nothing would work. To add to his grief and frustration, the miller discovered that a sudden and voracious plague of rats in his granary had eaten all his corn.

The miller had experienced quite enough. He sold the mill, deciding it was better to concentrate all his efforts on the other mill that he owned. His troubles were not over, however. His first mill was destroyed by fire, and he himself took ill and died very soon afterwards.

The cursed mill was then taken over by yet another man, a kindly and earnest soul who had taken a young gypsy boy under his wing. They managed to set the mill to rights, and it worked beautifully, making them a good living until the old man died. The gypsy boy left to find a job elsewhere, and another miller stepped in to run the mill. Although the machinery had been well maintained and everything appeared to be in good working order, the mill refused to work properly and the miller was plagued with problems. The gypsy boy was summoned to give his advice, and much to everyone's amazement, with a tweak here and a twiddle there, he managed to get the mill to work. Nobody could work out how he did it. And yet, no sooner had he left the premises than the mill ground to a halt yet again. The miller threw up his hands in despair and left.

The gypsy boy returned to the mill to take charge. As long as he was there, the mill worked perfectly well and he made himself a good living. But after his death the mill fell into disrepair. Because of the angry words of an old woman, long dead, nobody else could ever get it to work again.

The Curse of Alloa Tower

Alloa Tower stands bleakly empty nowadays, a haven for rodents and nesting birds and a magnet for vandals who have left their handiwork on the boards that cover up the doors and windows. The dereliction of the place adds to the air of grimness that surrounds it, but its proud tall walls and castellated turrets remain intact, as if making one last determined stand against the curse on the Erskines, Earls of Mar, the family who once owned it.

Exactly when the terrible curse was first uttered is uncertain; some sources believe it to date from the sixteenth century. At that time the Abbey of Cambuskenneth was destroyed by the Earl of Mar, and some people believe that it was the abbot who pronounced the curse upon the family. When it was

pronounced and by whom do not matter so much as the horrifying manner in which events followed to bring about the
demise of the Erskines, exactly as the curse had promised.

The curse promised the following things:

- The family would become extinct.
- The estates of the Erskine family would fall into the hands
  of strangers.
- One of the Erskines would live to see his home, a place where
  a king was raised, ravaged by flames. He would see his wife
  die in the burning house.
- Three of that man's children would never see the light of
  day.
- The great hall of his house would become a place for stabling
  horses.

Bibliography

Hellish Nell: Last of Britain's Witches by Malcolm Gaskill (Fourth Estate, 2001)

Not of this World by Maurice Fleming (Mercat Press, 2002)

The Unbelievable Truth by Gordon Smith (Hay House, 2004)

Spirit Messenger by Gordon Smith (Hay House, 2003)

'Best' of Both Worlds by Rosalind Cattanach (Pembridge Publishing, 1999)

A Sense of Something Strange by Archie E Roy (Dog and Bone, 1990)

Supernatural Scotland by Roddy Martine (Robert Hale, 2003)

Ley Lines and Earth Energies by David R Cowan (David Hatcher Childress, California, 2004)

News Sources

Sunday Herald (5 May 2001: Theatre call in exorcist to halt ghostly encore, by James Hamilton; 16 March 2003: The Exorcist Files by Vicky Allan)

The Guardian (2 May 2001: Exorcism: abuse or curse? by David Batty)

Christiantoday.com: (19 December 2004: Deliverance Group Recommends the Church of Scotland a Cautious Approach to Exorcism)

Haunted Scotland Journal (various dates, ed: Mark Fraser)